ADRIFT IN STORMY TIMES

by Rudolf Thill

edited by Dean Schwarz

Copyright©2004
Rudolf Thill and Dean Schwarz
South Bear Press
2248 South Bear Road
Decorah, Iowa 52101

All rights reserved
Printed in the United States of America

Library of Congress Cataloging
in Publication Data
1. Germany--World War II--nonfiction
2. Prisoner of War in US--autobiography
3. Hitler regime--nonfiction

Cover illustration by John Whelan

Layout by Zelda Productions
Decorah, Iowa

ISBN 0-9761381-0-7

TABLE OF CONTENTS

Chapter 1, One Ominous Day   7

January 30, 1933. The boy, age eight, observes worrisome changes in his Upper Silesian village and in the behavior of his parents as Hitler comes to power.

Chapter 2   Of Carp and Men at Christmas   15

The first Christmas under the Nazis… the joyous traditions are muffled by the ethnic tensions in the village.

Chapter 3   On the Village Road   23

The boy participates in a ceremony honoring veterans of the World War by marching beside the beautiful flag and by playing his drum.

Chapter 4   The Summer of '34   33

The boy's Uncle Max shows him sights in the world outside Upper Silesia including a momentary glimpse of Hitler riding by in a Mercedes Benz. All the thrilling adventures are numbed when he sees his uncle shout *Heil! Heil!* and salute *Der Führer*.

Chapter 5   Of Flags and Books   45

The boy's mother and father agonize over hanging the Nazi flag from their window, and the boy agonizes over his part in burning books considered poisonous by the Nazis.

Chapter 6   Oranges in Brown Paper Bags   57

The fourteen-year-old boy wonders why his Jewish schoolmates are absent on that November day. Columns of smoke from downtown Buethen distract students and teachers and cause an early dismissal, so the boy runs to the fire and sees the Jewish businesses being systematically destroyed. He cannot face his Jewish seatmate.

Chapter 7   August Days   69

The boy, now fifteen, listens to rumors in the town about rationing, and also listens to his own adolescent fantasies about girls. The Italian ice cream parlor allows him a chance to experience new flavors of ice cream and femininity.

Chapter 8   War   75

September 1, 1939—war with Poland is launched and the boy can hear the rumble of bombs just across the border. His father returns from military duty in Poland, and at the welcoming home party the boy's curiosity about women is suddenly turned to a wish to go to war.

Chapter 9   Capture   87

The boy, now a young soldier on the north coast of Africa, reflects on his experiences in the military while he tries to avoid capture by the Allies and go by raft to an Italian-held island in the Mediterranean.

Chapter 10   Prisoner Of War # 81G-16855   107

The soldier, now a prisoner, travels by train across Tunisia. He manages to ride on the roof with two English guards rather than being shut into a boxcar. He thinks back on his days stationed in France and being welcomed into a French family.

Chapter 11   Across the Atlantic   121

The prisoners are transferred from the English to the Americans, taken by truck to the great gray ship, and carried across the ocean—lice and all. At the Norfolk harbor, the lice are liberated and the prisoners are allowed their first warm shower.

Chapter 12   On the Train   139

From Norfolk the prisoners head toward the setting sun in comfortable coach cars and are served hot meals. But the prisoner must strain his memory of American geography to imagine where they are going—and to wonder how the war in Europe is coming.

Chapter 13   Camp Huntsville   149

Life in this camp would have been quite comfortable for the young prisoner were it not for his fellow prisoners who were Nazis. Their jeers and threats make this an ordeal, especially when he hears of the murder of two other anti-Nazis. Still he resolves to be his own man, to get a job in the office as a translator, and to maintain his friendship with twelve tattooed men.

Chapter 14   Which Way?   167
A two-day train ride takes him and the twelve men with tattoos through endless scrub-brush country. His limited knowledge of American geography does not help him determine where he is and where this train is going.

Chapter 15   Camp Fabens   175

At this small camp in Texas, the prisoner's days are filled with picking cotton and memorizing English vocabulary. His nights are filled with listening to his radio, reading his dictionary, contemplating the stars, and a one-time outing to a local football game.

Chapter 16   When Trains Cross Rivers   183

The cotton is picked, Camp Fabens is closed, and the prisoner joins many others on a train going east. Reflecting on his long personal tradition of spitting into a river and making a wish, the prisoner is determined to watch for the Mississippi, spit through the scant inches his window will open, and make a wish to return to this land as a free man.

Chapter 17   Camp Forrest   191

Tullahoma, Tennessee, the site of a huge camp holding thousands of prisoners of war, is at once a refreshing setting among tall pines and a fearsome camp among Nazis who kill anti-Nazis in the middle of the night. Until he is eventually put in an anti-Nazi compound, the prisoner fears for his life every night and finds solace by retreating into memories of childhood in the forests of Germany.

Chapter 18   Survival   199

Nine months after the end of the war, the prisoners are sent by train to New York and to a troop ship to be returned to Germany. A rough journey is made worse by the news that the German harbor is full and that the ship will dock in France. His fears are realized when boxcars carrying the prisoners are met by bayonet-bearing French soldiers escorting them to a prison camp of bare ground, barbed wire, and starvation rations supplemented with handfuls of grass. After two months he is able to get a job as a translator in the camp office where his life improves and he is promised an exact release date.

Chapter 19   Another Beginning   207

In the American Zone of Germany, the young man is discharged as a German soldier and released as a prisoner of war, but how will he earn a living? His English skills help him find profitable work in the Black Market. With the help of a cousin, he finds his mother and finds a job near her as a farmer's hired man… which he leaves in haste.

Chapter 20   Post-War Years and Beyond   215

He chooses to become a skilled laborer, a bricklayer, which requires a two-year apprenticeship. Finishing this, he applies for a job as translator for the Military Government. Later he meets Captain Ralph Cramer who invites him to come and live in the US.

Epilogue by Geraldine Schwarz   231

Appendix 1   Locations by Stan Zegel   241

Appendix 2   Geneva Convention Excerpts   249

Appendix 3   Maps by Mary Skopec, PhD.   255

1
ONE OMINOUS DAY

On that day, because of the cold, he could play in the kitchen, right on the kitchen floor with the flowered linoleum. In addition to the puffy flowers in cream color and green sword-like leaves, hot coals had burnt spots into the linoleum in a semi-circle around the front of the tiled kitchen stove. The spots looked like cat's eyes peering from the jungled flowers and leaves. Closer to the stove where heavier traffic had worn the linoleum to its rose sub-layer, even right down to the wooden floor directly in front of the stove, the spots seemed to lose their cat's eye-like appearance. For that they were much too numerous.

At "times like the-e-e-e-se," his mother would remark with a voice somewhat wailing and darker than usual, when unemployed coal miners swarmed over mountains of slag gleaning for something to burn in their stoves at home, or when the same men lounged on the village green playing cards, with matches for stakes, while tattered children herded an occasional goat and a few geese around them, the thought of a new linoleum was out of the question. It ought to be mentioned, though, that quite a few other places in the rectangular kitchen also showed considerable wear and tear. Among the worst spots were those around the table, where the boy's parents and he sat day after day to eat their meals, talk, study, and sometimes play games. Mother's remark of "times like the-e-e-e-se" was moreover used as an accusation of sorts for all cases of peeling paint, falling plaster, and darkening areas in the ceiling from kitchen soot and grime. The truth was that nothing could be done. The apartment they occupied was in the old village school, the teaching salary of his father came from the government, and village and state government were, to use a German expression, *kaputt. Da war kein Staat zu machen.*

Another favorite expression of his mother was "What shall become of us?" She would say that whenever some bad news about Germany would enter the house via the printed page or as a conversation piece, which was rather often during the first two years of the thirties. On occasion it would happen that the remark was accompanied by a sharp metallic click, followed by an even louder hollow-sounding clang, twice around, prompting the father to add, "When even the police are—afraid in Germany." The sounds came from the ground floor, where the local police were—stationed. In fact, the clicking and clanging of the doors was caused by unlocking and closing them. The heavier of the two opened into the house, the lighter into the police station. The station itself was manned by two policemen.

All the unlocking and closing of the doors was done with similar caution and speed by the two policemen, even though they were different in age, rank, and appearance. The younger of the two was rather boyish-looking, in contrast to the burly, heavy-set type. And while the eyes of the younger one, under the rounded fez-type police shako, tended to be quite shifty, those of the other had a pop-eyed quality about them.

Actually, the real difference in loudness of the clicks and the clangs and the pause between them was not so much due to any human factor, such as it was with the two police. The real difference depended on which one of the two doors was first opened, or whether a policeman was leaving the station and the house, or whether he was entering.

The boy had seen this: when the station-door was opened, from the inside for example, there would first be a cautious click, as the key would move the bolt out of the latch, and, as the door was opened ever so slowly, a pair of eyes would peek through the widening crack and scan the hallway. Factors of security were certainly involved in this. Only then would our policeman step into the hallway, gently closing the door behind him. The same would be repeated at the heavier house-door, with caution and hesitation and all.

However, when coming in from the outside, not only was the pause between the click and the clang, or the unlocking and closing of the door, much, much shorter, but the sounds were also much louder, quite like bolting a rifle for firing.

These also were some of the signs of the times: once our policeman was outside, standing with his shako right below the blue enameled house number 4, he would invariably assume the pose of the German policeman. This was true, without fail, for both of them: the black leather-legginged legs wide apart, the left hand almost akimbo grasping the belt in such a way so as to allow four fingers (minus the thumb) to tap a melody on the buckle, the right hand on the rubber truncheon, while the eyes, by now stern and authoritarian, would look down the village street, first in one direction and then in the other.

The boy played war that afternoon. That in itself was not unusual. Most German boys played war often enough anyway, from the Thirty Years' War with its horrendously nerve-tingling Swedish drink to the World War, usually by pelting each other with chestnuts, hard clods of dirt, even rocks from behind fences and ditches. During bad weather the game would be played inside, with the help of soldiers cast out of lead.

What was unusual that early afternoon was that the boy's father had gone to the only house in the village with electricity, supposedly to await some news on the radio. The father's absence from the afternoon routine, mother's withdrawal into the corner by the stove, where she sat looking rather askance, had upset the daily routine. No morality of 'work before play' today, as his father was gone and his mother, given to a torporific quality reminiscent of a female which Henry Moore would sculpt later, was too absent-minded to insist he first do the homework and take the cod-liver oil before playing. The cod-liver oil bottle stood between the two windowpanes in the corner of the window. A spoonful before going to school, a spoonful after coming home from school was the daily regimen, and always he would gag and choke over each spoonful, almost retch.

The boy played with a tank this afternoon and the usual number of lead soldiers. The tank had been a Christmas present. Its one great attraction was a spark-firing gun with a noise-rattling device. Soon after Christmas the winding mechanism had broken down—a loud snap marking its demise—and thereafter fire and rattle could be produced only by pressing the tank against the floor while moving it forward, or backward, at the same time.

The tank's spark-firing gun and the blotchy camouflage of earth colors covering all sides of the tank, from which a pitch-black German war cross with a brilliant white outline would shine forth, gave the boy a real sense of exhilaration. His imagination did the rest. It made out of the area in front of the kitchen stove, where spots had been burnt into the worn linoleum, a battlefield. The spots became shell holes, the sparks of hot coals, falling from the grate into the ash box, during their short flaming journey would be transformed by the boy's passionate mind into artillery, its distant flashes dancing over the battlefield. Outside, the wintry day appeared to age faster than usual. As fading daylight crept through the windowpanes, flattening ice flowers into dull shapes, it barely reached the far end of the kitchen, where the boy was playing war and the mother sat motionless.

The battle, it must be said, was between the infantry-supported German tank and enemy soldiers. From the village war veterans, the boy knew the enemy as French *poilu* and British tommy. And even though the veterans always spoke of the enemy with an undertone of respect, even admiration, the *poilus* and tommies were being badly beaten today. The furious tank attacks had left them in disarray, having been tumbled, like fallen idols, from their lead-based martial postures. But the German soldiers, with their protectively shaped helmets, were still picture perfect, firing standing up, or kneeling, or lying down.

That someone had stepped into the kitchen, neither the mother nor the boy had noticed. A raspy voice came from the door. It was that of the father, only higher than usual. As if probing the ground under his feet, he took some uncertain steps into the kitchen. "Martha," he said half way across the kitchen, underlining the name with a hand gesture of futility. "What is it?" When she got no answer, the mother repeated quickly, "What is it, Alfons?" and rose awkwardly from the chair. Then they embraced.

The boy had never witnessed his parents embrace or call each other by their first names. Always they would share with him the customary "Mama" and "Papa" for each other. Somehow, something had been happening that gave an indistinct, portentous meaning to father's earlier absence and mother's withdrawal.

Two more sentences were to pass between them, as mother broke the embrace and, sitting down on the chair, said, "How could it happen?" Father's reply was, "It just did."

That was all that was said for the moment. Not wanting to draw upon himself their attention, which could lead straight away to homework and cod-liver oil, the boy fell in with their silence and stopped playing war.

That evening mother served *Zur* for dinner, a sweet-sour Polish soup made of sour dough and groats, with pieces of steaming Cracow sausage served on the side. The dish was the boy's favorite, but rather less so his father's, who between spoonfuls of soup and bites of sausage, spoke up again. "There is still the Army, you must know." And after a pause, "Hindenburg and von Papen will put the bite on him." But Mama said, "Papa, what if you are wrong?"

The father seemed to catch his breath, as if giving fresh conviction to the next sentence. "Mama, on a day like this, nothing is better than your *Zur*."

The day had gone not only topsy-turvy, but at that moment the boy also knew that his father was not telling the truth. Avoiding his father's glance, the boy looked straight ahead to the place on the wall where a crucifix was hanging, of the kind that graced millions of German homes. Christ's head sagged to the left, in the direction of one of those handy tear-off calendars. Its big batch of still untorn papers, one for each day, was fastened against a larger cardboard with the image of the *Gleiwitz Wanderer,* delivering the daily newspaper of that region with gargantuan steps. The calendar showed the number 30 for the day, the name January for the month, and on the cardboard
itself, in a circle round the sun, the words *IN ANNO DOMINI*. In the blazing center stood 1933. On that day Hitler came to power.

Photo courtesy of Stan Zegel.

The schoolhouse of Pilzendorf, built in 1904 is where the author began his education. The lower grades were taught on the lower floor; older students through age fourteen climbed to the upper floor. The author's father was a teacher here, and the son attended until age ten, at which time he took the enterance examinations and went to *Realgymnasium* in Beuthen. For this he needed to walk to Klausberg, a village of 20,000 and take the train to Beuthen. No *Realgymnasium* existed in Klausberg because less than five percent of students went on to secondary school. The rest went to trade schools or became apprentices.

Adjacent to the school, at the right, is the old school that was converted into apartments. On the second floor was the Thills' apartment, located over the police station. The dirt road in front of the school was paved in later years.

2

OF CARP AND MEN AT CHRISTMAS

Every year when early Advent weather would sweep into Upper Silesia, into those former German lands hard by the Polish border, with the first real touches of winter, the boy's mother would bring up at once the matter of carp. A carp at home was as much part of the Christmas season as, well, gingerbread men and spritz cookies, tree ornaments and tinsel.

"I feel," mother would say, "it's time for the fish to get a good soaking." And almost in the same breath she would add, quite like an afterthought: "A real good soaking." With that she would roll and purr the 'r' in the *richtige* German fashion.

What she meant, back in those thirties, was that it was time for carp to be caught in the fishpond, which was a distance away from the village near a brickyard. And thus each year a carp would be brought home live and kept alive in the zinc bathtub until the day of the Holy Evening. Relieved of the muddy taste as the result of an extended stay in the bathtub, as mother believed, the fate of the carp was eventually sealed under a thick coating of bread crumbs; by the time the carp graced the table that evening, its color was a golden brown and the aroma of the crispy fried outside and the steamy, flaky inside, mingling with the scent of pine needles and burning candles, filled the kitchen where the family would eat the Christmas dinner.

There was no telephone back in those days, at least not in the village in which the boy grew up. It is anybody's guess, how the people in the village from one hour to the next found out on any given afternoon that the pond would be seined for Christmas carp. Yet somehow the news would pop, as it were, in the village and the word would reach the last of the houses at both ends of the rutted village street in no time. Within minutes groups of men with their children would be on the way to the pond, which lay beyond gently rising fields. Among the men were the coal miners and ironworkers, at home between shifts, and the few German teachers in the village.

In trying to understand the hurried exodus of the villagers to the distant pond, to say nothing of the strange behavior of both the Poles and the Germans, as we shall see, one should know that in the thirties things were often, in a manner of speaking, touch and go. Just take the Christmas carp as an example: either they were seined out of the pond on the right day, or it could happen that the waters would be frozen shut the next. But if caught too early, and if the days before the Birth Of Our Savior were without freezing cold in the air, the fish were likely to spoil. Big zinc bathtubs, in which the carp would be kept alive, most non-German villagers did not have. The Poles would butcher the carp on the spot, right on the grassy slopes of the pond, and then the fish would be taken home to let Mother Nature freeze and preserve them until Christmas.

But Christmas carp and their catch were not the only thing that touched the lives of these villagers in the thirties. There was a lot of whispering going on that times were changing: Weimar yielded to Buchenwald. Dachau, after an existence of charmed German small-town life of close to a thousand years, took on overnight still another more sinister meaning. In the land of poets and thinkers, of *Dichter und Denker* as the Germans once proudly thought of themselves, in this land... where religion had once attained the loftiest of expressions, the Cross was being twisted into the *Swastika*... from where music of unsurpassed beauty had come, now voices shrill with the excitement of bloodied knives and conquests began to drone... where its philosophers had probed profoundly questions affecting mankind, the Nazi mythmakers cajoled the crowds with racial flatteries and mind-boggling promises. The land of Luther, Bach, Beethoven and Kant, of Schiller and Goethe was now marching to the beat of a corporal drummer. *Heil* Hitler was the solution for everything.

Upper Silesian Poles were born survivors. Bred into them, after living for centuries under Austrian, Prussian, and German masters, were Slav qualities of resilience and toughness, which they displayed in turn by evading and avoiding the ways of the masters, of feigning as much as fawning, of yielding one day, only to resist the next. First, Germanization and now Nazification had an effect on these Poles in Upper Silesia, as 1945 was to show, like trying to beat water into shape with clubs. In that form of resistance the minority of half a million *Wasserpollacken* in the Third *Reich* was without match.

No sooner did the word of the impending catch reach the home of the boy, when the big zinc bathtub, in which the family would take turns taking the weekly Saturday bath, was hauled from the adjoining garret into the kitchen. The boy simply relished the thought of the bathless weeks until Christmas. On days when the flowers and crystalline shapes of ice on the windowpanes grew thicker and thicker, the tub with the carp in it was moved closer to the tiled kitchen-stove for the night. An extra shovel of coal kept the water from freezing as mother could be heard imploringly that, Lord forbid, anything should ever happen to the carp, at least not until Christmas.

For now both the boy and his father emptied several buckets of water into the tub, water pumped by hand from the well outside. And from now on until Christmas it became a daily chore for the boy to empty the water from the tub, bucket by bucket, down to the level where the fish could still swim upright; then he would refill the tub with fresh water from the well. However, on some days when from waste and the crushed oats that were thrown to the carp the water had turned very brackish, the carp would be given a complete change of water. First, the boy would corner the fish with a bucket at one end of the tub to scoop it up with one quick swoop, and then he did empty the tub completely before returning the carp to it with buckets of fresh well water. We should not think that all those changes of water, all those splashes sent up by the frantic carp, that all the wet floors and smelly waters in the face were just so much

Original drawing by Rudolf Thill

ballyhoo. The carp was for real. Besides, it gave the nine-year-old a sense of accomplishment.

By keeping to the dirt roads that extended like arms of crosses over the fields between the village and the pond—fields dark from the plow and fields greening with winter grain—it took about half an hour to walk (briskly) to the pond, even less when heading straight across the fields. It must be said that the Germans among the villagers always did the former, the Poles almost always the latter.

Stepping on "God's Acres" was the most reprehensible thing "these people" could possibly do, at least in the eyes of the boy's father. The father was a gentle and kind-hearted man; he was loving and he forgave easily. But in this matter of stepping on "God's Acres" he would come as close as ever to losing his temper: "Don't they… don't these people ever learn that their heavy boots trample the tender greens… break the fragile shoots?" And by drawing in his breath with a hissing sound so as to give suspense to the next thought, he would speak of "times" and "nature" likely to turn out both bad and angry.

As soon as they were out on the first stretch of dirt road, the boy could already see that the Poles were heading straight across the fields, even though the fields of new greens, from which next year's bread would come, lay bare and unprotected under the wintry sky. It had not snowed yet. He also saw that father's countenance grew dark. At every turn in the dirt road, when the sharp wind did not leave the lungs breathless, the father kept on muttering: "Where shall this all lead to?" The words hung like notes of staccato in the cold December air.

By now, the first Christmas under the Nazis, the men and the women in the village had had their awakening. Gone from their lives was the joyousness of the day each spring when the songbirds returned, or when the village storks hatched. Such days, even though they were still happening, were less likely to bring villagers out of their dark houses for friendly chats across fences or gatherings at the barn, where they had watched year after year the storks on the day of the hatch. By now, two of the villagers had been snatched by the *GESTAPO*, outside Nazis had staged the book-burning with furious abandon, and failure to display the Nazi flag on flag-days carried a deadly risk. But gone also were the days when the men, idled coal miners and iron workers, would play cards on the village green, with matches as stakes. For the mine was again taking the men "under day" three shifts daily, and the distant skies above the iron-works were glowing night after night from the unceasing flow of molten metal.

At the pond the Poles and the Germans at first stood separate from each other, with a touch of deference shown by the former. Whenever the handful of Germans moved, a step or two, over to where the Poles had a better look at the seining just getting under way, the Poles would yield, however imperceptibly and without any demur. But the children, the children would play 'catch.' With bursts of speed, body feints, sudden stops and starts they would race around the two groups of men, around their fathers, in circles or in a weaving pattern, much like the pattern of one of the wilder midway rides in the city.

Or they would streak out into the pasture, pursuer and pursued, fall to the ground and wrestle, boy with boy, boy with girl, with whoever was handy. Some would run to the far end of the pasture where a small herd of cattle was grazing. There the boys and the girls would stand momentarily, all gasping, and their breaths streaming into the cold air looked like some flags of quicksilver.

Back at the pond, the noisy chase and the wild pursuit would be resumed. Oh yes, what gave a note of caution to the running—a step shortened or a foot sidestepping something—were cow-chips that lay scattered in the pasture. As the seining began in earnest, the children scampered back to their fathers, their lungs short of breath and their eyes wide with anticipation.

The seine was a net with cork floats and lead sinkers designed to give it the right lay in the water. Extending from bank to bank, it would widen in the center into a train, like in a bridal gown. That train was supposed to sweep snugly over the bottom of the pond to gather up the fish. To make sure it did, a young Polish worker from the brickyard in his long gray underpants would wade into the frigid water, do some diving, and keep the train from balling up and overlapping, lest the fish escape. Two men at either end of the seine would now pull the net toward the other end of the pond where the men with their children were waiting.

In the language of the villagers, back then between the two wars, there were those "heavy calibers" of carp in the pond. The word perhaps was a leftover from the days when the *Krupps* called the biggest gun rather affectionately after one of the matrons of the clan. And so, what the "Big Bertha" was to brassy minds, the "heavy calibers" were, with undiminished Christmas fervor, to the villagers.

At first not much was going on. Nothing more than a slight tremor went through the corks, as the men moved the seine forward inch by inch. Their backs were taut, their muscles were straining, and their heels were digging into the soft bank like in a tug of war. About midway through the pond some fish were trying to swim back into the half of the pond from which they had been frightened away. They began to swim into the net. In fact some of the "heavy caliber" bumped right into it.

Now corks bobbed violently. Bounced back by the netting, the fish whiplashed their bodies forward and their tails lashed out, as they frantically sought to escape. Waves going hither and thither marked the attempted escapes and, where foiled, the fish jumped and their bodies would slice through the air like sharp knives. More and more the waters resembled the fabled witches' brew.

The excitement of the catch caught up with the men and the children on the bank. Giving up the protective, warming hands of their fathers, the children all at once began to scamper again, they leaped into the air and they clapped their hands. Among the men the thin line that kept the Poles and the Germans in their places was disappearing. Necks craned forward, they now stood together and shouted words in unison. They shouted words of excitement and of encouragement, Polish and German words of, what we call, strong language aimed in particular at the men at the ends of the seine, whose bodies by now were awash with perspiration. Expressions of *Weiter Scheisse* and lots of *Perunje* could be heard amidst the shrieks of the children. The noise now sounded like on a Sunday afternoon when in a close soccer game the home team scored the winning goal… with a difference: the Polish words here on the bank of the pond, where the Christmas carp were caught, bore unmistakably a German accent, and the German words, in the vowel-flattening ways of foreigners, sounded Polish. The strong words were shouted by the Poles and the Germans in each other's language.

A big batch of fish, some of the "heavy calibers" in it, was dragged up in the train into shallow waters and, with final tugs and pulls, up on dry ground. As if on a command, the men and the children rushed in to disentangle the fish from the netting, this jiggling and contorting mass of fish from the train. Working furiously, young and old began to sort the fish by tossing the "small fry" back into the waters for another day and by heaving the "heavy calibers" unto the pasture. There they became, when all else was done, Christmas carp in exchange for pennies.

By now the day was fading fast. While the boy and his father, who carried the live carp in a bucket, were still on the dirt road, the Poles and their children had already disappeared across the fields into the rapidly falling night, dead carp bleeding through wrappings of newspaper.

A December moon hung in the air. From the village church, or from a church somewhere on the dark horizon, the thin and languid sound of a bell could be heard. It pealed the message from the grim reaper. The pealing ceased with a final stroke, more like the half swing of the clapper into the bronze wall of the bell. Whimpering into the still and frosty night, it sounded as if the bell had died, too. "Who will be next?" That was all father said.

Below in the village the carbide lamps were burning with fierce incandescence. Later, as the evening wore on, the lamps would gradually take on tinges of yellow and rose, before going out altogether.

The rest of the way home on the dirt-roads criss-crossing their ways over to the village, the boy thought of only one thing: how from now until Christmas the carp would be in the tub in the middle of the kitchen. That very thought rose in him like a warming flame, here in the early night of a long, cold winter.

3

ON THE VILLAGE ROAD

It was the dirt road, running from the highway into the village, that gave the intersection the shape of a cross. The highway itself headed in opposite directions, like a pair of outstretched arms, where after two turns it went deeper into the heart of Upper Silesia with its coal mines and blast furnaces. As for the short extension of the cross, that stretch of highway eventually changed into a street in nearby Klausberg with tram tracks, storefronts, and a movie theater.

To the villagers, the highway was known as *chaussee*. The word was not even German; and yet what all *chaussees* had in common, in Upper Silesia at least, was that they were of asphalt. Concrete pavement was yet to come, later with the *Autobahn*.

As such the *chaussees* were really very smooth and sleek, in contrast to the village road which was a mixture of dirt and crushed rock: dusty and bumpy in the summer and more or less rutted after each spring thaw or after a heavy rain. What made the ruts so deep and so irregular were horse-drawn wagons. In fact, in the quagmire they had a tendency to wander from one side of the road to the other, as if the driver had imbibed one or two *schnapps* too many in one of the taverns along the way.

But *schnapps* or no *schnapps*, the small-time teamsters with their one-horse wagons got their hauling done when it counted. It was coal they hauled. For each house in the village about a load in the fall and one in the spring, or for the village about 300 loads in a year. Add to that the bundles of firewood for kindling fires in kitchen stoves and in all those *Kachelöfen,* so meals could be cooked and harsh winters would be kept at bay.

When not hauling coal, the men and their horses were usually in the fields. Fields had to be plowed and harrowed; manure needed to be taken out and spread; rye had to be sown by hand*,* always by the men, and potatoes had to be planted by the women and by the children. And if the heavens took pity and the lands escaped late frosts and untimely hailstorms, to say nothing of rain-drenched summers, then, at last, the time would come to bring in the crops.

Nearby, on large tracts of land, all work was done by powerful steam engines, by tractors, by an array of teams of horses, and, if necessary, by armies of workers. These lands, in name at least, belonged to *Graf Henckel von und zu Donnersmarck*. What they did was to hem in the village on all sides, in effect girdling it. For the people in the village the fields of the *Dominium* were good only for some gleaning of left-over stalks of grain and a few potatoes.

No one had to contend more with the adversities of the village road than the miners, in rain and in snow, in heat and in cold. On that road they rode their bicycles to the mine, where most of them worked "under days." Working *unter Tage* in a coalmine was synonymous with working underground, such as working at the head of a gallery.

With three shifts a day, there were always men on the road, especially when shifts changed. One group of men would leave, and the other would come home. Not that all of them came home at the same time. There were always the stragglers, especially on payday, and among the stragglers there were those who never quite made it, who, after spending too much time in a tavern, ended up beneath a shady tree on the *chaussee*, or in the ditch. There they would lie until their wives would come with a handcart and get them. That is, they would load the tipplers, bike and all, on the cart and haul them home, haul them all the way home on the village road. For recovery and for a purgation of sorts, the common remedy on the day after was lots of sauerkraut juice. Meanwhile, at least until next week's payday, the village had something to gossip about.

Others to use the village road were such tradesmen as the rag collector, the knife and scissor sharpener, the man who fixed leaky pots, and the dispenser of malted beer. They came, bell ringing, in ways peculiar to their trade. The rag collector plied his trade from a horse-drawn rickety wagon.

For the knife-sharpener, it was a bicycle that doubled up as a grindstone. The pot fixer pulled his own cart on which the secrets of his trade—an anvil, metal scissors, and a blowtorch—were stored. And then there was the man who dispensed malted beer, or *Einfachbier* (simple beer) whose own ways were not always so simple and uncomplicated. At least not with the distributor of real beer, a former socialist turned Nazi. And, finally, there was the truck from outside the village to make weekly stops at the grocery store and at the bakery.

Anything else on the village road was big news: like the doctor riding into the village on a bicycle to visit the sick; an ambulance taking someone to the miners' hospital; the horse-drawn hearse rolling into the village for a funeral; a truck of slogan-shouting *SA* men driving up and down the village road—before unloading books on the village commons; or the *GESTAPO* whisking a reputed Communist away, in the middle of the night.

In such matters as life and death, death was not a stranger. It was not a stranger when it came, slowly and haltingly, to the sick and the old; when it snuffed out the lives of the young who succumbed to galloping consumption; when it claimed men under collapsing mine shafts or in ravaging firedamps. With men going to the mine three times a day, with women taking to *childbett* in their own homes, with children being at the mercy of such killers as scarlet fever and diphtheria, death was never far. It was as near as the pealing of the death bell in the church steeple and the sounding of the siren on top of the mine tower.

Johann Sletta had left the house for the mine before dawn, as he had done for years. On the following day he was back, in a coffin. For three days his body lay in the room with the big clock, the framed pictures on the commode, and the heirloom sofa, and for three days, in between silent nights, there was wailing in the house. Wailing and praying. In Polish to *Matka Bosza*. In German to the *Mutter Gottes*. And in the afternoon before the funeral a house full of women mourners dolefully murmured the beads of the rosary in a mixture of Polish and German.

The boy could hear the wailing and the praying. His room faced the Sletta house. It was spring, the windows were open, and down in the garden the pear trees were in bloom. And in one of the trees a pair of starlings was getting ready to nest in a box the dead man had once built. It was the pair from last year, so *Herr* Sletta had told him. For the boy that was good enough. Had not *Herr* Sletta always known things and done things he was yearning to know and to do some day? Such as building bird boxes, raising pigeons, keeping rabbits; such as hatching chicks under a broody hen. Also, the boy remembered wintry evenings when *Herr* Sletta would pour lead into forms—the result of blazing coals and of molten metal—and let him have the lead soldiers. And now the good man was dead. The boy turned away from the window. He lay down on the bed and buried his face in the pillow.

Leading the funeral procession was the crucifer. Next came the priest. Third in the procession was the hearse. Its roof, topped by a golden cross, was in the shape of a canopy, which in turn was supported by four fluted columns. The coffin, covered with funeral wreaths and surrounded by white lilies, stood on a platform between the columns. A lone horse, the same old mare of a horse, was pulling the black hearse in a slow and halting gait, as if the animal knew that the grief-stricken are never in a hurry. Walking behind the coffin were Sletta's mother, Sletta's wife, and Sletta's daughter Hedwig, all in black. Then, marching in rank and file, were the miners in their coal-black uniforms and shakoes, with shiny silvery-looking buttons and crossed pick-axes. The rest of the procession was made up of people from the village. Among them were the third-graders of the village school, the classmates of Hedwig.

He had been at funerals before. It was at his grandmother's funeral a few years ago that he had experienced the finality of death for the first time. When her coffin was lowered into the grave and when mourners began, as part of the ritual, to throw shovelfuls of earth into the grave, only then did the finality of death hit home—to the hollow sounds of earth striking the wooden coffin.

There were nights after the Sletta funeral when, straining into the dark silence, he would mark in his mind the spots where mice rustled about, where birds fussed on their perches in the vine-covered wall outside his window, which way a train was headed as it rumbled in the distance.

Then there were nights when he listened to the faint buzz of bicycle chains and to the squeaks of springs, knowing that the men were on their way to the mine. Or he tried to pick up a word or two that passed between them down on the dark road. Then again he would count the number of bicycles going by, as the reflections of the carbide lamps flickered eerily across the room, fiercely white from fresh carbide or softly rose-colored from carbide on its last light. As it was, the reflections reminded him of the dead man, for a while at least. Then, more and more, he thought of Hedwig.

What he could not know was that there would come a time when she would arouse in him the first stirrings of masculinity. When, down in the yard, against the wooden wall of the shed, he would press his body against hers, while her arms would push him away one moment and pull him close the next, so he liked to think; when he was aware of nothing so much as her quickened breath, her flushed face, their trembling bodies.

In return, as it were, he helped Hedwig on the small plot behind the house with such chores as hoeing potatoes, picking potato beetles, raking hay into stacks, taking the goat out on the path between the plots to graze. And after work, on hot summer days, they would go to the pond to swim. He watched her undress. In the pale blue bathing suit, which matched the color of her eyes, she looked lovely. She still looked the lithesome, innocent girl, and yet he also saw that, since last summer, her body had been changing into that of a woman. Somehow he was seized by the desire to possess her. To possess her in ways he did not know how. It was in the water that he reached out for her, under the pretext of a water fight, and while she tried to wiggle herself free from his embrace, their bodies would touch and sometimes, for a few precious moments, she would yield and let him hold her close, her body against his. But giving herself to him she never did, not in the shed, not in haystacks, not in the tall grasses of June meadows.

By the time the war was two years old, she became a war bride. And after that there was nothing that he could do but keep his desire for her to himself.

There had been other times. There had been times when, oh, but to experience happiness was getting the first rabbit, the first canary, the first male thistle-finch; times when he got his first dog, his first bicycle, when he played the drums for the first time in public, in a parade no less. It was on a Sunday morning and the whole village had turned out. Actually, it was not so much a parade as it was the consecration of the colors, the consecration of a real flag with eye-catching emblems and heroic words. The flag in question was the new flag of the local chapter of the war veterans.

To choose the flag took all summer and most of the fall. For the members of the committee it was an arduous task. Not only were there different flags in different catalogues to choose from, but as an added challenge there was, for example, the emblem of the eagle in a variety of poses. There were eagles spreading their wings, ready to soar; there were eagles tucking in their wings as if they were about to pounce, with fierce eyes and sharp talons, on an imaginary beast of prey. Then there were eagles that bared their breasts while others bared their beaks. And then there were some that did both.

As for heroic words, they were apt to appear on the flags in any shape or form: on garlands, in inscriptive little ditties, on carriages of big guns, or wherever heaven and earth happened to be in the scheme of such flags. The boy's favorite flag showed an eagle in profile, a magnificent bird, with spread wings, a fierce eye and a yawning beak in which the tongue looked like a windblown flame. And garlanded in its talons were the words *Ehre—Treue—Pflicht* (honor, loyalty, duty).

For the boy, whose father was the commander of the local chapter, this was the most exciting of times. To be in the same room with the war veterans, in meeting after meeting, to sit with them at the big table and hear what the men had to say about the flags, about the relative merits of each one of the flags was thrilling enough. To be present when his favorite flag was indeed chosen in the end as the official flag of the 20-member *Kriegerverein* was like miracle. *War ein Wunder.* Besides, the boy had already been selected, as the son of the commander no doubt, to be one of two drummers of the brand-new drum and fife band, two drummers and four fifers in all.

By the time the flag issue had been decided, the six boys had already begun to practice on a pair of new drums and on four fifes. All practice sessions were held in the fields, on cow paths between fields of rye and potatoes, where no one in the village could hear them. Whether to spare ears or to save every last sound of the band for the first performance was never mentioned by the drum major. And the drum major, *Herr* Kubitzka, a balding man with a reputation of having fought in the battle of Verdun, was none too eager to offer an explanation. For Kubitzka, it seemed, the three conditions to good playing were not explanations but practice—practice—practice. And practice they did that spring, day in and day out, or at least whenever it was not raining. To get the boys together on any given afternoon, the drum major would simply start with his bicycle at the far end of the village road and, whenever he came to the house of one of the boys, ring the bell on his bicycle. Three rings at each house. And within minutes the boys were on the village commons from where they set out, with their drum major, for the fields to practice.

And did they ever practice! They practiced the basics, the first marches, they practiced playing separately and together, they played standing still and they played while marching. That's when the real trials began, as *Herr* Kubitzka's *Taktstock* was nothing less than exacting in terms of sharp entries, stirring finales, and precise endings. Anything else, in the *Kapellmeister's* words, sounded like goat manure dropping on a drum.

The *Taktstock* was fashioned by *Herr* Kubitzka himself—from a wooden cane, a spike from a German steel helmet, several ornamental cords, and a round brass tank from a kerosene stove. With the spike on top and the brass globe just above the handle, with colorful ornamental cords twisting and twirling around the gnarled cane, the *Taktstock* was eye-catching. In the hand of *Herr* Kubitzka, it was like a wand, the way it coaxed stirring marches out of the boy musicians. On the day of the consecration, the band was ready.

Meanwhile the flag had arrived. Its fabric was of a rich brocade. The flag, as a whole, was more impressive than he had ever imagined it to be. Every color, from the silvery background to the eagle's golden talons, from the red tongue and the fiery eye to the sated brown of the plumage was of sheer brilliance. And as if that were not enough, the plumage and the words in the garlands were standing out from the background as if aquiline fierceness had ruffled the bird's feathers and had lifted the brave words into something like suspenseful animation.

There were days when the boy felt like touching the eagle's plumage, when he felt like tracing the garlanded words in the eagle's talons, just once. He never did. As the flag stood in his parents' bedroom, in a stand, its fabric hanging in folds, the flag, like the monstrance at church, looked sacred. And just as the monstrance was touched and raised by the priest only, so was the flag to be lifted out of the stand and was to be carried forth for the consecration by none other than the three-men detail of the *Kriegerverein*.

To carry the flag from the parents' bedroom through the living room and the kitchen, down a flight of stairs before it was taken outside through the heavy house-door, did take some practice. Commands had to be shouted in the bedroom where the flag stood. Precise steps had to be executed as part of the ritual. The flag had to be maneuvered, had to be maneuvered deftly around sharp corners in the apartment where, in addition to the full length mirror in the bedroom, there were other dangers lurking. Dangers like Boecklin's *The Isle of the Dead* in the living room, or Mama's watercolor of the *Königsee* in faraway Bavaria. After three tries, not counting Mama's innumerable entreaties to "watch it" and to be "careful" and to "slow down," the three-men flag detail had everything down to perfection: the commands, the steps, and the maneuvers. For the flag's debut everything was ready.

On that Sunday, to the roll of the drums, the flag was at last brought down from the apartment into the open. There, on that portion of the village road between the school and the *Bürgermeister*'s house, the people stood waiting. At long last the flag was in their midst. In the bright sun it was all sparkle and as it swayed in the morning breeze the garlands agitated into streamers and the perched eagle seemed to turn into a bird of prey on the wing.

For the boy it was a glorious day. Father was shouting ringing commands. Mother, with his little sister in arms, stood proud and erect in the open kitchen window. The people, in their Sunday best, were craning their necks. Three rows of war veterans snapped to attention. And while he and his fellow-drummer were beating the drums, in a long roll, the flag was taken to the head of the column. They were ready to march.

And march they did, to the beat of the drums and to the tunes of the fifes, while Kubitzka's *Taktstock* rose to the occasion with an assortment of stabbing thrusts and freewheeling twirls. Down the road they marched, the whole village marched, past unpretentious gray stucco houses, past little barns with crowing roosters, past fenced-in yards that had been swept clean and had been weeded for the day. And as they headed for the church in the neighboring village, they passed fields of rye in which poppies were blooming and cornflowers were waiting to be picked.

As they marched past the red poppies and the blue cornflowers, they played the tune of an old German march. A young man must leave home and leave his love behind. As the boy beat the drum to the tune of the march: *"Muss ich denn, muss ich denn zum Städtele hinaus, und du mein Schatz bleibst hier"* (Must I now leave the little town, and you my darling stay behind)..." rat-ta-ta... rat-ta-ta... rat-ta-rat-ta-ta-ta-ta... he thought of tomorrow. And as he thought of tomorrow he was asking himself whether he would ever have to leave home for good. Tomorrow, first thing after school, he would ask his father to go out into the fields, for a walk. And there, as they had done so often, they would pick a bouquet of cornflowers—for Mama.

4
THE SUMMER OF '34

By the time he was ten years old, in the summer of '34, he still had not been out of Upper Silesia. Living in Upper Silesia, then, was like living in a country of dead-ends. To the east lay Poland, and to the south lay Poland, or about fourteen kilometers each way from the village in which the boy was living; and to the west, about seventy kilometers away, there was the border with Czechoslovakia. It was only to the north that the country was open. And here, in the ways of school maps, where rivers appear to flow upward and locations are reversed, Upper Silesia at the lower end of the map was joined to Lower Silesia at the upper end of the map. And to Germany beyond.

But all that was to change shortly. For in the summer of '34 the boy was to travel twice across the borders of Upper Silesia, both times in his uncle's Hannomag.

A two-seater and a cabriolet, with a rumble-seat in the back, the Hannomag in those days was one of the sportiest cars around. For colors, the chassis and the top were yellow and black, respectively. Or as his uncle would say, "As yellow as the yolk of an egg from a barnyard hen and as black as the inside of a chimney." And as for the grill, it looked more or less like the fantail of a pigeon, except that for feathers there were strips of chrome radiating from the hole for the starter-iron at the bottom to the Hannomag emblem on top.

That the Hannomag had a name was the legacy of *Tante* Henny. She had called it *Wichtel* (pixie). That was last year when she arrived, after an all-day train ride from Hamburg, at the railroad station in Katscher. They were all there to welcome her: *Onkel* Max, the boy, and the boy's parents. And, yes, the Hannomag was there and even two carriages, drawn by a horse each, were there. Obviously this was no ordinary arrival. Not when *Tante* Henny was coming as a bride, complete with her trousseau and accompanied by her parents, all the way from Hamburg, on all those trains from the crack *Fliegende Hamburger* on down to the jerky small gauge train that linked Gross Peterwitz (literally Great Peter's Joke) with Katscher.

What a feast the wedding between *Tante* Henny and *Onkel* Max was going to be. Days of preparation had already gone into it. One day it was a bower of fresh pine logs and green twigs that the men built all along the front of the house, a bower big enough for the wedding banquet. Next day the men were putting up a dance floor and a bandstand in the yard, while in the house the women were baking Silesian cake, with fillings of poppy seed and cream cheese, and reams and reams of butter cookies.

Finally, for the wedding roast, there was the killing of the pig. The boy watched the animal come out of the dark sty into the sunlit yard, grunting contentedly, to be coaxed and poked by a farmhand to where the butcher was waiting with an ax in hand. And just as the pig was holding still for some feed that had been thrown for a bait, the boy saw the butcher send the blunt side of the ax crashing into its head.

Stunned, the animal went down. It went down on its front feet, looking strangely obeisant for a moment, almost like a dog, before rending the air with terrible squeals. Then it fell on its side. Once more the butcher went to work, this time with a long, thin knife, which he drove with a twisting motion deep into the chest of the animal.

By the time the pig had squealed its last, with a few gurgling sounds, and had been scalded and scraped and gutted, the boy had the premonition that something grave was going to happen. Something from which there would be no escape.

That evening, while waiting for the train, the boy could hear its whistle a good distance down the tracks. At first he hesitated to link the sound with his premonition. But as the train got closer, there was no denying that the whistle sounded just as pitched and just as piercing as the squeals of the dying pig had earlier in the day. It was as if the sounds were part of the premonition.

And so the bride arrived. She was blond and beautiful. Adding to her fragile appearance was a slight lisp in her speech. All around her, amidst a flurry of words of welcome, there were hugs and kisses; and as for the kiss she gave him, he was very much aware that she held his face in her hands very tenderly, before pressing her lips on his.

After the bride's trunks were loaded, the party was ready to go: the pair of parents on the two carriages, the bride and the groom in the Hannomag, and the boy in the rumble seat in back of them. It was during the short ride home, in the open car, that the boy heard her call the Hannomag *Wichtel*. And *Wichtel* it was to be from now on.

That evening the boy played with the toy rooster she had brought him. It was in a wooden cage from where it would come flying out, perched as it was on a swiveling piece of wood, whenever the latch that kept the door shut was pushed down. At the same time the boy kept mimicking the rooster, crying *kikeriki* to himself, as if this was one way to keep the premonition from his mind.

Next day it came back to haunt him. Out in the yard he saw that the spot where the pig had been slaughtered had turned dark. Dark from the blood that had gushed out of the wound and had splashed on the ground before the butcher was able to catch it in a bucket. Besides, the house still smelled sweet and steamy and spicy after the stirred blood had been mixed together with some boiled meats for the blood sausage…

In less than a week *Tante* Henny was dead and buried. She was buried in the graveyard, which as the crow flies, was not all that far from the railroad station. It was the dread *Kopfgrippe* that had killed her. And there was talk that the bride must have caught this terrible head flu during the long train ride from Hamburg to Katscher.

In fact, she fell ill on her wedding-day, just as the picture of the wedding party was about to be taken. One moment it was the photographer who (for the umpteenth time) emerged from under the dark cloth (that was draped over the big camera) to direct a head this way and another head that way, or to compliment the bride on how lovely she looked, or to tell the children, who sat cross-legged in the front row, to hold still, and the next moment it was the bride who fainted. Fainted as if she had been struck by some blow out of the clear blue sky.

In the end, the wedding picture was never taken. The band never played. None of the champagne bottles were uncorked, and the toasts remained unspoken. Instead, the doctor came and rushed into the house and word came back that the bride was still unconscious; that she had a fever, and that the fever was so high that, for cold poultices, they took ice-cold water from the tub in which the bottles of champagne were chilling.

Out in the yard, under the bower of evergreens, some of the guests finally sat down for the wedding banquet. Mostly in silence. Or if they talked, they did so with hushed voices. All the boy could do was stare at the slices of roast pork before him, with generous helpings of red cabbage and applesauce, and with a dumpling the size of his own fist. Then he gazed out into the yard and saw that someone had raked fresh sand over the spot where the animal had died. By now the word *Kopfgrippe* was going round and round, if only in whispers, adding to the boy's premonition that the wedding was turning into a wake. That same night the bride died.

By next summer her picture was on the tombstone. It was a small photograph actually, the kind that the so-called *photomatons* in Germany were turning out by the millions, as the Germans showed themselves only too eager to have their picture taken. All that was required, for a few *pfennig* at a time, was to sit still in the booth, in front of one's own mirror-like image, press the button, and presto, after a faint hum in the cabin, out would come the picture, feeling moist and warm to the touch as if freshly incubated.

The picture on the tombstone was framed in beveled glass, giving it a larger-than-life quality. If nothing else, it was a reminder how beautiful *Tante* Henny had been: the radiant eyes, the delicate face, and the hair falling in waves on her shoulders. At that moment the boy remembered the last time he had seen her. Her hands were folded and her eyes were closed, as she lay, dressed in her wedding gown, in the coffin.

Hers was not the only picture in the graveyard. There were others, older ones, showing the dead in their former lives in poses like mustachioed men sitting in wicker chairs, with the right hand resting on a cane; or women leaning on flower stands. There were also pictures of husbands and wives, sitting side by side in quiet repose.

Some pictures on the tombstones were of the boy's ancestors. Generations of them had been born and had died in this Upper Silesian town near the Czech border. In between they had pursued their lives as best as they could: as shopkeepers, as artisans, a few as farmers, and one as an entrepreneur of sorts.

The stories about them were legend. The entrepreneur had started out in the forwarding business as a wagoner, with an old horse and a rickety old wagon. While making the first delivery in his newly-founded business, the horse had collapsed and had died on the spot.

Then there was the story of a great-grandmother, the one who had given birth to thirteen children. What made her story rather unusual was the way she had delivered some of the children. On the day in question, she would still go out to work in the fields in the morning, together with her husband, and only upon feeling labor pain would she go home where, with the help of the midwife next door, she would deliver the child. And if on that day the sun was still high, she would go back into the fields where her husband and some of the children were still working, to show the newborn.

Year after year, on the loess rich soils of this ancestral farm, they had raised banner crops of wheat and sugar beets. Some of the credit should go to the children. In the spring, they could be found walking the plowed and raked fields with clubs in their hands, striking at clumps of dirt to render the soil "as fine and as porous as flour."

Other stories included a grandfather of die-hard republican convictions. As such he made no bones about his contempt for the *Kaiser* and his cohorts. Nor was he wont to hide his scorn for imperial pomp and parades. On days, then, when, in his words, "the imperials would strut like peacocks across the stage," he would shut all doors in the house and shutter all windows... against the blare of bands and the clap of marching boots that came drifting up from the town square. And if any of his sons, in a fit of boyishness, did so much as flex a knee or sway a hip, punishment was swift. The offender was made to face the wall and repent on bended knees—on the hard floor.

Then there was the other grandfather. He was kind and gentle and, by all accounts, he was the kind of a man who went through life without having an enemy. His children he admonished to do "what was right and fear no one". To which we should add, other than God. The God-fearing man and devout Christian that he was, he never took anything that was not his, and he was never wanting to give freely. Moreover, as the owner of a bakery, he practiced the perseverance of his trade by being the first to rise in the morning and to lay in a fire, and only then to climb the three flights of stairs leading to the attic to waken the help. And by the time the first batch of bread was baking in the oven, he would don his dark suit and go to church. The good man went to church every day in his life, except on the day that he was to die. Here in the cemetery, the boy noticed that there was no picture of his grandfather on the tombstone.

It was Sunday, the first of the boy's vacation with his uncle. For this summer vacation he had gone ahead of his parents. To get there he had travelled from the Polish side of Upper Silesia to the Czech side, or all of the seventy kilometers, on several trains, until in Gross Peterwitz he at last had changed into the small gauge train for the final ride to Katscher.

The boy loved to stay with his uncle. Staying with his uncle meant to live in a world of men and machines. Of sweaty grime. Of men giving orders. Of men swearing. It meant that, as his uncle as master brick maker roamed all over the brickyard, the boy would never be far from his side.

Not that his uncle was in any way doting. For that, his uncle was much too busy, especially on workdays, when machines would break down, automatic dispensers releasing coal dust into the kiln clogged up, or else ran wild. Also, cables would snap, lorries loaded with clay would derail, steam engines driving the machinery to mix the clay would lose pressure. Once pressure was lost, then all the subsequent pressing and cutting of the clay into raw bricks would come to a halt, and so would all steam-driven operations in the brickyard.

These, then, were some of the harsh realities of daily life. But harsher still were some of the injuries the men suffered, of which the harshest were the injuries that maimed for life. There was the man whose body had been cut down to a torso by a lorry, after it had careened out of control. On sunny days the man would sit outside in a wheelchair, and he would wheel himself around in the yard, unless he was busy waving to passers-by or was talking to children.

Then there was the worker whose face had caught the brunt of an explosion, which left it scarred and disfigured. The boy noticed that the color of the man's face never changed. Thus the face always looked as red and as raw as fresh flesh, while the eyes, awash in tears, had the saddest of all expressions.

Then there were workers whose hands had been mangled or whose fingers had been cut off. And even the boy's uncle had not escaped the harsh reality of the brickyard. A machine had wrenched off part of the right arm. As a result, he wore a prosthesis from the stump of the lower arm on down, where, for a hand, the prosthesis had a hook. Or was it a claw? The boy could never make up his mind between the two, except that by now the artificial arm had begun to exert a strange fixation on him.

In fact, he was aware of nothing so much about his uncle as the hand. How it hooked into something. How it clawed at something. How it held an object in place. How it pushed things to the side. And how, with the help of a special mechanism at the end of the lever, it shifted gears in the Hannomag.

In the end, though, it was not even so much how the hand looked and what the hand was able to do that mattered, but something else. It was something that was new and different.

This summer the boy had begun to wonder how his uncle would give the Nazi salute. Would he, in shouting *Heil* Hitler, raise the right arm? Raise the arm that for a prosthesis had a stump and for a hand had a hook or, for that matter, had a claw?

Or would his uncle raise the left arm? And bare his good hand for the Nazi salute. What we should remember was that by now, in the summer of '34, all other salutes in Nazi Germany had become suspect. Thus the Lord's greeting was suspect, so was a simple *Guten Morgen,* or *Guten Tag,* or *Guten Abend.*

Shouting *Heil* and raising the right arm had become, in public at least, the salute of the Third *Reich*.

These were not just some idle ruminations of a ten-year-old. For one thing, there was that recent newspaper clipping, complete with a picture, which Uncle Max had sent to the boy's parents. The picture showed his uncle with one of the venerable generals of the World War. Indeed, it showed him saluting General von Mackensen at a gathering of Katscher war veterans. And in that military salute the right hand with the piece of metal was shown to come right up to the temple and touch it. And again, the boy was not sure whether to think of the piece of metal as a hook or as a claw.

The boy also remembered his mother's reaction: "What if Mack, the general, thinks that Max, the soldier, has lost that arm in battle?" That's what the boy's mother had said to father. "Shed blood for the fatherland." And with the same wry expression she related how her brother had spent the entire war at some supply depot far from the front, and how the family had sent all those *Fresspakete* containing whole sides of bacon and all those rings of smoked sausage from at least a dozen butchered pigs to Max… to "lubricate" his safe post.

The same picture was to produce yet another kind of rumination, again between the boy's parents. It was in the form of a question, a question that could not but sound alarming. At least as uttered between the boy's parents it sounded alarming. The question was whether Max had become a Nazi. For proof there was in the lapel of the dark suit the latter was wearing the image of something like a badge, like a Nazi party badge. But because of the profile view of the badge in the picture, the image was badly distorted and quite blurred, and the question had remained moot.

Not so for the boy. Not on this Sunday anyway. He looked at the dark suit his uncle had on and what he saw was that there was no Nazi party badge on the lapel. None whatsoever. Unless, of course, his uncle was wearing a different suit than the one he had worn in the picture. Or unless his uncle made it a custom to display the party badge on certain occasions only… and the badge was tucked away in the breast pocket. Be that as it may, because of his parents the boy liked to think that Uncle Max was not a Nazi.

They were leaving the graveyard. The boy and his uncle had gone there after church to visit the graves. It was noon now, and the day was turning stale with heat. Suddenly there was the voice of his uncle: "How would you like to see the *Führer?*" In the stillness of the graveyard, the words sounded strange. They were like a false echo to the memories of the dead.

Presently his uncle continued that the *Führer* was coming to Breslau… for the National Choir Festival.

By the time they were in the car, and by the time his uncle had tapped the steering wheel of *Wichtel* with the metal-tipped hand, in a kind of drum-like roll, Breslau and the *Führer* were a cinch. That's how his uncle put it. Then the latter suggested that (for the trip later in the week) they drive across the border to fill up on gas. "It's cheaper over there," his uncle said. "Besides," he continued, "they have *Pilsen*... and from *Amerika* they have *Coca Cola.*"

For the boy it was the first time into a foreign country. He did not quite know what to expect. Several things, though, crossed his mind: things like interrogations, searches, and the likelihood of coming face to face with border guards with dogs. But if the boy had any fear, he did not show it. Instead, he asked whether he could ride in the rumble seat. From there he watched his uncle shift gears, as the round piece of the artificial hand would slip over the knob at the end of the lever with a click, to make the short moves from one gear into the next. Meanwhile, the wind was taking his breath away and his eyes began to water; finally, from what he had heard, the border was not all that far away.

And it wasn't. It came into view with flags and turnpikes and guardhouses, but not much else; and as far as he could see, there was no one around. Neither was there any sign of traffic. The flags were hanging limp from the poles, two on the German side of the border and one on the Czech side; and the guardhouses, at either end of the turnpikes, looked like empty boxes. It was strange. The border looked like a deserted stage.

However, they were across before he knew it. What happened was that his uncle in his *Wichtel* was known to the guards on both sides of the border. What the guards also must have known was his uncle's weakness for *Pilsen* beer, especially on hot and humid days. For the words *Pilsen* and *Durst* was all that was said good-naturedly between his uncle and the German border guard... to be repeated in Czech over on the other side. And with that they continued to Troppau.

In some ways Troppau was like Katscher: from the kind of villas that kept their distance from the street by standing deep and discreet in well-tended gardens to the blocks of houses with slate roofs and street level shops. And as for the streets, after mingling with each other, they all ended at the four corners in the town square.

It was in the town square, in the beer garden of a restaurant, where they spent the afternoon and evening. Over *Pilsen* beer and *Coca Cola,* to say nothing of *bratwurst* with *sauerkraut* and bread. For the boy, it was his first taste of *Coca Cola.* It tasted rich and delicious and it left him pleasantly dizzy.

There were other impressions. Czechs of all ages were sitting at tables, eating and drinking. They made for a lively crowd. Also, there was an orchestra that was playing dance music. Couples were dancing. And then there was the woman his uncle was dancing with.

Dancing and dancing. And the boy's eyes never strayed far from the woman's body on which his uncle's hand would come to rest. It was the hand about which he wasn't sure whether it was a hook or a claw. Fast dances would see the hand on the woman's waist. But with languorous tangos, as with all slow dances, the hand would start coming down on the woman's shapely body with a movement that was about as caressing as it was cloying.

The boy never found out how well his uncle and the woman knew each other. Not even whether they knew each other before they started dancing together. And not only dancing. Once, in the middle of a dance, they linked arms and left and did not return for some time; and all the boy could think of was that they must have taken *Wichtel* to fill up on gas, for the drive to Breslau.

They were back in time for one last round of dances. For this round of sentimental melodies and slow rhythms, the string of lights in the beer garden was getting dimmer and dimmer as the orchestra played softer and softer, and finally, as if on a cue, the lights went out and the violins were left playing the last of the music.

By the time the lights came back on, his uncle was alone and the woman, to the relief of the boy, was gone. Later the boy was told that she had left two bars of chocolate for him. "One for the drive home, and one for the trip to Breslau," his uncle said.

By next weekend, they were on their way to Breslau, in perfect weather. "*Führer* weather," his uncle kept saying while the right hand with the piece of metal was tapping the steering wheel or was making sweeping gestures. What his uncle was saying stirred new suspicions. To suggest that someone other than the Good Lord was the bringer of bright sunshine and blue skies was like mouthing a sin. To the boy it was. Besides, there were his parents who never used the name *Führer*. With them it was always "*dieser* Hitler," or "*dieser Mann.*" And once more the boy was faced with the question whether his uncle was not, after all, a Nazi.

Breslau was like an anthill. The city was swarming with people. Flags flapped in the wind. Sound trucks blared martial music. The *SA* was out in force. So were the police. Now it was only a question, where to find a place from which to see the *Führer?* For some reason his uncle did not inquire with the *SA* or the police. Instead his uncle decided to fall in with a group of Breslauers who seemed to know their way… until they all ended up on a wide sidewalk facing a boulevard… where people were standing shoulder to shoulder… ten or more deep… waiting for the *Führer* to drive by… in the open Mercedes-Benz touring car… from right to left… or from the airport to the *Kongresshalle.*

The boy felt dwarfed in the crowd. People were towering above him, were standing on their toes, were craning and stretching their necks, and seemed to be seething with expectations.

It started as if on command. Suddenly, at the far end of the boulevard, thousands of shouts went up *Heil… Heil… Heil.* And from there the shouts travelled like wildfire… down the boulevard, sparking new outbursts of *Heil… Heil… Heil…* in frenzy after frenzy, until everything was one continuous roar.

For the boy it was now or never. To judge by the roar, the Mercedes-Benz must be passing by this moment. And still he had not seen anything, even though he had done everything to catch at least a glimpse, from standing on his toes to craning and stretching his neck.

In desperation he looked at his uncle. What he saw changed the world for him at that moment. His uncle was shouting *Heil* again and again, his right arm he had thrust forward in the Nazi salute, and in the lapel of his coat he wore the Nazi party badge.

Afraid that their eyes might meet, the boy looked away. He looked in the direction in which all the arms in the crowd were pointing. By now they were pointing to the left. And it was at that moment that, through an opening in the crowd, he saw the figure of "that man" pass through the piece of metal, be it hook or claw, like an apparition. And was gone. And all the figure did was to stand in the car and raise the right hand.

That was all there was to it. To the boy it was.

5

OF FLAGS AND BOOKS

There was no faster way to come to the attention of the Nazis and, through them, to the attention of the *GESTAPO* than not flying the *swastika* flag on certain days.

Such days were the *Führer's* birthday, the 1st of May, and the Nuremberg Party Day, to say nothing of Third *Reich* plebiscites when the whole nation was asked—after the fact—to give its approval to some of Hitler's more adventurous moves. Not to fly the flag and not to vote in a plebiscite, or even worse, to cast a NO vote on a ballot specially marked for voters known to have been one-time communists, socialists, or liberals, spelled trouble. Moreover, for anyone daring enough to be critical of the Nazis, the answer was nothing less than the concentration camp. *Ins Kozentrationslager verschwinden* (to disappear into a concentration camp) became dread words in Germany. In the vocabulary of evil, the names of Buchenwald, Belsen-Belsen, and Dachau became dread household words. At a minimum, they imposed on the average citizen of the Third *Reich* three requirements: to keep the mouth shut, to use the "*Heil* Hitler" salute in public, and to fly the *swastika* flag.

Until Hitler came to power, there were no Nazis in the village. For the one hundred or so coal miners and their families, for the handful of one-horse peasants who hauled coal on the side, for the two innkeepers, for the grocer, for the butcher, and for the baker there was no earthly reason why any one of them should have joined the Nazi movement. In fact, for these *Wasserpollacken,* as the people of Polish descent were known in Upper Silesia, to embrace Nazism was about as remote as, say, for a black American to sidle up to the Ku Klux Klan. And as for the four teachers in the village, all of German descent, two were members of the Catholic Center Party and two were known to favor the German National Party. Among the latter was the boy's father.

It was the *swastika* flag that was to cause something like a disagreement between the boy's parents. As arguments in such disagreements go, they were not all that heated. Actually, they were rather subdued. But in arguing the question whether to get a *swastika* flag, now that the Nazis were in power, so that on flag days it could be flown from the house in which the family lived, the boy noticed that his parents called each other by their first names. Such use of first names was the exception to the affectionate *Mama* and *Papa* with which his parents ordinarily addressed each other.

"Alfons," his mother would say to his father, "we cannot be too careful with the Nazis… they frighten me." And what she had to say about the flag was this: "Hanging a dumb flag out of the window… is a small price to pay for secure days and for nights free of worry."

Demurring, his father would reply, "Martha, believe me, the Nazis are mere *Eintagsfliegen* (one-day flies)." And for good measure he added such proverbial afterthoughts as "no soup is ever eaten as hot as it is cooked," and "no tree has ever grown into heaven."

Mother was quick to answer with her own brand of proverbial certainties. "Foresight is better than hindsight," was one. "One must howl with the wolves," was another.

The boy kept wondering about the proverbs, as they seemed to say first one thing and then another... as Mama's argument for the flag and Papa's argument against the flag were equally convincing. At second thought, though, the whole exercise of proverbial wisdom was baffling. What if both arguments were wrong? What if the answer to some arguments was that there was not always a good answer, as the following proverb seemed to suggest: *Man weiss nie im Leben, wie es kommt, und dann kommt es im Leben immer anders, als man denkt.* (In life one never knows what will happen, and when it happens, it happens differently than one thinks.) That proverb, incidentally, was a favorite of both of his parents, even though in this case it went unused.

Other disagreements between his parents had either been settled quickly in one way or another, or had gone away in their own good time. Thus, with the first berries in the garden, with the strawberries and the currants and the gooseberries, it was always the same: Papa was all for eating them, right then and there, while Mama was already thinking about conserving them for the winter. The same was true for the last of the berries, except that by then maternal foresight and vigilance had already produced rows and rows of glass conserves, as rich in color as a painter's palette and as abundant in fruit as a cornucopia.

Or speaking of another disagreement, however slight, Mama would surprise Papa feeding honey to ants in the garden (to observe their habits), while the weeds went unpulled; and so Mama would say to Papa that he was not at all practical, which prompted Papa to say to Mama that she was not at all poetic since ants to her were nothing but a pest.

Or take cobwebs. To Papa they were a thing of beauty, plain and simple. What was not so plain and not so simple, at least not to the boy, were father's lyrical outpourings about cobwebs, seeing in them something like the apotheosis of the divine order, the quintessence of all patterns, the trap to end all traps. And as if to prove the last point he would wait—often for a long time—until a fly or some other flying insect would end up in the web.

In the meantime weeds again went unpulled and caterpillars were left to ravage berry bushes and cabbage plants—and while Mama, as in the case with the ants, was not completely opposed to Papa's ways, she did make it clear that between his poetic vein and her practical side she stood for something like a mixture of the two. "Can't you, Alfons," she would say, "pick a few weeds and a few caterpillars on the side while watching your beloved creatures?" The boy meanwhile tried to think of a proverb that would do justice to both the practical side of his mother and the poetic vein of his father - and could not come up with any.

As it turned out, the Nazis in no time changed the country into a dictatorship. The word for the change was *"Gleichschaltung"* (political coordination). It was the most innocuous word for the most vicious assault on a democracy ever. It busted the unions, bashed the parties, abrogated all civil rights, in fact it left the democratic constitution of the Weimar Republic a dead letter. In its place the Nazis put up their version of a totalitarian state, it erected the *Führer-State. Führer befiehl, wir folgen Dir* - or charging the *Führer* with leading them and following him were to become the slogan, if not the driving force, in Nazi Germany. Everything else was suspect and had to go.

The first villager to disappear into a concentration camp was a young miner, known to have been a communist. It was rumored that he was seized at night by the *GESTAPO* while returning home from work and that he was whisked away. And only after days of anxious waiting was his mother informed that her son "had been taken into a *Konzentrationslager* for his own protection."

His name was Josef. Father remarked about him that he had been the best player of *Schlagball* (a German version of baseball) he had ever seen, adding darkly that something must have gotten into the young man. What it was, why Josef disappeared into a *KZ,* was never explained; except that the village was abuzz with talk that some daredevil of a miner had rigged up, under cover of night, the red flag on the tower of the mine. There the flag with the hammer and sickle was discovered in the morning.

Father remained adamant about the *swastika*. As a substitute he suggested they get the black-white-red flag of Germany. But to mother that flag was about as useful as hanging out a washcloth, adding: "That was Weimar, and the Weimar Republic is *kaputt."* To which father replied, "Well, there is still President Hindenburg and the *Wehrmacht."* It was not until after two more events had taken place that father relented.

One was the visit of the county leader of the Nazi Party in the village, where as *Kreisleiter* he was only known by his last name; and that name, to the glee of not a few, was Jewish. Absalon [sic] came straight out of the Old Testament. It was also said that Absalon looked and acted like Göring, big and rotund and swashbuckling.

Kreisleiter Absalon and his cohorts in their *SA* uniforms of brown shirts, brown jodhpurs, chinstraps, shoulder straps, leather belts, and leather boots arrived in two open Mercedes-Benz cars. With the black cars trailing, they walked down the village road with the sureness of fighting cocks. And whenever they encountered someone on the road, or saw someone in the garden, they raised their right arm and shouted *"Heil* Hitler." As uniformed Nazis they looked every inch the brawlers of earlier street fights. Now they had come to show that the road in this village, like all roads and streets in Germany, belonged to them. They had come to intimidate the village.

And some people in the village began to tote the new line. The burgomaster, a former *Sozi* (social democrat), was one of them. He joined the Nazi party in a hurry and began to wear the party pin from one day to the next. What the *Bürgermeister* also did was to show his new colors by flying a big *swastika* flag on all possible occasions from his house and to line up *swastika* paper flags in each of the street-side windows. There they would remain until bleached white from the sun, before being replaced.

The march of the Nazis down the village road and the change of the *Bürgermeister* into a "beefsteak" Nazi (brown on the outside and red on the inside), as such political converts were called, eventually ended the argument between his parents. Father relented. They were going to have a flag, a small one, and Mama would sew it and it would hang, not from the kitchen window, but from one of the small windows in the pantry.

When finished, the flag was in some ways different from the official one. The official *swastika* flag was blood red in color; it had a circle of white in the center and in that center, equal in parts and in spaces between the black and the white configurations, stood the *swastika*. It stood poised at an angle of 45 degrees.

Mama had bought the material for the flag as "remnants" at a store in Beuthen. The red cloth turned out a shade too dark, being wine-red, in fact; also, for lack of two large pieces of red material for either side of the flag, several pieces of red material had to be patched and sewn together; and as for the *swastika*, with its double zig-zag-zig geometrics, it ended up quite thin and small under Mama's scissors, besides falling backward on one side and forward on the other. And yet for all the imperfections there remained the consolation that the material had not cost all that much, and that in the small pantry window, under the low overhang, the flag would not be all that conspicuous. What the boy also noticed was that Mama for once did not mention the store in Beuthen where she had bought the "remnants." And Papa, not wanting to hear perhaps that in all likelihood the remnants for the Nazi flag had been bought in a Jewish store, did not ask.

Sticking the flag into a bucket full of rocks was the boy's idea of holding its pole in place inside the pantry and of letting its cloth hang from the small window. And so from the spring of 1933 until he left for the army in the summer of 1942, he was to wrestle with the *swastika* flag on flag days by jamming it into the bucket full of rocks and by securing it with wire and nails. And once the war was on and plebiscites became a thing of the past, the number of flag days in the embattled Third *Reich* became fewer and fewer anyway.

As soon as the *Kreisleiter* and the *SA* men showed up in the village a second time, they went straight across the village meadow to the soccer field. On that warm and sunny Saturday afternoon they found village life at its best: young mothers showing off their newborn, the old coming out with a grandchild or two, the kibitzers standing behind the goal, and the boys, under the watchful eyes of the girls, emulating the ways of the men in the game of soccer. And soccer was king: in the heat of playing, as the men dribbled with the ball and sent the ball flying toward the goalie with powerful kicks, and as the boys scrambled after every ball that went wide, in return for the privilege of kicking the big ball back to the big players... there was no one, at least not among the players, who saw the Nazis. They had come out of nowhere. Suddenly they were standing in the middle of the field, around the center spot, where ordinarily the games were kicked off.

What the men saw was that *Kreisleite* Absalon was making sweeping movements with his arms, round and round, while turning on his heels, only to step back and point at the center spot. In fact, the *Kreisleiter* kept stepping back and forth several times while making stabbing gestures at the center spot, as if driving home a point. In response, the brown-shirts with their billed caps nodded in agreement, clicking their heels.

The players had stopped scrimmaging. Instead they kicked 11-meter penalty kicks. It gave them time to watch the Nazis, furtively and stealthily, as if as defenders of the home turf they were watching some invaders. And when at last the Nazis started to leave the soccer field, along the sideline, to return to the two Mercedes-Benz cars out on the road, the players feigned indifference. Then as before, only louder now, they shouted words of encouragement to each other with each kick—in a watered down dialect of the Polish language, in what was known as *Wasserpolnisch*. And there could be no doubt that the Nazis must have been aware of the gesture of defiance, namely that the men were not speaking German. Also, as the Nazis returned to their cars, there was no one on their side of the village meadow: not one woman with babe in arms, not one of the girlfriends of the local soccer stars, not one kibitzer, not one elderly man or woman with grandchild in hand. They had all drifted over to the other side of the meadow.

After the big cars with the Nazi standard on the right fender had driven off in the direction of the *chaussee*, there was a great deal of guesswork and some head shaking as to what all the posturing and gesturing had been about. In the hissing and airy sounds of *Wasserpolnisch,* a language the boy understood fairly well, he could hear remarks by the players that on that center spot "they" (the Nazis) would put up a pole and hang the flag ... "they" would put up a plaque for the *Märzgefallene* (a sarcastic reference to all those "March Dead" among the Nazis who, as recent converts, belatedly claimed to have suffered persecution during the years of struggle)... "they" would put up a loudspeaker for all the new loudmouths. And what did the boy think? Hearing the men talk the way they did gave him a feeling that, come what may, these men would never change all that much.

It was not until the following week, again on a Saturday afternoon, that the Nazis showed what they were up to: they had come to burn books.

It began during the small hours of the afternoon. Three trucks roared into the village. Two went straight to the soccer field while one, carrying storm troopers, drove down the village road, slowly and haltingly as if stalking wild game. Two storm troopers straddled the cabin, the rest stood on the open truck, and whenever the truck stopped, one of the storm troopers would shout through a megaphone such messages as "Germany has awakened… let the flames cleanse German literature… the day of reckoning is at hand ... this afternoon… on the sports field."

Just where a week earlier the *Kreisleiter* had made his stabbing motions, they built the pyre. From the back of one the trucks they removed dry sprigs to pile them high over the center spot, then heaped split wood on top. Finally they placed wooden props (the kind that were used to shore up shafts and galleries in the mines) all around. When done, the pyre looked like a tepee, at least to the boy it did.

The books came next. They were on the second truck. By now there were more boys on the scene. And in their eagerness for a fire and with words of encouragement from the storm troopers, the boys began to reach for armfuls of books right off the edge of the truck, to where the boots of two storm troopers kept kicking and shoving them. And as the boys put the books on the ground, in a circle round the pyre, they made sure that each book came to lie face up. That's what the leader of the storm troopers had told them. In the end, there were two circles of books of all sizes and of all colors going round the pyre, waiting to be burned.

Off to the side, at the far end of the soccer field, a group of villagers had been gathering. They were mostly men. The boy could see that his father was among them. For a moment he felt like running to him. But since none of the other boys did, even though the fathers of some were also there, he held back. He kept telling himself reassuringly that he had done his chores on that Saturday, chores like laying in a fire in the kitchen stove in the morning and bringing up more coal, in addition to taking up the rug and the runners for a cleaning. Then, after giving the rug and the runners a thorough beating, down in the yard, his mother had said that he could "play" for a while. Shortly thereafter the trucks had arrived.

The fire that was about to be lit was not the only one in Germany. During that first spring and summer of Nazi rule there were hundreds and hundreds of such fires lit all over Germany, all lit by the Nazis, all lit to burn books. It was the worst outbreak of book burning ever, in the land of Gutenberg no less. Thrown into the fires were the works of writers, dead or alive, who had failed the Nazi test on grounds of race and ideology. Such writers were called a battery of names, from "corrosive" to "subversive" to "poisonous." Among the writers were some of the best in the German language. Thomas and Heinrich Mann were among them, so were Bertolt Brecht, Kurt Tucholsky, Sigmund Freud, Arnold Zweig, Franz Kafka, and Heinrich Heine. In Jack London and Upton Sinclair, the list included two Americans. The pyromaniacs' favorite was *All Quiet On The Western Front* by Remarque. So was *Under Fire,* the other anti-war book, by the Frenchman Barbusse.

Torches set the tinder on fire. Soon the pyre was a mass of flames. For the storm troopers it was the moment to reach for the books, to part their covers, to rip the books apart if at all possible, and to let go. That way the books tumbled and fluttered into the fire like wounded birds. That way they burned better.

Once again the boys pressed forward to finish what the storm troopers had started. It may be tempting to ask what it was that triggered the frenzy of the next few minutes. What set loose the wanton destruction? What aroused, under the cajoling of the Nazis, the zeal with which the boys kept throwing and throwing books into the fire?

All that can be said is that, once started, the frenzy kept feeding on itself. Thus book after book, whole flurries of books sailed into the fire, stirring up showers of sparks and scattering aloft clouds of charred paper. And as more books landed in the cauldron of burning and glowing and smoldering books, a column of black smoke rose high into the sky. Drifting in front of the sun, it caused the day to turn dark.

They were down to the last books in no time. For the finale, the storm troopers made the boys take turns for one last throw. In his hands he held a book of poetry. Golden letters graced its dark blue cover. The book looked like the one he had seen at home. Suddenly he was seized by a feeling of guilt. He could not bring himself to look in the direction where he had last seen his father. Now it was his turn to throw. And as the book sailed into the flames, he saw it bounce around several times, pages flipping, before coming to rest. Then, lying still, it buckled and heaved as if coming to life, and at last it turned crimson with flame.

He would always remember the moment: when he looked again for his father, he was gone. It was the first time in his life that his father had left him, without so much as a word or a wave. He ran home. There he found him sitting at the kitchen table, reading a book. Before him on the table were more books. Mother sat at her favorite place at the kitchen stove, looking forlorn. Neither spoke a word.

He only knew that the silence was worse than being scolded... than being told that he should not have done what he did... than being taken to task for burning books... than being queried why he had not come to his father when he saw him... than being reprimanded for letting himself be used... than being made to answer what had gotten into him, what had possessed him... than being told to say he was sorry.

By now he was aware of the connection between the book his father was reading and the fire. Between the books on the table and the fire. Between the books his father was keeping in several bookcases in the attic, to which they would sometimes go to read, and the fire. Overcome with shame, he felt a wave of heat surge through his body - as if he himself was on fire.

He was also aware of other things that had been happening lately in the village. In class his teacher would sometimes spend whole periods pacing back and forth from one side of the classroom with the cane on the wall to the other side with the large windows, gesturing and talking to himself while the class sat in silence. Sat in rapt silence since even the slightest noise or the slightest movement would bring upon the offender, boy or girl, the fury of the cane. If there was one word that was driving the murmured sounds of *Herr Lehrer* Laake forward, driving them forward as if by the cracks of a whip, it was the word "Nazis." And sometimes the word "*verdammte*" (damn) could also be heard. Among the third graders there was little doubt about the connection between the two words.

After damning the Nazis, it always happened that their *Herr Lehrer* would get hold of himself. He would suddenly stop, wipe his glasses, check the time on his pocket watch and before going on with his ranting, or return to teaching, or before dismissing the class, whichever came first, he would turn to the class and he would say, with an air of indignation, "*Wenn das nur unser Führer wüsste!* (If only our *Führer* would know that.") And for the sake of posterity, we should know that the Nazis never caught on with the feigned indignation of this staunch Catholic Centrist.

In a way, the boy did. The boy knew that the indignation was feigned, if only because of what he had overheard. Although his parents were always cautious with their remarks, especially in his presence, he did get the idea: his parents feared for his teacher, feared that his rantings would land him in a KZ, feared for his young wife and the two little girls. In fact, there were times when his parents expected the GESTAPO to show up at his door any day or (what was more likely) any night to take him away. As it turned out, the GESTAPO never laid a hand on him. What may have saved the ardent Centrist was something that was coming into vogue in Nazi Germany: it was the practice, the trick, to voice one's indignation over excesses of the Nazis in the name of the *Führer*. To pretend, as the boy's father put it, to be more *führerisch* than the *Führer* himself; or, to use a proverb of long standing, to be "*päpstlicher als der Papst* (to be more papal than the pope himself.")

Which brings us to the church. Why its *Herr Pfarrer* (Monsignor) decided to keep the war veterans' flag out of the church was anybody's guess. What had happened was that on that Sunday the war veterans were marching once again to the church, led by the flag and by the marching band of two drummers and four fifers. And like the first time when the war veterans of the village had marched out to the church for the consecration of the flag, everything was going off with parade-ground precision: from the presentation of the flag over the roll of the drums to the lively march tunes of the fifes ... until they reached the church cemetery. There the veterans were met by the chaplain who told them that they would not be able to bring the flag into the church and that, moreover, the drums and the fifes would also have to stay behind. And when the boy's father as commander of the *Kriegerverein* reminded the chaplain that last time, following the consecration of the flag on the church steps, they were allowed to bring the flag into the narthex, the chaplain replied that he was merely conveying the wish of the *Herr Pfarrer*.

That Sunday the boy musicians and the veterans of the three-man flag detail remained at the church gate. There was no way they were going to go to church and leave their instruments and the flag behind, not even if one of the veterans was to stay behind as watchman. Somehow they were all in this together, except for the drum major who with his baton had marched right past the man of the cloth. And so, with their drums and their fifes and the flag the men and the boys settled down at the gate to await the end of the service.

It was during mass on that Sunday that the priest prayed for the *Führer*. Not that the men and for that matter the boys had been aware of the inclusion of Adolf Hitler in the prayer. For that they were too far away from the church. But after being denied to bring the flag into church, if only into the narthex, the sense for danger had been aroused in these men. That sense for danger was never far from these war veterans and coal miners.

As the sounds of the organ and as the Latin chants in their sharp modulations were rising in the sanctuary, to reach the outside through open windows, the men talked about dangers they had faced. Dangers they had faced in the last war and in the mine. And they talked about how to meet these dangers. For the flag carrier the best answers for the worst dangers in war and in peace were, as he put it, an empty helmet, an empty stomach, and a full birdcage. Each amounted to this:

An empty helmet, raised on a bayonet, ever so cautiously above the parapet, so as to imitate a soldier about to peer into no-mans land, is the quickest way to find out whether enemy sharpshooters are lurking on the other side.

An empty stomach during an attack on enemy lines is the only chance a soldier has to survive a bullet in the guts.

A full cage (with a canary as it turned out) is the best insurance against methane gas in the mine.

The men talked in German. No doubt it was due to the fact that they had experienced the war in the Kaiser's imperial army. They fell silent during the consecration of the host, when they bared their heads and made the sign of the cross in response to the bell. It rang three times. And after hearing the thin sound of the bell the boy kept wondering whether that bell, ringing for the consecration of the host, and whether the bell announcing the death of a villager, were one and the same.

They marched home that Sunday without fanfare. The men knew that with the church denying them to bring the flag inside, there would henceforth be no other place to march to. And if there was any hope that the *Herr Pfarrer* might reverse himself, that hope was dashed when the men found out that the congregation had prayed for the *Führer*. In fact, all churches on that Sunday had started to include the *Führer* in their prayer. All in return for the Vatican's signing of the Concordat with Nazi Germany. And in that respect nothing changed until the end of the Third *Reich*.

On that Sunday the flag was returned to its customary place in the bedroom of the boy's parents. There it was to stand, year after year, never to be taken out again. A cover, looking like a hood over the head of a man condemned to death, kept the flag's brocade with the eagle under shrouds. And the drums and the fifes? They were to fall silent.

There were a few times when the boy felt like removing the hood from the flag, if only to see whether the eagle still looked as fierce as ever. But he never did.

6
ORANGES IN BROWN PAPER BAGS

Throughout the night of November 9, 1938, and the next day, repression of the Jews in Nazi Germany turned into violence. The *Kristallnacht*, or Crystal Night, gave but the first hint of the holocaust that lay ahead.

From where he was sitting, in a class of fourteen-year-old German high school students, he could see a column of smoke over downtown Beuthen. The column rose straight into the sky, where it stood like some exclamation mark before drifting off in the direction of the Polish border.

A short time into Latin, the boy began wondering why the column kept doing such strange things as blowing puffs, even balls, of black smoke one moment and trails of gray smoke the next. The former would billow round and round some imaginary centers, one skyward journey after another.

The boy wasn't at all sure what to think. If there was one point beyond which his mind was reluctant to go, it was whether the fire in downtown Beuthen had anything to do with the absence of the Jewish students. In fact, in his class five were absent, and Pinschover, with whom he shared the desk, was one. But at stake was something more than just absences.

To watch the column—with sly glances over the shoulder—took some caution. It was, however, not the kind of caution necessary when cheating on an exam. In that case the eyes had to be especially furtive in scanning the paper of his deskmate. Or the hand had to move ever so cautiously toward the Faber pencil box with the translations or the formulas squeezed inside. With the column of smoke he merely had to turn his head sideways, about half way over his left shoulder, in order to see it in the window.

Earlier, on the way from the depot to school, he had seen several trucks with *SA* troopers. The trucks, on which the men were standing, were waved through the intersection by a policeman with gestures betraying great urgency. Each truck carried about two dozen storm troopers. Although the men were holding on to the cage-like framework of the trucks, from which the tarpaulins had been rolled back, they swayed back and forth, like marionettes, each time the motors shifted into higher gear, as the trucks roared through the intersection. They were headed for downtown Beuthen.

Morning classes that day went from Latin to math, and from English to history, with recesses between classes. The class in German was not until after noon. On that November morning Pinschover did not show up, nor did any of the other Jewish students at the *Horst Wessel Realgymnasium*. Named after a pimp turned hero by Nazi propaganda, the school was one of three public high schools for boys in the city. That the absence of the Jewish students, the rush of the *SA*, and the antics of the smoke swirling and merely drifting into the dull sky were somehow related could no longer be doubted. But how, no one seemed to know.

Or pretended not to know. The teachers (the *Studienassessoren, Studienraete*, even the *Oberstudienrat*) kept mum and said not a word on that day outside their disciplines. Not that such a word unrelated to Caesar could be expected from the Latin teacher, who in his dealings with students was as impersonal as he was a man marked in his physical appearance. A wooden leg from the hip down, which gave his walk a hump at once slightly pivoting and rather creaky, was one legacy of the war in this class. Another reminder of the W*eltkrieg* was the scarred face of the math teacher. A large eye-patch, almost half the size of a mask, barely covered the worst of mutilations. It might be added that the math explanations of the disfigured man had something of the ruminations of an embittered soul in them. And this day was no exception. Even the most engaging of the teachers, the English teacher, lapsed into droneful soliloquies about the use of "to do." Boredom was creeping into the class, rumors and wild talk during recesses notwithstanding. By the fourth hour the *Oberstudienrat*, who seldom missed a chance to crunch his knuckles and to let chalk-dust fly in his "drum and trumpet" approach to history, did something the class had never seen him do before: the portly man sat at his raised desk all hour long and stared out the window.

By now the fire in downtown Beuthen had been burning for all those hours of Latin, math, English and now history, filling the non-descript sky alternately with gray and black smoke, as if being stirred into life, over and over again. The boy had seen fires before. No fire had ever burned like this one. The worst, an inferno of flames, cinders, and smoke had reduced a flour-mill of several stories into a burnt-out shell entirely too quickly, or so he thought. And however much his ears had retained the booming sounds of heavy mill machinery crashing through fire-ravaged floors, until there were no more, and however sharp the visions of a sea of leaping flames were before his eyes, the mill fire was in the moribund nature of things not without logic. Even the fires he and his friends had been setting year after year playfully in the fields surrounding the village, using dry potato stalks as fuel, had a close kinship with, say, rules of combustion—to say nothing of roasting potatoes in beds of hot ashes. This fire in downtown Beuthen was entirely different, if only because it made no sense whatsoever.

He thought of Pinschover. They had been deskmates for over three years by now. How the son of a Jewish shopkeeper and the son of a German village teacher came to share the same desk had actually been decided during the first few minutes of school over three years ago. What had happened was that the classroom teacher seated the ten-year-old freshmen-*sextaner* in the order in which they arrived. And Pinschover, the son of a Jewish shopkeeper in fresh fruit in the city, and he, the son of a German schoolteacher in a village happened to enter the classroom, which was smelly from freshly waxed floors, at the same time. The two were still sharing desks during the *Quinta* or the second year, the *Quarta* or the third year and now the fifth month of the

Untertertia. It was almost mid-November 1938.

Pinschover, moreover, seemed in favor of the arrangement that had kept the two together, even though for the other four Jewish students the days of sitting with a German classmate were long past. Times were changing. Schoolmates began to jeer Jewish students. Some teachers showed their racist ideas in such ways as ignoring the latter completely. Sharing the desk with a Jew, year after year, in the *Horst Wessel Realgymnasium* was bound to have an effect on a fourteen-year-old German boy from the village.

If he cared about anyone else among the Jewish students, it was Behrend From the start the latter had been class primus in every subject, except art and sports where he was as untalented as he was awkward. Frankly, the class rationalized Behrend's superior performance with sweat, pure and simple. However, in math, Behrend simply awed everybody. With only minutes into new and unfamiliar areas, his right arm would go up and stay there, with left-hand support in an age-old expression of mastery and boredom, until the teacher nodded permission to the *Wunderkind* to work the problem on the blackboard. It was always done with the greatest of ease, almost as if in his veins flowed the blood of Leibniz and Einstein.

Mid-way during the fourth hour, while the history teacher kept staring out of the window, right at the column of smoke, the boy was beginning to feel a sense of loneliness. Without Behrend, in front of him, who would have shielded him from the strange stare of the teacher in whose glasses the window was sharply reflected, and without Pinschover to his right, he felt as if everything in class—the creaks of the prosthesis, the soliloquies, the stares, the boredom—had been heading his way all morning long, for a rendezvous he did not seek.

Pinschover was thin and of gangling growth. His head tended to be raised slightly to the side, as if trying to smell something. And Pinschover almost always smiled. It was a smile that flickered in his eyes like a delicate flame. Perhaps in reality it was only a defense of sorts against Jew-baiting Germans. The two boys had come to an agreement that, for an orange a day, the one would protect the other. For the boy from the village, where oranges were a Christmas rarity, the daily orange, which came in a brown paper bag, was precious beyond description. And it should be noted that no one ever laid hands on Pinschover

As his hope for the orange was dwindling, his sense of loneliness was aggravated by a longing for Pinschover It was a longing borne out of all those torments and triumphs of school life, when words of consolation and admiration are expressed for bad grades and for good grades, homework is copied at the last moment, drills are done from word lists in Latin and English, in the give-and-take normal for deskmates.

His memories were adrift now. Uneasily and painfully he recalled a recent day when the religion teacher had caught him with *Der Stürmer*. That the most vicious of anti-semitic publications, showing (among other vilifications)

lascivious and leering Jews victimizing German girls with blue eyes and blond hair, would make the rounds in religion was largely due to the fact that the Jewish students were automatically excused. For the rest of the class it was thus much easier to pass the *Der Stürmer* from desk to desk, underhanded of course. Some German students had already been caught and punished over the distraction *Der Stürmer* offered, even though they hid it under the desk for quick glances only. When his turn came, on the day he remembered now only too painfully, the massive figure of Herr Kaplan appeared, as it were, out of nowhere. One moment that figure was still a safe distance away, the next it was towering over him. Before he knew it, the paper was torn out of his hand, he was pulled up forcefully by the shoulder and told to stand. Then the chaplain walked back to the raised desk, flung *Der Stürmer* on top and returned.

Legion of Shame
Ignorant, lured by gold - They stand disgraced in Judah's pay.
Souls poisoned, blood infected - Disaster broods in their wombs. (*Der Stürmer*, #37, August 1935)

Teacher and student were now facing each other. It was a situation—from ear pinching over the rod to slaps—with which all pupils and students who ever went to school in Germany were familiar. At the *Horst Wessel Realgymnasium* the teacher of religion in this situation was downright feared. The punishment, a slap into the face, was more like the crash of muscle and bone into facial flesh. Moving in closer, raising his arms slightly, for better leverage, the man of the cloth stared him down angrily and began to feint and to fidget with both arms for the slap that could be thrown by either hand with equal force. For man and boy it came down by now to split-second timing, pitting reflex against reflex, or slap against evasion.

The hand that crashed into his right cheek had such force that it both surprised and dazed him. Only a moment ago he had felt the breath of the angry man. It was hot and it was bad and it reminded him of village dogs hot from the chase, and wet from rain. Distracted, the slap caught him, in boxer language, flatfooted.

He slumped into his desk, sensing only the blurred image of black cloth and the curve of a gold chain on a closely buttoned vest. His cheek felt as if it was on fire.

To the pain came the shame and the anger. Anger at himself for having been caught with *Der Stürmer* in the first place; and anger for having been suckered into the slap; anger also at the religion teacher for inflicting the pain and the humiliation for what he felt was no great offense. *Der Sturmer* in the last analysis was no crib-sheet; in fact, didn't it enjoy official Third *Reich* status! And lastly, how in this world of class solidarity could a fourteen-year-old be expected to stay aloof from the game of passing something from desk to desk?

With the anger also came the shame. When Pinschover returned to class after religion, the boy tried to hide the bruised and burning side of his face. Although no words were exchanged, he felt his Jewish deskmate knew, and for once he didn't feel right getting an orange that day. When at last the bell for the lunch break rang, Pinschover as usual reached under the desk for the brown paper bag, held it out to him unopened, saying, it's all right. "*Stimmt schon.*" Thus on the day he was caught with *Der Stürmer* his Jewish deskmate, relinquishing his own, gave him an extra orange.

It also happened that from this day on the boy's awareness of some of the things he did was taking on, like the beam of light passing through a prism, an added dimension. Such things as marching with the Hitler Youth and singing "and when the Jewish blood squirts from the knife" reminded him, here on the dusty village street, of Pinschover in the city. What would he, who gave him an orange every day, think if he ever heard him sing that line "*und wenn das Judenblut vom Messer spritzt.*" Moreover, he remembered the expression in Pinschover's face the moment the bag with the two oranges was passed, that the smile was gone. In those eyes was only sadness.

More black smoke was billowing into the dull November sky. The glasses of the history teacher, who kept staring out the window, reflected the column of smoke in a nervous flicker. Suddenly the school custodian stood in the door, just long enough to announce that after this class school would be dismissed for the day. The class received the news in silence, sensing somehow that something unusual was happening in the outside world. Also, the voice of the Hausmeister was barely above a whisper and the dapper man appeared strangely somber, as he stood hunched in the doorway as if embarrassed to step into the classroom.

School dismissals happened for two reasons only: for excessive summer heat and for Fuhrer speeches. On this November day one was as much out of season as the other was, for lack of fanfare, out of question. For *Führer* speeches were announced by the *Herr Hausmeister* well ahead of time, say a day or two, and then with the voice of a former drill-sergeant. "Tomorrow," the voice would boom, "the *Führer* will speak." All this and details of time the man would give with a great deal of posturing and infinite elocution, which only ended with a click of the heels and the announcement that after the all-school assembly for the" *Führer-Rede* there would be no school that day. "*Die Schule ist aus*."

A speech by the *Führer* easily meant two hours of assembly. Students, from the lowly *sextaner* to the lofty *primaner*, would file in that order into the assembly hall and stand at attention during the singing of the national anthem and the Horst Wessel Lied. Secretly he envied the Jewish students in school who did not have to attend all-school assemblies for the *Führer* speeches. For the speeches were invariably long and full of ramblings and rantings, crackling radio noises and waves of thunderous applause. Thus it went from one hour to the next, while the students of the *Horst Wessel Realgymnasium* listened with rapt attention, or at least pretended they did.

On this day the school custodian with his meek-voiced announcement of school dismissal had come and gone, and *Herr Doktor Oberstudienrat* for the rest of the hour said not one word, not even a word about an assignment in history. He merely sat there and continued to stare ahead, in the direction of the window framing the column of smoke. Class was dismissed with a futile wave of his hand.

The boy ran the half mile from school to the intersection, where earlier he had seen the *SA* troopers on trucks, as fast as he could. A glance at the sky over downtown told him that the fire was still burning. It belched more smoke than ever.

Church clocks struck the noon hour. Early dismissal gave him an extra hour before catching the train that took him to a station near the village where he lived. To reach the fire, in the city square or close to it, he headed for Beuthen's oldest shopping street. It was a narrow street with small shops on both sides. From where he entered the street, it would take him past storefronts to the city square.

His eyes met a sight he had never seen before. Half way down the street, up to a slight curve, a dozen or more shops appeared to have been blown up, or out, or something. Books, papers, kitchen utensils, toys, flowers, food in cans and fresh fruit and vegetables, clothing, toiletries, even pieces of furniture and some musical instruments lay in a sea of devastation on the sidewalks and in the street, together with shards from broken windows. The devastation—broken, mutilated, smashed, scattered pieces—reminded him of oxen flayed in the village butcher shop, when after slitting bellies bloody gore would plop on the concrete floor.

As he made his way through the debris, mostly by keeping to the middle of the street, his senses became numbed in a strange way. He was barely able to realize that the shops, raked with destruction, were all Jewish. From this realization, his mind was forced to see the casuistry of truckloads of *SA*, the absence of the Jewish students, the erratic behavior of the column of smoke, the strange ways of the teachers, and dismissal of school. He thought of the orange he had to miss that day. Ahead lay the shop of Pinschover's father.

In the street were *SA* men. They were standing around with arms stemmed into their hips. Or if they took steps, stiffly as if measuring the extent of the destruction, broken glass crunched under their iron heels. From the black boots to their brown breeches, to brown shirts, to billed caps held in place by leather chin straps, to black leather belts and shoulder straps with hooks in front and in back, and to the red arm-bands with the black *swastika*s in circles of white, the *SA* looked like men in harness.

At the sight of the destruction, numbness gave way to a feeling of agitation. What was he to make of musical instruments terribly mutilated, of pianos with gutted sound-boxes, smashed keyboards, when at home the most valuable heirloom was the Grothrian-Steinweg? How was he to reconcile piles of scattered food with the sternest of parental admonitions to never waste food? How was he to square his father's passionate love for learning with the fury with which books had been swept off the shelves into piles of litter?

Dazed, he drifted deeper into the street. In a fabric store hundreds of rolls of material in all colors were left in shambles. And he saw, in a sudden flash, his mother bowed over the sewing machine, using and re-using every piece of fabric before letting him have torn and tattered remnants for the rug-man…in return for crusty mana bread.

The *SA* had an air of icy calm about them, not unlike the air of relaxed predaciousness toward prey brought low. Less sure, displaying in fact an expression of startled disbelief, were housewives with shopping bags, coal miners between shifts, day laborers, office workers, students clutching briefcases.

The fury of destruction had not spared the shop of Pinschover's father. Neither had the fury spared the apartment above the shop, to judge by the broken windows in which the sheers had been caught on the jagged piece of broken glass, flapping like the wing of a dying bird. There was no sign of life. In the shop below lay trampled and squashed all kinds of fruit on the floor. Apples and oranges had rolled out of the shop, across the sidewalk, into the street. He felt like picking up some of the fruit, at least one orange. Or he could kick at least one or two along the gutter, away from the stare of the *SA* trooper. The stare unnerved him. He did nothing.

Ahead lay the city square. He saw at a glance that on this day everything about the square was different. Except for one firetruck and two police vehicles, the square was empty of traffic. As if staged for a gigantic outdoor performance, there were three groups of people. First there was a cordon of police standing along the sidewalks. Behind the police were thousands of German spectators, standing several rows deep. And lined up in rows in the center of the square were the Jews, several hundred Jewish people facing the synagogue. The synagogue was burning.

Storm troopers were still escorting Jews into the square, either singly or in groups. He saw one elderly orthodox Jew, with beard and locks, who had to be supported by two *SA* men. They dragged him the last few feet to a stretcher and plopped him there. Stretcher and wheelchair cases formed two rows in front of the burning synagogue.

Smoke was belching from the synagogue. Jewish parents gripped the hands of children. Among the Germans, women wiped their faces. *SA* boots clicked on cobble-stones. The whistles of trains wailed in the distance. A flock of pigeons circled nervously near the burning building.

The boy was able to make his way around the square by keeping close to the storefronts. Several stores had been pillaged, although here in the square the debris had already been cleaned up. *SA* stood in the doorway of each Jewish store, including the Schüftan store. It was mother's favorite department store and the boy was thoroughly familiar with her story: how each time she shopped there, Herr Schüftan would personally greet her, complete with name and the profession of her husband, and unfailingly inquire about the well-being of each member of the family. As of late, however, the *SA* had placed a permanent trooper there displaying a sign "*Deutsche - Kauft nicht beim Juden*." (Germans-don't buy from the Jew.) Mother would only say that she missed buying from Herr Schüftan.

At the store the crowd was less dense, perhaps because of the *SA* at its back. He was able to squeeze through the crowd to the front, past coats smelling of mothballs and rustling Rose Mary beads. The synagogue was straight ahead.

It was a building of massive walls of brick and stone that rose squarely into a domed roof. Smoke was billowing out of the building, right through an opening in the pitched portion of the roof, a narthex-like extension below the dome. Through the door and the windows, forced open and smashed, he discovered why the fire had acted so strangely all morning long, with all those thin trails and nervous puffs and swirling balls of smoke ranging from light gray to very black.

Several fires were flickering and glowing on the floor, in a tangled heap of charred objects. Silhouetted against the fires were several storm troopers. From time to time they would be moving about, their dark figures outlined against the glowing and flickering fires, as if performing a savage ritual. The men took cautious steps toward the fires, heaved a bucket or two of some fluid at them and, having rekindled the fires, retreated backwards. Burning darkly and sluggishly, flames would send black smoke billowing through the roof. And in the sky the column of smoke was again doing its antics. By the time it had thinned to a trail, the men inside the synagogue repeated their cautious advance and quick retreat, emptying buckets of the fluid. Outside, the fire-truck stood by idly. Now the boy knew all there was to know.

He looked for Pinschover, scanning row after row of Jewish men, women and children. Their faces were expressionless. Only the children from time to time lifted their faces toward their parents, as if asking for an explanation.

Pinschover stood in the last row. His hand clutched a brown paper bag.

Church clocks struck the half hour. The boy had just enough time left, he discovered to his relief, to reach the train. He squeezed through the crowd, hastening along buildings with more ransacked stores, and he thought of the next day, wondering whether he would ever see his deskmate again. He never did.

7
AUGUST DAYS

Times were changing. Among the rumors there was one about impending war with Poland. Then there were all kinds of uncertainties about the future, from talking about the introduction of rationing to figuring out how far the manufacture of *Ersatz*-materials was going to take the German economy astray. One example was the appearance of *Ersatz*-soap on the market taking the place of old-fashioned bars of soap; or when *Ersatz*-fabric by the name of *Vistra* took the place of genuine cloth.

Talk about irate women when they found out that the new soap was smelly and came without foam; or when the new *Vistra* blouses and dresses would shrivel and shrink under the first drop of rain. Or when copper prices were going through the roof. Or when people were stocking the larder with sides of bacon and bundles of hard sausage. And what about the boy who found himself at the center of the storms of puberty?

Even the weather showed itself fickle. On some days thunderclouds would be gathering in the western sky and remain there wan and-motionless as if stillborn. And then again on any other hot and humid day the thunder clouds would lose no time to lash out at the village with pelting rains and driving winds… before rumbling off towards the Polish border.

In the meantime the fifteen-year-old had gone through storms of his own. With his intense feelings about women came nagging questions… whether a child was born through the mother's navel… how a woman got herself into the state of "hope," the German idiom for being with child. In fact all he knew about human sexuality, in the jargon of the street, was often bawdy and not at all clear. And even after brooding about the question he was still not sure how to be together… how to be really together with a woman.

In the so-called water-battles in the pond, the boys and the girls were on opposite sides, which was as natural as their bodies were different: bare-chested the boys and soft and budding the girls under their wet swimming suits. For the battle both sides stood up to their bellies in water. It gave their arms better leverage, as the combatants would shoot jets of water into each others' faces, every time their arms with cupped hands skimmed over the water. And amidst the splashing of water and shrieking voices there would come the moment when the boys closed in on the girls and tried to touch their bodies in an embrace. Sometimes the boy would lie awake long into the night and relive the moments of the embrace.

Among the other attractions for the boy that summer was women's underwear. Wherever it was hanging out to dry he was especially keen on the colors. His favorites were tones of flesh and shades of blue, especially in town where on sunny days they could be seen in the garden of a villa. Twice a day, before and after school, he walked past the villa, and whenever such panties were hanging there he could not help but indulge in this question: which panty belonged to which woman. By the time his imagination had gone full circle he still was not sure which one of the pieces belonged to the three girls and to their mother. He was to remain a stranger to the women in the villa. It is also true that he did not know much about them. Occasionally he would spot them in the garden, however indistinct. He also knew that the dog, a white spitz, obeyed to Pfiffi. And on some days behind the lace windows piano music would drift out into the street.

On one of the last days in August he saw all four of them. They were window-shopping in Beuthen's busiest street. What he also noticed was that they were engaged in amiable talk, if only small talk underlined by little hand gestures. Their walk was graceful. Somehow the four appeared to be worlds apart from the rush of pedestrians on the sidewalk and the jam of traffic in the one-way street. They stopped in front of the ice cream parlor. He watched how the three girls took turns, like in a rehearsal, to speak to their mother, and how after some hesitation and pleading the mother finally yielded and walked into the parlor. He followed them shortly.

Tutti frutti was the latest hit with the ice cream-loving Germans. It had come to Beuthen in a roundabout way via the Pact of Steel between Hitler's Germany and Mussolini's Italy. Here in the parlor a lively Italian couple was busy scraping *tutti frutti* ice into balls to be served singly or with other flavors combined. The colors were always bright, and each color was served with a *buono* by the Italians. After the girls and the mother got their treat he bought with his last money a single serving of lemon ice, as yellow as the plumage of a canary. He found an empty place near the table where the four were sitting. Right above the bubbling shopkeepers hung the picture of the Duce. It showed him with bull neck, jutting chin, and a cockily poised head in a pose of indomitable will and resolve. By now the expression of will and resolve were household words on both sides of the Alps. In this picture the dictator's grandstanding was from the balcony of an Italian palace in front of a wildly saluting crowd.

Meanwhile the girls kept passing the cups with the balls of *tutti frutti* to each other, tasting each of the flavors of the Mediterranean world with dainty licks while humming little sounds of delight. With the colors of the *tutti frutti* came thoughts of their underwear, and with the shape of their comely bodies in front of him he indulged in the most luring of imaginations. Small talk from the four was drifting to his table in a potpourri of words: Willi Birgel... organdy blouse for me... rides for Germany... more tutti frutti... Soederbaum in the film... believe me... dance next time... not in fashion... why can't I... old enough... etc.

A member of the *SA* stood in the door of the parlor and began to jingle coins in the red "winter relief" can. It stopped all conversation in the parlor. Moments later the jingling stopped too. Into the ensuing silence came the voice of one of the girls: "Doesn't Papa come home today?"

"He doesn't," said the mother.

"Wasn't he calling this morning?"

"Yes."

Once again all conversation in the parlor was interrupted as the *SA* man in the door started to shake the red can again. It was something that happened in tens of thousands of places all over Germany on the last Friday of every month. But the *SA* man this time had no taker and for a change stepped out into the street. After a moment of silence the boy heard the youngest girl say, "What did Papa say?"

"He sends you his love."

"What else did he say?"

Before the mother could answer, the second girl asked if there was anything wrong, and between licks of *tutti frutti*, the third of the girls blurted out, "There must be something wrong with them over there," and nodded in the direction away from the door. It could only be the Polish border a few hundred yards away on the east side of Beuthen's Bahnhof Strasse.

The mother's voice trailed away: "Business is off… things are bad." Standing outside the door the *SA* man shouted, "*Heil Hitler*," as somebody dropped a coin into the can. And even before the jingling started up again the mother told the girls hastily that their father would return tomorrow on the two o'clock express train from Berlin.

It gave the boy a jolt. His own train, a local that took him home each day after school, was due to leave in five minutes. And only if he ran the length of the Bahnhof Strasse from the parlor to the depot at the far end of the street did he have a chance to make the train. He rushed into the street. The air was heavy with fumes from automobiles and fumes of the asphalt street under the sun. Horse manure reminded him of his village. If he missed the train he would not reach his home before evening, and he longed to see his rabbits who were in hutches in the garden and watch his pigeons fly.

Against the streams of cars, trucks, and horse-drawn wagons of coal that were choking the street, against the stream of pedestrians on the sidewalks, it was difficult to make headway. Darting through the crowd he ran as fast as he could towards the depot, past shops with their sweet and spicy and smoky and fragrant odors.

He reached the depot with moments to spare. He was lucky, one of the gates was free and, holding up his student card, he passed quickly and rushed down the concrete steps leading into the tunnel. In his headlong rush through the tunnel he sensed that something was different. The sounds of the Polish locomotive on the Berlin/Krakau express were different. Instead of the nervous vibrato of hissing steam and the rapid tempo of metallic clicks with which the engine was usually primed for the start, there was only a long drawn-out gargle coming from the engine. And as for his own train as he reached the platform, it only stood there. Silence surrounded it. Conductors shouted no orders. Even though the train was at least seconds overdue. He found an empty compartment. Standing in the open window, he looked over to the express train, by now five minutes late. The locomotive was still only gargling. As usual the train had the

Titian-red dining car and the azure-blue sleeper in addition to the gray coaches. Travelers could be seen standing in the wide-open windows of the coaches, or sitting at tables with vases of flowers in the dining car. But what was unusual about the train was a group of men who, despite the heat, wore trench coats and hats. There were also several railway police on the scene. Their shoulders were hunched forward towards the men with the trench coats as if they were expecting orders from them. Just as he thought of the latter as *GESTAPO*, his own train started with a jolt. He fell back into the corner as a rush of air swept over him through the open window.

At Bobrek a few minutes later the maze of tracks slowed down the train. On one of the tracks to the far side, where a spur was branching off into the lands hard by the Polish border, another train came into view. It was a freight train. Tarpaulins covered the freight on flat cars, creating shapes that were rather odd. On the flat cars it was one bulk after another and each bulk had a distinctive shape. The boy thought they looked like covered guns. As the train stood ready to head off into the lands hard by the Polish border, a stream of smoke belched forth nervously from the stubby stack of the locomotive.

The boy closed his eyes. From the rush of wind sweeping over him, and the rhythm of the wheels vibrating through the wooden seat, he felt the surge of the train taking him closer to home. After his close encounter with the women in the parlor and the strange impasse of the trains at the depot, he looked forward to his rabbits in the garden and his pigeons in the loft above his room. There, with his rabbits in the garden and his pigeons in the loft, he would find peace and respite from the turmoil of these August days.

8
WAR

Swarms of Heinkel 111 and shots of champagne. Original drawing by Rudolf Thill.

It was during the pre-dawn hours of September 1, 1939, that undeclared war was launched against Poland. The attack was not a total surprise. Two days later Britain and France declared war on Germany. The Second World War had begun.

Until sunrise on that Friday, or until the gunners and bombardiers could make out their targets in the first daylight, the peaceful calm of early morning would hover over the village.

Meanwhile the animals were the first to stir. Heaving their bodies up from straw-covered floors, where they had rested during the night, horses and cattle would sometimes bump against wooden boarding in their small stalls. Once on their feet, they began to forage on hay and oats left over from the previous evening. Actually there were only a few horses and head of cattle in the village, for feed and land were perennially scarce. But whenever the animals did bump against wooden boarding in the stalls along the dusty road, it sounded as if bass drums were being struck.

Aside from the hollow and dark sounds, there were others. Dogs began to bark. Cocks crowed. Goats bleated in staccato. In the lofts pigeons turned to cooing. Sparrows fussed in rafters. Songbirds came to life with faint runs on melodies they would sing fully throated later on. The sounds rose muffled and often hesitant into the last darkness of early morning.

The boy awoke as if lightning had struck the house. The room was bursting with noise. It flashed through his mind that there must be two or three thunderstorms raging at once. Next, it all sounded as if whole packs of dogs were rattling furiously at their chains. At last he perceived the noise more like a roar, a revved up and ominously resonant roar, that came from the outside through the open windows into the room.

Moments later he stood under the chestnut trees in the yard, his heart pounding. A sense of fear and excitement had taken hold of him. He did not dare to step out from under the canopy of trees. Nevertheless he saw, first in the western sky, that planes were flying eastward.

The planes were indeed flying on a course somewhat oblique to the village below. But as soon as they were directly above it, they banked slightly and then flew straight east, as though the village road had given the pilots a cue. Formation after formation of Heinkel bombers appeared to be on the final run for some target nearby.

Before the sun's first rays were to slant across fields and meadows, the propellers of the planes at their higher angle and altitude had picked up the reflections. The result was tens, nay hundreds of little suns whirring and whirling like circular saws, two to each plane. Ahead of the suns, in the translucent noses of the planes, were men lying in nearly crouched positions. Slightly above and behind them, in the cockpits, he saw the capped heads of additional crewmembers. The men in the noses and cockpits of ribbed steel and Plexiglas sections looked like some primordial pupae in strange new cocoons.

The last formation was flying by. Again its pilots slightly banked their planes before roaring on. On the underside of the wings were the German military insignia of white crosses with lined, open-ended extensions on a black background. While banking, sunlight struck the crosses. The roar dimmed. Then there was silence.

Something in the boy told him to stand his ground under the chestnut trees. He kept listening, as if expecting the return of the roaring Heinkels momentarily. But except for the din of the engines lingering in his ears, which cleared almost right away, there was nothing but silence around him. Nothing stirred, not even the animals. Within seconds, sounding at first like rumblings of gathering storms, the echoes of detonating bombs could be heard, echo after echo of deep-dark rumblings. The war had begun with a roar over the village and with the detonations in Poland, moments apart.

However, there had been signs and rumors of an impending war. Two had actually given the fifteen-year-old some anxious thoughts. One was that his father had just sent word to the family not to worry if they didn't hear from him. His father was serving with a Wehrmacht reserve unit at the Polish border. The second sign had been even more alarming, since its impact was visual. It had brought him face to face with the grim destructiveness of war. Only last Sunday then, right after church, he and his friend had gone on bicycles to Schomberg, a border village. Schomberg had been shelled by artillery earlier in the week.

What he saw were portents of the violence to come. Though as yet comparatively scant, the evidence was real enough. Three or four houses had their roofs torn open, leaving gaping holes with jagged and splintered rafters around the fringes. The force of the shell-bursts had blown most of the tiles of red clay in every direction. They lay around mostly shattered in gardens and yards. In yet another spot either a barn or a tool-shed of weathered lumber had received a direct hit. From the torn remains there was no telling which it had been. Only the markings of the gabled roof could be seen running at tent-like slants on the wall of the adjoining brick building. Above that line the bursting shell had sent metal fragments into a wall painting of sorts. As a piece of outdoor advertisement, it showed a smiling patriarch about to quaff a foaming glass of beer. Schultheiss beer went with Upper Silesians like wine with Rhinelanders. And sharp fragments had left the face pockmarked and scratched. One piece of metal had gouged its way into the glass of beer the tippler was holding. It looked as if the beer was about to run out.

Talk among the curious had it that several Schomberg men, coming out of a tavern, had charged across the border under cover of darkness. We must understand that such words and many more besides were merely whispered in Nazi Germany, if that. At any rate, the Poles had responded with a round of artillery. As the curious stood around in several groups, a man with beer on his breath pointed out the "Polish positions" to the group the boy was with. They were, as a matter of course, right across the border, no more than a few hundred yards away. Straining his eyes to the limit, the boy could only make out a cluster of ordinary houses with red roofs and gray stucco walls. Dense greenery of bushes and trees softened the boxy and straight lines. There was also a poplar-lined road leading to a local coal mine. The Polish flag flew on top of the steel turret with the giant wheel.

The crowd that milled through Schomberg's main road on that sunny Sunday afternoon was not too different from an ordinary crowd after church, except that it was certainly larger and that more than usual the crowd was given to a lot of whispering. Although the road had been cleared of debris and had been swept, tiny glass splinters sparkled in the bright sun. Women in colorful dresses pushed baby prams. Men in Sunday suits of heavy dark cloth led children by the hand. Boys pushed bicycles. Young men and women walked with arms around eachother's waists. Taking one last look at the farcical and mangled face of the tippler, of Herr Schultheiss, he heard the coal-husky voice of an Upper Silesian: "Hope he gets to drink his *pivo*."

The most anxious of premonitions during the recent propaganda blitz, for the boy certainly, was the matter of English support of Poland. His admiration for the people on the Isles had been nurtured over the years by his father. For this village teacher, the ways and manners of the English were virtually synonymous with all kind of desirable traits. He never tired of telling his favorite stories. One had the band of the "Titanic" play "Nearer My God To Thee" to the end, until its members were swept to their death by the icy waters of the Atlantic. When extolling English discipline, the anglophile related how queuing English never fail to respect "first come" rights. The favorite story involved a Hyde Park orator, a London policeman, and a German tourist. Mindless of the Bobby on the scene, the man on the soapbox railed against the government downright fiercely, or so the German felt. Just as the German thought of arrest and the rest of the consequences, the Bobby asked the crowd to move to the side a bit, so others may join or walk by. All that with perfect politeness.

Besides, the boy was doing well in English in school. He already grasped some understanding of the language over Radio London and "The Times," at least the half open front page visible each day with every issue at the newspaper stand of the Beuthen railway depot. Thus English was giving him the kind of gratification, that five years of Latin, obsolete and dead Latin he thought, had never given him. He found himself in a quandary, when Nazi propaganda panned the English more and more the enemy of the *Reich*.

The war produced new words and expressions: *Blitzkrieg*... *Sitzkrieg*... *Kesselschlacht*... west wall... *Panzer* offensives... *Stukas* dive bombing... total annihilation, and so on. Not to be outdone, the home front (*Heimatfront*) had its own legions of heroes. One of them was the art teacher in school, nicknamed Mr. Mustard. This Herr Mostrich had earned his name by being the target of just about every prank known to students, from aiming paper-missiles fired from slingshots at his back to setting off black powder in class. In the prank that gave Mr. Mustard his name, the class had smeared blobs of the stuff on the chair on which his posterior eventually ended up. He sat there unblinking and unflinching, minute after minute, while the stuff oozed through to tender skin. All the class could do was to keep from bursting into pandemonium.

With the war, *Herr* Assessor Weiss was a changed man, or so it seemed. Gone were his timid ways and cowardly reactions. Facing the class of eighth grade *Obertertianer* squarely, with arms stemmed into his sides, the art teacher and pin-wearing member of the Nazi Party would now theorize about the war and such things as geopolitics with the certainty of an armchair expert. And by the time *Herr* Weiss spoke of the glorious future to which the *Führer* beckoned Greater Germany, including this class of flimflam students, the falsetto voice quavered and the fish eyes stared. If the ranting and raving had one effect, it was that, for the time being at least, the class let up on the pranks. With classes being dismissed right after each special victory announcement from the *Führer* Headquarters, which came in droves, school was getting pleasantly shorter and shorter anyway.

The campaign against Poland was over sooner than expected. Hitlerite Germany and Stalinist Russia divided the Polish spoils. Soon the victorious army was in a great rush to return to the thinly defended western border, only this time it moved on rail and highway through Upper Silesia from east to west. Naturally, lightning war and sudden victory had aroused feelings of relief and euphoria, even among Upper Silesians. But most of them kept a sense of wariness and harbored a case of resentment. What had happened was that the soldiers of the *Reich* were slurring Upper Silesian women, at least according to gossip and rumor. From passing trains and mobile convoys it was shouted. On walls and solid fences it appeared as graffiti. Soldiers in drink babbled it. The slur allegedly went thus: "*Jetzt verlassen wir Euch oberschlesische Sauen und gehen zurück zu unseren Frauen*" (Now we leave you Upper Silesian sows and return to our women). When the soldiers got ready for the attack on Poland, the native belles had at every opportunity bestowed their female charms perhaps too generously. Now they felt shamed and angered, while deep and lasting rancor was borne by the men.

It was a warm and bright Sunday afternoon when father's return from Poland was the cause for a garden party. Among the customary delicacies were assorted cold cuts, meat salad with capers, a sheet of Silesian cake with chunks of buttery crumbs on top, and fruit punch spiked with cognac, no less. How the bottle of cognac had made its way from France to the village is anybody's guess, for the time when the Third *Reich* went dizzy with French spirits still lay ahead.

Regardless of the source and the occasion, alcohol at gatherings of friends did two things. It loosened tongues and, for the children, it bent parental toleration in favor of eavesdropping and late bedtime.

That afternoon the sun was still very bright, though it was early October. The brilliance of the sun filled the sky where the boy had first spotted the planes. On this Indian summer day, the grasshoppers were chirping, the air smelled of burning potato-stalks, and silky strands of gossamer floated everywhere.

Among the guests, who sat in a half-circle around the table with the punch and the delicacies, was Behrla. Behrla was visiting her sister, the wife of another teacher who lived in the apartment downstairs. What was rather unusual was that Behrla was called only by that name, her last name, just Behrla, no more and no less. Now, there was no doubt that she was beautiful and that she had engaging manners. It was said that she had never married. The boy's father kept remarking that that was beyond anybody's understanding.

To the fifteen-year-old, Behrla had always held an attraction. It was the simple and unaffected attraction a schoolboy feels when asked about school by a beautiful and mature woman. In time Behrla would ask other questions. Once she asked him, and he remembered the moment vividly, whether he could dance the slow waltz. Another time whether he had a girlfriend. Beuthen, where she lived and he went to high school, would enter with mention of a movie or two. Finally, on the Sunday of the party, she remarked how well the suit he was wearing looked on him. From that moment, for the rest of the day, he looked at her with different eyes.

She sat next to his father. The punch which the boy helped serve was beginning to show its effect. "That must be the cognac," said mother. As voices grew louder, the conversation became more animated among the guests, Behrla and father included.

It was his first opportunity to watch her as a woman for whom he now longed. She was in her most alluring form. As yet he had no real idea what would go where if he ever got together with her. What drew his eyes to her, more than anything else, was the way she sat in the chair. Her legs were parted wide enough to reveal perfectly formed thighs. Under the flowery dress of muslin they seemed to glow from within. It dizzied him to think that, where those gleaming thighs came together, there must be the answer to his yearning.

Glasses were being refilled. He shook slightly with excitement and could not help spilling some punch. Politics were now dominating the conversation. Raising his glass, the third teacher in the party spoke up sharply: "What do you think about our party bigwigs planning to protect our women?" He was known for his centrist views from the days of Weimar.

"Paul," his wife with the bun in her hair tried to hush him. "Haven't you heard the announcement by Goebbels and company that party members will be around for the rest of the war to fortify the home front, ha… ha… ha?

"To escape the real front," Behrla's brother-in-law mocked with a smack of his lips.

"Not a bad idea," said father and looked intently at Behrla.

The exchange among the men had obviously exasperated some of the wives. Clasping their mouths with one hand, they pointed with the other around them, mostly into the sky, and stared at their husbands in turn. One of the wives blurted, "Don't you… don't you know that they are everywhere? "

"The Nazis can look me up where the pepper is growing," countered one of the men proverbially.

Now the owner of the brickyard demanded to know: "Do you know," he said with a sweep of his hand, "what the biggies did to my car?" When his inquiry met with silence, since by now the fate of the car was known, he raised his bushy eyebrows a notch and with glaring eyes, magnified behind thick glasses, he hissed, "They took it." He fell back into the deep garden chair and motioned for another glass of punch.

"I think of our BMW day and night." The voice of the matronly looking woman wailed on: "I can't help but worry."

The boy's mother was now passing trays of cold cuts and bowls of salad. Coffee and cake would come later. All were hearty eaters. Moreover, the punch with the cognac had whetted their appetites. They helped themselves freely, the men and the women at the party under the chestnut trees. All but Behrla. Even mother's hortative reminder "long eating brings long life" had no effect. Behrla firmly refused to have any more food. With her perfect rows of white teeth she barely nibbled on a piece of bread.

The conversation now turned to more prosaic things, from the Indian summer with its glorious days of warm sun and blue skies to supplies of coal and firewood for the winter. The rationing system sparked small fires of indignation, again about the bigwigs.

He had eyes only for Behrla. Her face was turned to his father. Well proportioned and delicately carved, it bore its beauty with tender comeliness. He longed to be close.

It surprised him that Behrla and his father were talking about the war in Poland. Moreover the conversation settled on the San River in eastern Poland where the soldiers of the German and Russian armies had met for the partitioning of the unfortunate land.

"How do these… Russian men look?" inquired Behrla.

"Absolutely no soldiers, I must tell you," was the answer with a touch of the officer in it. She leaned over, as if trying to make sure she caught the next round of explanations.

"In a war," said father edgily, "they have no chance against us."

"You are sure?"

"Absolutely."

"But what if…"

Her voice was cut off by the wave of his hand. As if to apologize, father raised his glass to her in a silent toast. Both sipped the pink punch. "There is no IF," said his father who had just come victoriously out of Poland.

What followed were the familiar remarks about the Russians, sounding so quintessential: how they made an even more miserable impression than the vanquished Poles; how they shouldered their rifles with pieces of twine; and how, worst of all, they showed complete disrespect for their officers.

He was not able to see her reaction to these words, for by now her face was almost completely turned to his father. Once more the boy, the fifteen-year-old admirer of a woman more than twice his age, felt his masculinity stir. Her breasts were softly outlined by the muslin of her dress. The triangular shape of womanhood, with the shapely thighs and the gentle curve of her lower abdomen, was glowing dimly under that dress.

Suddenly it struck him that Behrla and his father perhaps meant more to each other than all the casual course of events at the party, who sat with whom, who said what, who showed the effects of the punch spiked with French cognac. And with that voice in him, his mind edged closer to seeking the causality between pupae of men and their bombing of a Polish target, between the one-time *Herr* Mostrich and current *Herr* Assessor Weiss, between the Germans and the Russians at the San River, and lastly between the glow of thighs and silk of Behrla's womanhood and the rough fabric soldiers wore. And he thought of the slur.

He watched Behrla intently. Momentarily her legs drew together sharply. Her eyes glowered with indignation at him. He felt their sting.

Father's voice seemed to come from a great distance: "You must not worry, Behrla," he said and touched her arm. "Not about the Ruskis."

Still feeling the piercing, offended look of her eyes the boy stumbled backward. All he wanted was to get away from women with thighs of alabaster and eyes of steel, and for a moment the boy yearned to be in the war.

9
CAPTURE

By now the soldier knew he would have to go it alone. He would get away from the highway on which the Africa Corps was fleeing in a hail of bullets and bombs and head for the coast. On the coast, on the side of the peninsula that faces the sea, he hoped to find a chance to escape.

The thought had first occurred to him during the turmoil of retreat. On that morning of May 6, 1943, as the Allies were launching powerful drives at key points of the front, the Germans retreated everywhere. Within hours retreat turned into flight, flight into rout. It was lightning warfare with a vengeance, it was *Blitzkrieg* in reverse. For Rommel's Africa Corps it was the beginning of the end.

Why the sudden collapse? What was it that made Rommel's troops crack in a matter of hours? What caused the army to run, when only a year ago it stood poised at the gates of Egypt? Why the headlong rush for Tunis, on a few miserable roads where enemy planes were certain to rain down death and destruction?

Lately, the war in this corner of the world had not gone well for the Germans. They were hungry, ammunition and fuel were in low supply, leaves had been canceled, mail was down to a trickle, and the popular Rommel had been replaced by a general the soldiers had never heard of.

Moreover, by now it was an open secret that the lanes between Sicily and Tunisia had turned into a graveyard for Axis ships and planes; and that here in Tunisia the Italians were having second thoughts about the war. For by now the *Itaker,* as the Germans called their Italian comrades-in-arms with some derision, were abandoning their units for the more remote areas of the hinterland, such as the Medjerda River valley, to wait for the end of the war.

For their part, the Germans were reacting to a grim situation with their own brand of humor, saying to each other: *Avanti Kameraden, es geht zurück.* (Forward, comrades, we are retreating.)

In the larger scale of World War II, there were even more ominous signs. El Alamein and especially Stalingrad had dashed the notion of German invincibility; words like *Russischer Winter* and *Stalin Tank* and *Stalin Orgel* ("Stalin Organ" or rocket launcher) had taken on a dreadful ring; official terms like *Frontverküerzung* and *Frontbegradigung* (shortening of the front and straightening out the front) were generally known to be but a cover-up for retreat; and as if the gathering storms along the eastern front were not enough, in the west, in this spring of 1943, sunny skies over Germany echoed with the dark thunder of American bomber formations. Goebbel's latest boast of "total war" was starting to come home.

In North Africa the Germans were making a stand in Tunisia. After retreating from El Alamein and after reacting to American forces landing in North Africa and the Allied occupation of Tunisia, that was all they could do. The landings had taken place in November of 1942; and even though at first the

Germans were able to foil Allied attempts to drive them into the sea, the tide of war was against them.

By the following March the Allies stepped up the pace of combat, sending sharp attacks into the German lines and harassing the defenders with tank and artillery fire. Meanwhile, the Spitfires and, as newcomers, the Lightnings had been taking on the Messerschmitts. Superior numbers were to prevail.

By April the *Luftwaffe* was practically finished. From that moment on, the planes with the stars and the planes with the rings were to roam the skies over Tunisia virtually at will, bombing and strafing.

On land the final onslaught began with the roar of artillery. All night long, in several sectors of the 150-mile-long front, enemy guns raked the German lines with deadly fire. At dawn the tanks came crashing forward. Outgunned and outnumbered, the Germans at this point were no match and fled.

Within hours on that sixth day of May 1943, on the few roads leading away from the front, the Africa Corps was swept up in a maelstrom of retreat. And retreat breeds rumor. As rumors go, it was the standard version for an army facing capture: that salvation lay just ahead and that an armada of ships and planes was waiting at Tunis to evacuate the Africa Corps, to the last man.

And so, every last wheel and track of that army, from Volkswagen to Tiger tank, was swept up in the rush to reach Tunis. And tearing into the fleeing columns with deadly accuracy were the Spitfires and the Lightnings, the Marauders and the Mitchells, and in the end, just before Tunis fell, the Liberators and the Flying Fortresses.

He heard the news of the fall of Tunis on radio Belgrade, during a lull in the flight. Breaking into the strains of martial music was the voice of the German announcer—and a grave voice it was—to report that the defenders of Tunis, out of ammunition, were hurling rocks at the attackers to the end. Similar heroics were claimed for the rest of the Africa Corps. Then the station of *Lilli Marlene* fame played more martial music and the columns, as if driven by their own momentum, kept grinding ahead on the last road open to them. That road went straight into the dead end of the Cape Bon peninsula.

For the battery, what was left of it, the flight ended in a ravine somewhere on the peninsula, just off the road.

Almost at once the soldier became aware of the voice of the captain, even before the last of the engines had been turned off. The voice had a strange way of sounding both high and low pitches, like a two-tone whistle, either shrill with a dark undertone, or dark with a high, shrill vibrato. Either way, he had always found the voice grating.

In this situation, Captain Schmitz's voice was to fluctuate even more. One moment, when giving the order to prepare everything for demolition, without that darker undertone the voice would have been lost in feebleness. The next moment, when ordering that all vehicles be drained of gasoline, Schmitz sounded like a man with something like a chest tone of conviction, the high overlying pitch notwithstanding.

The soldier was surprised that the demolition charges went off more with hollow-sounding thuds than ripping explosions. Nevertheless, the charges blew open hoods and tore doors ajar, although none of the vehicles—two self-propelled guns and six trucks—caught fire. And as he looked at the gun he had been serving and riding on from the front all the way to this ravine here, he could not help but feel both a sense of loss and relief. The gun and its armored carrier had been his home, but now that it was gone he felt free to think more and more of escape.

Presently the captain ordered the men to fall into line and to stand at attention; into single line, since there were only about forty men left. The victory salute by *Herr Hauptmann* Harold Schmittz was nothing short of perfection. Sounding brassy, but with that nasal twang, Schmittz shouted victory for the alliterative *Führer, Volk,* and *Vaterland,* three times, and in turn the men shouted back *Heil.*

Next, the captain began to deliver himself of a diatribe against Germany's enemies: "These damnable Allies," Schmittz cried out in a near falsetto voice, "will never—will absolutely never—wrest victory from our beloved fatherland." His face was showing contempt. "Never," the captain continued, "will the pepper-sacks from across the Channel—will the gangsters from across the Atlantic—will the Bolshevik hordes from the steppes—set foot on German soil. Never, ever will the Jews be once more able to…"

At that moment several terrifyingly powerful detonations drowned out the captain's voice. The men felt the ground shake and tremble, as the horizon erupted in a mass of dirt and dust. Instantly a string of fireballs shot into the air, one after another, and soared in violent convulsions of flames and smoke into the azure African sky. Their momentum spent, the fireballs then billowed into dark gray clouds, glowing brilliantly along the edges, while tons of debris were starting to fall back to earth, like cloudbursts. Over and over, the boom of the detonations washed over the men like big waves.

The men shifted on their feet. "My God," somebody said in a hushed voice, "it must be an ammunition dump blowing up."

Captain Schmittz looked downright awkward. Reaction to the explosions had left his body in a rather strangely twisted stance—half turned to the men and half facing the clouds behind his back—staring at the clouds over his hunched-up shoulder. Otherwise, from his jodhpurs on down to the tip of his boots, the captain was still all-front with respect to the men. All in all it looked as if the explosions had put an end to the captain's grandstanding.

In the sky the clouds began drifting away. The soldier followed their drift. Were they driven by winds coming from the sea? There was indeed a damp smell in the air. The sea must be close, he thought, and the sea he must reach, if he was to have any chance to escape captivity.

Harold Schmittz meanwhile was regaining his composure. Standing once again squarely before the men, the C.O. kept clearing his voice. When at last the words came, rather slowly and haltingly, they were to form a string of Third *Reich* exhortations: one must sacrifice—must always endure—must not give up—must be tough—must be of steel—must never doubt in final victory—must be faithful—and, above all, must follow the *Führer*.

Facing the men straggle-legged and stemming both arms unto his hips, the captain by now was his own self. Presently his voice was telling the men, of all things, that according to the latest reports the Italian fleet and the *Luftwaffe* were on their way to evacuate the entire Africa Corps. "To the last man!" the captain shouted, taking a step toward the men. "After fourteen days of home leave," the captain went on, "you men shall rejoin the *Führer* in his heroic struggle against the enemies of the Third *Reich*." And finally, after something like a dramatic pause, Schmittz burst out; "We shall all fight together—side by side with the *Führer*—until final victory."

Schmittz gazed at the men as if to measure the effect of his words. Then something strange happened: under that gaze the men began to click their heels, one after another, from left to right, right down the line, ramming their steel-rimmed heels together as if standing inspection on some parade ground far from the war. When the soldier's turn came, he, too, clicked his heels.

In turn Schmittz was to shout, "Long live our beloved *Führer* Adolf Hitler," and then, saluting smartly, he turned on his long-shafted black boots and strode to the command car that had been waiting for him. In the open car *Hauptmann* Harold Schmittz came to stand in something like the *Führer* pose: next to the driver, ramrod erect, stern-faced, with the left hand on the windshield. It was the *Führer* pose all right, except that in the back of the car there were several pieces of luggage and two canisters of gasoline, left over from the trucks and the guns, piled high. Schmittz was about to depart.

But not without one last bit of drama. As the car started to move, Schmittz, with glove in hand, suddenly pointed frantically at something beyond the demolished trucks and guns and shouted "Go to Pantelleria... to Pantelleria" before cupping his mouth with both hands and yelling, *Rette sich, wer kann!*

The men stood like dazed. The last thing they had expected to hear from their C.O. were a strange name of God-knows-what place and words telling them to save themselves. This "Save yourself if you can"—as all would agree—was the stuff out of which high sea drama was made, for passengers on a sinking ship before they jumped into the sea. But here on land...?

The men reached for their cigarettes and passed them around for a puff at a time, like in a ritual. Even the nonsmokers, coughing and hacking, joined in.

The soldier inhaled deeply the smoke of the Superieur, savoring the calming effect. As it was, the captain's last-minute antics had produced, by a strange coincidence, the name of the island over which he had been racking his brain since the news of the fall of Tunis. Now he knew that his hunch was right. He was certain that he must go to the coast, where he hoped to spot Pantelleria. To Pantelleria, to the island held by the Italians, he must make it if he was to have any chance to escape captivity.

With the name came recollections. From high school history he knew that the island in ancient times had been a Carthaginian colony and as such had guarded the straits between Sicily and Carthage (near modern Tunis); he also recalled that the island was volcanic, lay more or less close to Cape Bon, and hence should be visible from the coast; finally, he could not help but recall propaganda claims that had touted the island as the Axis answer to Malta.

The men had not spoken a word since their commanding officer had left them. In the sky the last of the clouds, by now tatters, had been blown away by the strong winds and once again the luminous blue of the African sky was arching high over the land. At this moment he became aware of nothing so much as the deep silence around them. For once it was without the sounds and echoes of war.

Two nights ago, at the front near Medjez el Bab, the battery had come under fire in one of the worst bombardments of the war. From the first he had feared for his life. The guns had gone off with a tremendous flash and with a deafening roar, and had turned the night into hell. And since that night, since surviving the ordeal, he felt somehow drawn to the bombardment with the kind of eager reflection peculiar to survivors of a catastrophe.

Thus, he remembered the drumfire of shells howling and shrieking before exploding with terrible crashes. Crashes so close that they would shower him from time to time with clumps of dirt, causing him to reach back to feel for a tear in his tunic, for something warm and wet underneath.

He remembered the gagging smell of exploded gunpowder and the choking effect of dust as the guns, in salvo after salvo, kept raking the earth all night long.

He remembered how, in fear of his life, he had clutched the ground, had clawed into its gravelly surface in a desperate effort to pry loose from his foxhole the last possible centimeter of protection.

And he remembered that he had felt like being touched by death whenever the shock wave of a close shell had brushed against him, like an ill wind.

His memories of that night were suddenly cut short by the sound of a plane. Seconds later he saw the plane come in low, barely above the horizon, then bank and go down for what appeared to be a landing. The plane's bulky fuselage and its snub-nosed three motors left no doubt that it was a Junker52, the workhorse of the *Luftwaffe.*

The men had not seen a German plane for days. Drawing closer, they looked in the direction where they had seen the plane go down. Some slapped each other on the back, with words such as "airfield" and "evacuation." But other than that, the men just waited.

Looking for a cigarette in his bag, the soldier came across the Bible. It was the same Bible, bound in blue cloth, that someone had given to him in Naples before leaving for the war. It caused his memories to be stirred anew. He remembered that, at some time during the bombardment, out of sheer fear of death and—yes—fear of damnation, he had taken the Bible out of the bag, had put it in front of him, and had pressed his face on it. And while around him the night was going berserk with the screams of the shells and the cries of the wounded, while the night was ablaze with the flashes of guns firing in the distance and with the fires of burning vehicles nearby, a feeling of great inner calm was to come over him, in which God, the God of his childhood, stood at the center. To this loving and caring God he prayed that his life be spared.

And he made confession. He confessed that he had strayed from the church (like playing billiards in the village inn instead of going to church); that he had stolen (by taking apples from orchards of French farmers in the Bretagne under the cover of night); that he had coveted (the young wife of a neighbor who had gone to war); that one night he had vandalized the garden of the village Nazi bigwig (for taunting him over his long sideburns); that he had stood by (while an SS man had terrorized a French shopkeeper with a drawn pistol); that he had not been chaste.

There was no way of knowing whether he had killed, regardless whether killing in a war was sinful or not. He knew that he had not killed outright, such as bringing the foresight and the notch of the carbine, or of the machine-gun, in alignment with the body of an enemy soldier, before pulling the trigger. What he had done was to slam magazines into the chamber of the 20 mm gun, while the gunner behind the gun sight had fired at low-flying enemy planes and, once, at enemy tanks. But the mark of a kill, a white ring around the barrel, had eluded them.

Standing on top of the ravine, the men kept waiting for the Ju52 to reappear. In the distance guns began to fire, reminders that there was still a war.

The sound of artillery brought back still more memories of the bombardment. Toward morning the guns had burst forth with renewed fury, in salvo after salvo, as if angered by the prospect of daylight. Then, as suddenly as they had started, the guns fell silent.

An eerie calm was to settle over the battlefield. Dawn broke. In the first light of the new day, coming up pale and jaundiced in all those clouds of dust, the battlefield was a scene of utter destruction and desolation. The *wadi,* or dried-out riverbed, into which the battery had moved a few days ago, was virtually gone. The fury of the bombardment had blown away its banks and had filled in the riverbed with loose gravel. There were craters everywhere.

Black smoke poured from burning vehicles. Other vehicles, by now burned out, were smoldering. Among the casualties were several self-propelled guns of their battery. He saw that his gun was not one of them. Apparently it had escaped a direct hit.

He bolted out of his foxhole toward the gun. The driver of the gun's carrier was already there. Matthes must have stayed with the gun during the ordeal. Together they shouted the names of the two other crewmembers. They got no response. The makeshift tent, where the four of them had played blackjack right until the onset of the bombardment, had been blown away. So had the foxholes. For that matter, there were no signs of life around the other guns farther down the *wadi*, except for the gun at the far end, where one of the crew pointed toward the enemy lines. What they saw was chilling enough. The slope between them and the enemy was crawling with tanks. And the tanks were advancing, in a stop-and-go pattern, toward the German lines.

By rocking the carrier back and forth, to get out of the gravel, which the exploding shells had piled against caterpillar tracks and the two front wheels, Matthes managed to free the vehicle and they got away.

They raced all the way back to the supply base. There the "jackrabbits of the rear," as supply troops were called in German army slang, for once showed themselves to be generous, showering each crew member of the two guns that had made it out of the *wadi* with "iron" rations: a whole salami, two loaves of hard army bread, chunks of Dutch chocolate, and a pack of Superieurs. All in return for news about what had happened. For the men of supply were aware of the bombardment, having heard its distant thunder. And the captain, who had spent the night at the supply base, a short time later gave the order to head for "defensive positions," with his command car in the lead.

Of all the sights on that road to Tunis, from the wounded to the dead, from grotesquely torn and twisted pieces of equipment to charred vehicles, he knew he would never forget the sight of the little Arab girl. Her body lay prostrate on the pavement, near the edge of the road, face up, in a pool of blood and in a mass of spattered brain. The face had been flattened onto the asphalt, as if a big tire had gone over it, and as such it looked like a pressed flower. Kinfolk were grieving around the body with loud and piercing cries and with wild gesticulations. They were on their knees and kept rocking their bodies in heartrending frenzy. For once the columns slowed down and went wide.

What reminded him of the little girl was the sight of another Arab. He and his mule had come out of nowhere, slightly to the left from the ravine, and were getting ready to plow. And plow they did, a small patch of land, as if there had never been a war.

At last the plane lumbered back into view. Flying low, it headed back in the same direction from which it had come. And he thought of the sea, of Pantelleria, and of home.

Again there were rounds of backslapping and shouts of *Flugplatz* and *Evakuierung* (airport and evacuation). What he also noticed was that the elation of the men was mutual, that the men of supply and the men of the front, usually at loggerheads with each other, were standing together. They were getting ready to leave for that imaginary airfield ahead of them.

All he was able to envision was a landing strip in the middle of nowhere, with soldiers, desperate for a place on a plane, crowding around the makeshift strip. And he was convinced that only officers had a chance. The rest would stay behind and serve as cannon fodder for enemy bombs and bullets.

He walked away without saying a word. He simply could not bring himself to say good-bye, to shake hands—least of all with Matthes—for a very simple reason. He was afraid that he would break into tears.

Matthes and he were more than just fellow crewmembers of a gun. They were close friends. They had gone to the French cinema together, had shared the last cigarette, the last piece of bread, the last drop from the canteen. Together they had gone to army bordellos and one day, back in Naples, they had climbed Monte Vesuvius.

But what counted most in this friendship between the 18-year-old high school student from the Upper Silesian village and the former taxi driver from Berlin were the latter's ready casuistry about army life.

A veteran of the Russian campaign, where he was busted in rank for breaking into an army food store, Matthes had nothing but contempt for the inane ways of German militarism. His favorite targets were recruit-baiting corporals and sergeants, whose pastime it often was to subject the lowest in rank to such "extra duties" as polishing boots with spittle and cleaning latrines with a toothbrush. Another "extra duty" was to send them through the paces of doing push-ups and knee-bends, and of making them run the "rounds," always to the point of collapse, and sometimes beyond. All that in Holland and in France, where the 18-year-old had been stationed with the German occupation forces in the summer and fall of 1942. At that time the real war was still only in North Africa and in Russia.

To Matthes, under four eyes, he would vent his anger, knowing that the former sergeant had nothing but contempt and scorn for the tormentors. And what Matthes had to say never failed to assuage his feelings. Thus, speaking of the *Wehrmacht* (literally "Armed might" or Army), Matthes never failed to call it the *Wehmacht* (Woe maker).

Furthermore, Matthes told him in so many words that the whole lot of recruit-baiting corporals and sergeants ought to have their asses kicked. And sometimes, after looking around to make sure nobody was listening, Matthes would add, in a low voice certainly, "Don't be surprised, if some of the bastards will end up with bullets in their backs—at the front." The one exception was Harold Schmittz. "That idiot is not even worth the powder of a bullet."

Leaving Matthes behind and going it alone was the most difficult decision he had ever made. And even though he had pleaded with Matthes to go with him, he felt strangely at odds with himself. As it was, Matthes had turned a deaf ear toward the idea of trying to escape on a raft or a boat. The fact was that Matthes could not swim. Matthes was terrified of the sea.

For a moment or two, as he walked away from his friend and from the men of the battery, he hoped for a shout, or shouts, urging him to come back. But nothing happened. All he was aware of was the noise of his own footsteps on the ground, footsteps that were taking him farther and farther away from the ravine and leading him deeper and deeper into these lands of mostly scrub and bush.

Suddenly he felt very lonely. It was the most abject feeling of loneliness that had ever come over him. It was like a dead weight. His steps slowed.

He was not sure he could go on. He found himself slumping under a bush.

But loneliness was not to stay alone for very long. Soon there were other reflections, premonitions, fears.

The fear of captivity was one of them. It was never difficult to imagine watchtowers and armed guards, barbed wire and fences, gang labor, measly meals and mean treatment. They were part of what men in war sometimes think about. What was different, at least here in Tunisia, were the extreme claims and counterclaims both sides had been making about Allied captivity.

On one side there was the German claim that, in the wake of a recent incident on one of the Channel Islands, the English had put all German prisoners of war into chains. The claim was made in an order of the day and Captain Schmittz had read the order.

On the other side there was the Allied leaflet.

He had kept the leaflet. It was in the Bible. It had blown into his hole after it had been dropped over the German lines with thousands of other leaflets.

On that day the Marauder bombers had been coming straight on, bomb bays open, and it had looked like the battery, which had gone into position in a cactus grove, was going to be bombed. And since the bombers were flying above the range of the guns, the crews had taken cover in their holes. In a second he would see the lead plane fire the flare which was the signal to drop the bombs, and from that moment on, the eyes would be glued on the dark bomb bays, out of which the bombs would come tumbling down momentarily, and then do half turns before streaking down head first toward the ground. And after that there was nothing one could do but press one's face into the dirt, hold one's breath, have one's life go by in a flash, and hope one's life would be spared.

As if in a replay, he remembered seeing the flare arch away from the lead bomber in a streak of brilliant, dazzling phosphorescent light. At this moment, instead of tumbling bombs, he saw something else. He knew at once that what he saw were not bombs. What he saw reminded him of birds, swarms of white birds, that kept swirling in ever widening circles downward, twirling and twisting at the same time as if frightened by the planes above them. What he saw were leaflets.

The leaflet he had kept in the Bible. Now he put it in front of him. It had a drawing on each side. Under the heading *So* ("This?"), the drawing showed a helmeted German soldier drowning, crying *Hilfe* (help).

The other drawing, under the heading *Oder So* ("Or This?"), pictured a German prisoner of war returning home, safe and sound, as his wife and his two children, a boy in *Lederhosen* and a girl in pigtails, were welcoming him back with open arms. And looking on in this alpine setting of house and garden and fir and mountain peaks was the sun, all smiles.

But what was most startling, if not confusing, about the leaflet was that it gave several assurances to its holders if they signed it and if they surrendered without resistance. It promised humane treatment, ample food, adequate quarters and even satisfaction of sexual needs.

There could be no question that the claims and counterclaims about captivity had put him in a quandary, especially so in view of their extreme nature. What had remained fresh in his mind, though, was the kind of relief he had felt, grateful relief, when the Marauders had turned around to fly back to their bases, after dropping the leaflets. On that day the *Sture Achtzehn* (stubborn eighteen), as the bombers were called by the Germans, did not return with a load of bombs.

By now he had decided to spend the night under the straggly bush. With his bayonet he scraped loose the ground and scooped out the dirt with his hands until he had enough of a hole. Into that hole he placed the tarpaulin. For the night he would wrap himself in his blanket. But first he would eat.

For once he had plenty to eat. He had bread, salami, chocolate, and in one canteen he had red wine. He cut the bread and the salami into thick slices, unbuckled the canteen, and then he fell upon the food. .

The food came alive on his tongue, rich and spicy, and he washed the bread and the salami down with quaffs of heavy and aromatic wine. In between he ate pieces of chocolate, and then he had more bread and salami, drank more wine, and as his spirits lifted he began to hum. Humming, while eating, had invariably drawn the remark from his mother that, lest he quit humming, he would end up marrying a crazy woman.

The sky was turning tangerine. Hovering low on the horizon was a band of clouds. Or, he was asking himself, was it a band of mist drifting in from the sea?

That night his mind was astir with memories. He thought of home and of home leave. And the memories of home and the pictures of what he would do during these fourteen days of leave went together somehow like clockwork.

He would get up at dawn and go to his pigeons. They were in a coop in the attic, above his room. He would feed and water them and then, by waving a flag from the hatch in the roof, he would keep his flock of racing homers flying in circles around the house, as if it were again time to train the birds for a race.

On one of the days he would whitewash the inside of the chicken house with a solution of lime and water, against lice. And he would do the same with the rabbit hutches that were lined up against the wall of the old barn, out in the garden.

Meals would be feasts: for breakfast crisp rolls from the village baker across the street, with butter and home-made strawberry marmalade; for lunch home-made rye bread with a spread of freshly rendered bacon and hot milk; for dinner such favorites as potato pancakes, fried barley sausage with fried potatoes, sourdough soup with chunks of sausage, and, finally, on Sundays roulades of beef, or a pork roast, with potato dumplings and red cabbage. And every afternoon mother would serve coffee and cake, either Silesian butter crumb cake, or pastries of fresh fruit out of the garden.

Between meals he would work in the garden, hoeing and weeding, in return for words of praise from his mother. Later he would go to the ponds to scare up frogs and, on windless afternoons, watch big carp break the still surface of the waters in their search for food.

Then there would be the nights. Summer nights in the village were the nights, above all others, when the boys would get together with the girls, or at least they would try to, like other generations before them. And boys and girls would as often as not end up in bowers, in barns, on lonely country lanes, in stacks of hay where they would wrestle, in so many ways, with their desires and their fears.

At daybreak he was once more on his way. Suddenly there was this donkey coming out of nowhere. It was coming at a trot as if it was going some place. Then, as their paths were about to cross, the animal slowed down and, turning in his direction, sidled up to him. Now it stood, perfectly still, in a posture of obedience. Its low back was like an invitation for a ride.

He had seen natives riding these donkeys, riding them in a fashion while keeping their balance and straddling them; and while this picture flashed through his mind, he mounted the donkey and they were on the go.

After about an hour's ride, the animal suddenly stopped. In a manner of speaking, it stopped dead in its tracks. He got off its back, talked to it, tried to push it ahead, raised his voice, but did not beat it. The donkey did not move.

Finally he gave up, took his bag, and was on his way again, heading hopefully for the sea. The last time he saw the donkey, it still stood motionless where he had left it.

The sky was cirrus. Already in the air, in the strong wind, were the small noises of leaves. His thoughts were with the sea and sometimes he felt that the sea was near. But at other times he was almost sure that he would never see the sea.

Then, as he came up on a hill, there it was before him. It was vast and uncompromising and it was in a state of movement. Madcap waves, coming over the horizon, were racing toward the land. At some point they would heave into swells and, before running up on the beaches, would break into a frenzy of froth and foam. He had seen the sea before, but never like this. He stood transfixed.

It was on the shores of the Zuider Zee that he had seen the sea for the first time. On that summer day the sea was all sparkle, as it caught the sun in myriad reflections: White clouds were sailing in the sky, like grazing cattle, and lush pastures behind earthen dams stretched far away. In this tranquil setting of sea and land, it was the Netherlands at their best. But that calm was to be shattered by airplane noise and by bursts of gunfire. Here at the headwaters of the lake, the battery was out on target practice. A *Junker52*, towing a sleeve for a target, would fly by the gun emplacement, in pass after pass, and the guns would fire. Tracers would tear into the sleeve, leaving it in shreds; another plane would come with a new sleeve, and the guns, sounding like barking dogs, would fire again.

Next, at the other end of Europe, he was to come face to face with the Mediterranean. First, with the Bay of Naples, whose grandiose panorama he would see in one direction from a park bench in Bagnoli, and from the piazza on Capri in another direction. Finally, he saw the Mediterranean from an airplane window. On that day the battery was flown from Naples to Tunis.

He remembered that he had barely climbed on board the plane with other gunners when, as luck would have it, the plane's turret gunner told him to take over the machine gun on the left side of the plane. Of Belgian make, the gun was mounted in a window next to the door, and so was the gun on the other side. The windows were small and were the only ones in the cabin. But regardless of size, for him it meant that he would be able to see the outside.

Soon the vast expanse of sky and sea was before him. In this world the blues ranged from deep dark above and below, to pale along the horizon. And it looked as if the sky and the sea were being torched together with a hot flame.

Flying in loose formation were some other planes, ten Ju52s. With flapping wings and wobbly rudders, with wings tugging at ribbed fuselages and propellers reflecting changes in speed and pitch rather nervously, with all the herky-jerky movements in that helter-skelter formation—the planes in this ethereal setting of water and air looked more like mechanical marionettes doing strange theatrics.

The men, meanwhile, were eating their iron rations, as if on command, even though it had been hammered into them that, as their name implied, "iron" rations were to be consumed only as a last resort. For one thing, the men were hungry. For another, they had just heard from the pilot, however bombastic in tone, some dire news. "*Meine Damen und Herren*," the pilot had announced, "be merry and enjoy the flight—for it may be our last." And, making a throat-cutting gesture, had added with a sizzling sound, *"Scheiss* Spitfires."

He remembered Sicily's coast coming into view, rugged and girdled by the sea. Next there was the flat panorama of weathered mountains. He kept looking for signs of life. A road, perhaps only a path, a river, all very small and very delicate, were meandering like threads in a work of filigree. In that triangle between wing and fuselage other signs of life came into view. Fields of golden yellow and dark green, looking like patches in a piece of stitch work, alternated with a village here and there that was crawling up the side of a mountain. Pressing his face against the gun, so to be near the window, he wondered what life down there would be like.

The men were done eating. The fact that they were full was dulling their senses, if not fears. They settled deeper and deeper between piles of gear, that lay in disarray on the floor of the cabin, and let their bodies rock and sway with the motions of the plane.

They were a mixed lot. In his crew, besides Matthes, were the cautious Swabian and the easy-going chap from Cologne.

In another mix of human nature, there were on these planes the dandies, the dullards, the toadies. But there were also the decent, the ones who in Dutch and in French towns would step from the pavement into the street to let native pedestrians pass unhindered, and who, on buses and trams and trains, would offer their seats to the elderly and to the women.

As he remembered it, the shots were fired without warning, in several bursts, with the turret gunner yelling, "SPITFIRES!" At the same moment the engines gave out a roar, the plane banked sharply, headed down, and he saw the gray sea come up like a wall.

He never saw a Spitfire. Neither did he see again the Italian Macchi 202 and the German Messerschmitt 110 that had been flying escort since Sicily. Nor was there a sign of the Ju52s. Flying between the sea and a cover of clouds, by ducking under the one as much as skimming over the other, they were now flying alone. He was convinced that the sudden cloud cover had saved them. And so until landfall he gazed at the propeller-rippled surface of the sea and the amorphous cloud cover outside right through the concentric circles of the gun sight, as if caught in a cobweb.

Now on this hill he stood transfixed. Before him was the stormy sea, with white caps and with foaming surfs, looking something like a huge half globe, and Pantelleria was nowhere in sight. If it was out there, it was lost in the haze that was blurring the horizon.

The beach was empty. That much he could see. All of a sudden he felt he could not go on. And so at the base of a dune, on the side where it was sunny and calm, he dug a hole, settled down and undressed.

He had lice, body lice. He had had them for some time. They had sucked him sore, especially around the abdomen and on the inside of the thighs. Not sore like in a rash, but sore in that the tormentors had left his body with hundreds of tiny lesions, either dark brown, where scabs had already formed, or in the color of fresh blood. Feeling his anger rise, he turned to pick them.

He knew where to look. Favorite places were the knitted underwear and, on the inside of his trousers and tunic, the seams, especially under the fabric forming the overlap to the seams. With the lice came the nits.

What he did was to press the back of his thumbnails over the lice and the nits, louse for louse, and nit for nit, squashing and cracking each one in turn. In the absence of hot water, he would rub sand or dust along the seams of his uniform, and shake each piece vigorously. He got the idea from his chickens at home, which, after taking a dust bath, would shake themselves to shake off the lice.

Soon the backs of his thumbnails were covered with bloody slime. He felt the need to go into the water and cleanse himself of lice and of slime, of grime and of dirt. The water, swirling around him, felt fresh and clean. Then he went back to pick more lice.

Holding the underwear against the sun, he saw that the fabric of woven loops was crawling with lice. Not that the lice would scamper. What they were doing, on close inspection, was to start to move their legs, slowly and tentatively, as if awakening to old instincts. He saw at once that all the squashing and cracking of lice and nits would be wasted. The lice, ranging from transparent to dark gray, were all over the fabric. Clinging. And sticking to the fabric were the nits.

All of a sudden he heard himself screaming, "GO TO HELL!" The sound of his own voice startled him. He ran to the water's edge. There he dug a hole, filled it with wet sand, stuffed the underwear into it and piled more wet sand on top.

To judge from the sun, the beach swept to the western sky in a gentle curve. He could see two figures in the distance. He watched and saw them going back and forth with something like boards to the water's edge. Were they building a raft? Then they were rolling a drum, again to the water's edge. He decided to find out.

They were indeed building a raft. The two were paratroopers in their camouflage fatigues, and, like him, they were of the lowest rank. They said they had "organized" the truck and the material for the raft. Drums, planks, ropes, chains. And they had come here to try to escape to Sicily.

The raft was as makeshift as it could be. Made up of four empty oil drums, two on each side alongside a beam, the drums and the beam were tied and lashed together with ropes and chains. Without saying a word, he lent a hand as if he had been part of the building from the start. Together they placed boards across the drums and started to rig them into place, for a deck of sorts, and tomorrow they would finish. Tomorrow they would sail. But because of enemy planes, they would not sail until dusk.

He told them of Pantelleria. They said they knew of no such place. They would wait and see. But it was already clear that he would sail with them. "All good things are three," the fellow-Silesian from Breslau had said.

That night, in the hole they shared, they talked mostly of home. His uniform, dusted and shaken, felt warm. He divided more of his iron ration with his new comrades, and once more the food and the wine came alive on their tongues, together with the sharp and intoxicating smoke of the Superieurs. Behind them the sea was noisy with distant breakers and with waves running up on the beach. And from time to time, sobbing and gurgling, noises came from the raft, as the water swirled between and around the drums and the planks. While they listened to the sea, they talked of home and of girls. Finally there was silence. He was alone with his thoughts.

He had seen her almost daily, last summer, before he went away into the army. She was from the neighboring village and he would ride the bike to her house. From there it was only a short ride to the forest, where they would push their bikes down a path to a clearing to while the afternoons away. They talked about school, about themselves, and, in the furtive ways of shy lovers, about their longings. It was in that clearing, on a night when the moon was full, that they were together for the last time. Their hearts were heavy with thoughts of parting. They lay there, side by side, and after a while he saw that she was crying. Tears, catching a glimmer of the moonlight, were running down her cheeks. She would sob from time to time. He wanted to tell her that he loved her.

But more than anything else he wanted to wipe away her tears, smother them with his kisses. Their lips touched. They kissed long and passionately and only the moon, full and mellow, was witness to their love.

Here in this hole by the sea he thought of her and longed to see her. Her last letter had included the opening lines of Eichendorff's poem about a moonlit night:

Es war als hätt der Himmel	It was as if the moonlight
Die Erde still geküsst,	Had softly kissed the earth,
Dass sie im Blütenschimmer	To blossom into midnight
Von ihm nur träumen müsst.	With dreams of love and mirth.

Turning to the side he repeated the lines, silently he thought. But the Breslauer, who lay next to him, asked whether he was praying? And he found himself mumbling that he was.

Toward morning he woke with a startle—THE RAFT! It was the first thought that shot through his mind. For missing in the noises that the sea was still making were the raft's sobbing and gurgling sounds. Had it been swept out to sea? Was it lost? Next moment he was on his feet and he saw that the raft, left dry and high on the beach, was still there. He sat down and waited for the dawn.

Pantelleria rose out of the sea like a mirage. It rose high above the waters, in soft undulating outlines, out in the sea, where he had guessed its location all along. The first light of the rising sun was giving the island a roseate glow, was giving it a real and mysterious quality. The island appeared at once distant and near, as if its reality was still somehow in doubt.

By noon the raft was ready. Moreover, with their bayonets they had whittled away at three boards to make paddles. And for a sail they had jammed a pole between the planks and the drums, tying tarpaulins to cross bars. Their thoughts turned to their chances of reaching Pantelleria, or Sicily, if blown off course; and they pondered their chances of being spotted by enemy planes, of being shot at. But they said nothing. Nor did they say anything about the planes flying off shore, high above the sea.

But Pantelleria was adding reality to its existence, as it were, with faint suggestions of earthen colors and distinctive shapes. And the island looked indeed close. The two paratroopers and he said that much.

Whatever they were, they came like gray phantoms out of the sea; first straight ahead on the horizon and then keeping a course parallel to the coast. They were warships and they were running at some speed, to judge from the white around the bows, and they were in line. And just when he thought that they were Italian men of war, a flurry of lights went off on every one of the ships, from bow to stern, and split seconds later large caliber shells came over and exploded at some distance beyond the dunes.

For the briefest of recollections, before the echoes had died away, he thought of the windmills at Schiphol airport. These windmills on stormy nights had been making similar sounds, big, swishing, gargling sounds. He had heard the sounds more than once, usually when he was on guard duty from midnight to four, while going up and down a row of dummy planes. And in another one of the recollections of Schiphol he saw one, two Dornier 88 bombers, on two consecutive days, take off, roll over, and come down. Each flight had lasted mere seconds and had ended, upon impact, in a fireball.

The warships, the shelling, and the recollection of the plane crashes had brought the war close again. Earlier he had thought of going back to get the underwear, even make a fire to heat some sea water for a wash and, for a luxurious drink, warm some drinking water from one of the two canteens he had. They would eat, all three of them, wait for dusk, and then they would sail. He became aware that the waters were back between the drums and the planks of the raft, gurgling and sobbing. There were no other sounds around, at least not at the moment.

And yet he found himself straining more and more for certain sounds of war. Sounds like the squeaks and rattles of tanks. Likewise, he found himself scanning the horizon, especially beyond the dunes, for such signs as clouds of dust from advancing armor. Somehow he had the feeling that things would not last until night.

And then it happened. Coming down the beach, at great speed, was a car, open like a command car, except that it looked like a jeep—it was a jeep—with two German soldiers in it. All they did, in driving by, was to shout *Sie kommen* and they were off.

There could be no question what was coming. Soon enough the squeaky metallic rattle, sounding almost like the twitter of birds, was in the air.

For the next hour they tried desperately to float the raft out into the open sea. As long as they had ground under their feet, they made headway, a few feet at a time, by pushing the raft forward. But about half way out to where the surf was, they lost the ground under their feet, and now headway was measured in inches, as they resorted to the paddles, or used their legs to splash and to kick the raft forward, in something like propeller fashion, against the incoming waves. To gain mobility he took off his waterlogged uniform. Several times they came close to getting out of the surf, if only the raft would ride over the swells, just once, to gain the open sea. But each time the raft would be driven back by powerful waves, by real breakers that would come crashing down on the raft and on the men in towering cascades of water. More and more the men came up short. In the end, exhausted, they gave up.

They lay flat on their backs, on the planks, and underneath them, between the drums and the planks, the waters once again made sobbing and gurgling sounds. The raft was drifting back. He was aware of its gentle motions and if he had one thought, it was that the raft could go on drifting forever. Then there was a bump. As the raft ran aground, it turned slowly, tilting ever so slightly. "THE BAG!"—"HIS UNIFORM!"—it shot through his hand. Gone. Washed overboard. And all of a sudden he was very much aware that he was naked.

That was how he came face to face with his captors. As he waded toward them, with his hands raised, he saw they were British, except for one soldier. That soldier was black and he stood in front of a tank, with drawn pistols in both hands. His eyes seemed to betray fear, if only because the dark pupils in the white of his eyes kept shifting constantly. And as he came to stand in front of the black soldier, as if drawn to him, their eyes met, if only for a moment. But that moment was long enough to allay somehow the fear that the pistols in the hands of the black soldier would go off. Thus they faced each other: the German prisoner and the black soldier, naked the one and dressed in a somewhat gaudy uniform the other. And it flashed through the prisoner's mind that the only other black man he had ever seen in his life was in a circus in Germany, a long time ago.

There were other soldiers. In their khaki shorts, in their short sleeved shirts, in their Tommy helmets, they looked very British, very much at ease, very *salopp,* as the Germans would say. It was not even so much that these soldiers were sloppy in the sense of the original word, before it was taken over into the German language; it was simply that these soldiers were quite themselves, quite at ease, the way they were standing in groups, here on the beach, between several vehicles, chatting and smoking, scarcely paying attention to the three German prisoners.

It was another Briton, a sergeant perhaps, who was obviously in charge. Short and stocky, this sandy-haired, mustachioed sergeant was going about his business with an authority at once natural and direct. It took only a wave of his hand to have the black soldier put the pistols away, and another wave of his hand to have the prisoners take down their raised arms.

Then this Briton went to a truck and, after getting what he wanted walked over to the three Germans. When he came to the naked prisoner he handed him, with the hint of a smile, a blanket. [See Appendix 2, article by William H. Forman, Jr.]

10

PRISONER OF WAR

81G-16855

After all the uncertainties and fears about captivity... he was now a prisoner of war. For a moment he thought of the only prisoners of war he had ever seen in his life. They had the letters KG on their back, which stood for *Kriegsgefangener*. On that day, they were on the highway near the village, filling potholes with asphalt. For them, on that treeless stretch of highway, it was a day of hot asphalt under a hot July sun, with no shade and no cooling breeze. What he also remembered was that the prisoners had kept their tunics on, soaked as they were with perspiration, and so had the guards.

On his mind were other thoughts as well, rather like half memory and half question. In a curious way they were about as unreal at this moment as the facts of captivity were real. But they were there, nevertheless, shortly after he had surrendered. What he did was to ask himself, amidst a host of memories, how much of the English language he was going to understand, now that he was a prisoner of war.

He had never met an Englishman before, much less spoken to one. He had seen English men and English women in pictures and occasionally in the movies; and among the foreign newspapers at the newsstand in the hall of the railway station at Beuthen there was the "Times." Each day, on his way home from school, he would try to read at least the headlines, being careful not to anger the man behind the counter too much for getting into the way of customers.

Furthermore, he may have seen English travelers on the Berlin-Breslau-Krakau Express. If the Express arrived on time, which it almost always did, he had five minutes before catching his own train. In that case he had to run from track 1, where the Express was always pulling in, to track 8 via an underground tunnel. But in the meantime he had enough time to walk past the gray coaches and the dark blue sleeping cars of the Express, past the shiny red dining car, while straining to hear the sounds of foreign languages. What he heard was mostly Polish. But sometimes, as passengers leaned out of broad windows or stood on the platform, he would hear either French or English, or both.

As for English, with each year of school-English he had become more and more curious, if not impatient, to find out how well he would do in that language. How much, in fact, he would actually be able to understand and speak it, in a real situation with real Englishmen.

For a substitute he would tune in radio London. But listening to an enemy station was a crime in wartime Germany; therefore he would listen only when alone, which was not very often, and then only at a volume barely above a whisper.

What he discovered was that his understanding of the spoken word, as it came to him over the airwaves, produced at best mixed results. Sometimes he was able to understand the announcer quite well, especially in the case of war news with familiar terms and names. At other times, though, the stream of words would be beyond his grasp and then nothing made much sense. Then the language of Shakespeare, which high school students in Nazi Germany were still required to read, if only excerpts from the "The Merchant of Venice," would turn more or less into gibberish.

Later that day, his first day as a prisoner of war, he was taken away. Riding with him on the open truck were the two paratroopers with whom he had tried earlier to sail away in the makeshift raft to avoid capture.

With them on the truck were two English guards. They were two rather crusty, rough-hewn soldiers of Montgomery's army who could not have been more carefree. Thus, instead of keeping an eye on the German prisoners, they turned their backs on them, leaned over the truck's cabin, and not once stopped talking. And not even after more prisoners got on the truck, at a place outside Tunis, did the two change in any way. They still leaned over the cab, still let their rifles hang loosely from their shoulders, and went on talking. What had changed, though, was that from now on their truck was part of a convoy that was headed for Tunis, for the first Allied victory parade of the war. However, the prisoners did not know that and neither, it seemed, did the guards. He had been standing all along behind the two guards, trying to eavesdrop. If anything, the conversation between them sounded like banter, boisterous and jolly. Meanwhile, he did his best to understand more than the most basic of English words, words like "the" and "a" and "in"; and although he was straining hard to understand what the two were saying to each other, he was getting nowhere. In fact, save for some basic words, words disconnected from any meaning, he understood more or less nothing.

There was, however, one more word that was to catch his ear. It was that certain "f… word," and it came up in almost every sentence, in a variety of ways. Besides, it sounded quite like the German word of the same meaning. And so until Tunis he was aware of nothing so much as this "f… word," which made him think that the two were talking mostly about sex, however incomprehensible and unintelligible everything sounded.

For a while the truck was travelling over the same road the battery had taken three days ago. That is from the ravine on the Cape Bon peninsula, where the men of the battery had demolished the trucks and the last of the guns, back to the intersection outside Tunis from where they had continued their flight after hearing of the fall of the city. Momentarily, he saw the trucks and the two guns of the battery in the ravine, hoods torn open and doors blown ajar, and everything about them looked the same, except that by now the wrecks had attracted some Arabs. Poor and destitute, they were apparently looking for anything that could be pried loose.

There was more wreckage; there were more bomb-torn, bullet-riddled vehicles, fire-blackened shells of trucks, abandoned guns; along the road there was all kind of debris that had been left behind by a fleeing army. This road was the cemetery of Germany's Africa Corps.

Here and there in tangles of wreckage, German soldiers with Red Cross armbands could be seen; some were carrying stretchers. In other piles of wreckage there were more Arabs, looking like scavenging ghosts in their long, flowing robes. By the time the trucks reached the palm-lined streets of Tunis, everything changed. Out in the streets were large numbers of people. They were there by the tens of thousands, crowding the sidewalks, lining the boulevards, standing behind wooden barriers; they were all along the route the convoy eventually was to take, which was through the heart of the city. Alarmed, he asked himself what it was, other than curiosity, that caused such a massive outpouring of people?

Soon the answer became obvious. These people were in the streets to show their anger and hatred for the Germans. Most of them did, even though there were some who apparently did not. And since there were no native Tunisians in the crowd, at least not Arabs in long flowing robes, the display of emotions was confined almost entirely to the city's population of European descent.

Shouting, screaming, spitting, making throat-cutting gestures, tossing human waste in the direction of the prisoners, throwing rocks at them, showing their behinds (some women did)—the crowd was in a state of rage, while the prisoners, standing on the trucks and looking defiant, were being driven by ever so slowly.

However, in the same crowd there were some who were crying, who were making imploring gestures towards the prisoners. Though fewer, they were just as intense and volatile in showing their emotions. In fact, it was all very strange. Here they were, people of the same city, standing at arm's length from each other, who were either very angry or very sad. He sensed that those venting their anger were French, while those displaying grief were Italians. At the same time he was shocked to realize how much of the anger and how much of the hatred were directed against them, the prisoners, when, as soldiers of the Africa Corps, they had done not much more than lose the last round of the war in North Africa.

At first there were just a few, then there were more, and finally there were whole groups of young men running in the street, circling the truck… when the guards took alarm and fired several shots into the air. One who fired was the guard next to him. Eventually the convoy speeded up and headed out of the city. Ahead of them lay the camp.

The camp was in an open field behind a railway station. It was the size of several football fields. Rolls of barbed wire went around it, and inside, on bare ground, were several thousand prisoners. When taken into the camp he was given a number. It was on a piece of paper. The number was in the high digits. It was the number of his so-called "century."

The centuries of one hundred POW's each were meant to organize the prisoners into something like units. Thus, as a member of a century, the prisoner was to keep to a certain area in the camp, receive his daily ration of biscuits and tea, and eventually leave the camp for the train at the depot.

He feared that with the high number it would be days, if not weeks, before his century would be called out for the train. He felt restless. But there was no place to go except to cross and re-cross the camp while he looked for a member, or members, of his battery. He found none. All he found were men on the ground, men who were waiting, brooding, sleeping, picking lice, playing cards, talking in low voices; they were of all (except officers') ranks, who had nothing but idle time on their hands. In their former world, where rank and the power to command had been the capstone of existence, captivity had turned the world of these men upside down—at least for the time being.

But he was to see the two paratroopers again. They were back with their unit, in which all members were wearing camouflage fatigues. They were the only ones who did so in North Africa. In this camp they were keeping to themselves.

Back at the place of his century, he unpacked his bag. It was still wet. He remembered that within minutes after surrendering, the bag and the uniform had washed up on the beach; and the sergeant, who earlier had handed him the blanket, had motioned to him to retrieve the pieces.

Also wet and soggy were the Bible and the last loaf of bread. The leaflet, which had figured so much in his thoughts about captivity only two days ago, was now a piece of wet, limp paper. He thought of escape. But this time it was to be escape from open latrines, from filthy grounds with swarms of flies and fleas, escape from the torpid thousands on the ground. This time escape meant getting on a train as early as possible.

As he opened the Bible, careful so not to tear the pages, his eyes fell on stories he had known since childhood. The memories and the pictures of these stories from Noah to Isaac to Sodom and Gomorrah, or from the ark to the sacrificial altar to the fires, gave him a feeling of God's presence in all things, then as now. And he felt, however fleetingly, a sense of consolation.

He still had some salami and a few chunks of chocolate, plus a loaf of bread, soggy though it was. But the Superieur cigarettes had dissolved into bits and pieces of wet tobacco. Clinging to the inside of the bag, he began gathering the precious tobacco bit-by-bit and piece-by-piece. Later he would roll for himself a cigarette with paper torn from the leaflet. Then he would take off his damp uniform, fold it under his head, and finally he would wrap himself into the blanket and, smoking the cigarette, await the night.

Mentally, he thought he had prepared himself for his first night in a prisoner of war camp. He was prepared to see men stumble around prisoners sleeping on the ground, as they were making their way to the latrines; he was expecting the stench, a mixture of human waste and chlorine, to get worse (since at night stench always seems to); he knew that among the bundles of men, right around him, there was going to be some snoring and occasionally, in the middle of nightmares, some groaning and some half-cries; and he expected the night to be chilly. But for what he was not prepared, nor would he ever become reconciled to them, were the bright lights. Because of them he found little rest and when sleep finally came, he slept fitfully. He could not know that ahead of him were more than a thousand such nights—all under harsh and blinding prison lights.

By morning he had made up his mind. He would try to walk out of the camp with one of the centuries due to be called out for the train. And he would get on that train and ride it to wherever it would take him.

Feigning a limp, he joined the last rows of men heading out. He got through the gate without being checked by the guards for his number. He was at the train.

Like the one on the day before, the train was made up of boxcars. Fifty men, or half a century, to a car. The men with whom he had been walking out of the camp had mentioned that figure. In this there was nothing unusual, as boxcars with the *40 Peronen—8 Pferde* (40 persons—8 horses) signs were the customary mode of transportation in the German army, at least for units on the move.

He was among the last trying to get on the train. But with hundreds of prisoners ahead of them, who had already scrambled for places, the boxcars appeared to be full; especially since the prisoners, anxious for fresh air, were crowding the space in the open doors. As he hastened along the train he realized that if he did not find a place on his own (as there seemed to be no one in charge), he would have to return to the camp. And the train was about to leave. From the locomotive smoke was belching straight into the air, a sign that the engine was being primed for the first forward motion of its wheels; also, guards were already on the roofs of about every fifth or sixth boxcar. Just as he was coming to the last car, the train began to move. The car looked empty. He jumped on it.

It took his eyes some time to adjust to the dim light inside. Only then did he see that there were men sitting on bales of straw, or hay, along the sides. Their uniforms had red stripes down the sides of their trousers. In a flashback of memories he recalled to have heard as a boy, with something like fascination, that the stripes were the mark of staff officers. But until now he had never seen a *Stabsoffizier*. Now he was in their midst.

He felt awkward. Still, he did not snap to attention by clicking his heels and by reeling off his name and the name of his unit. He did nothing like that. He just stood there, with his back to the open door, holding on to a handle inside the frame of the door, while in front of him the officers were sitting on the bales, with heads bared and with hands on their knees. Open tunics showed white shirts. Thus, the lone soldier and the row of staff officers were eyeing each other, both now prisoners of war.

Eventually some of the officers started to settle back against the wooden walls of the boxcar, causing their bodies to shake even more with the jerky movements of the train; some were closing their eyes. Then, into the noise of the train, came the voice: "*Sagen Sie mal, Sie köennen doch nicht hier bleiben.*" The officer had scars in his face. One was slanting across his left cheek. The other scar was also slanting, but it was shorter and it ran across the chin in a cleft. No doubt, such facial scars were from the days of student dueling. They were supposed to be the signs of bravery and distinction among certain *Akademiker*, or Germans with university education.

But his mind was already made up. He was not going to stay in this boxcar anyway, not with all those red-striped officers. He would get out at the next stop and, somehow, he would find a place on that train. Even if ordered by any one of the officers to stay as an orderly, he would never kowtow again: not after seeing how low the high and the mighty had been brought these last few days; not after everybody, regardless of rank, had become a prisoner of war.

At the next stop he did find a place with the guards. In fact, there was no way he could have found a place anywhere else, not with so many prisoners crowding the doors. In looking up on one of the boxcars, there were these two English guards on the roof. They looked back. Then he heard himself shout, "May I come up?" One of the guards said something, which he did not understand. But both guards nodded. After climbing the ladder, which was at the front of the boxcar, he was on the roof. It was of metal, curving slightly toward the sides. On that roof, with the guards, he had found a place for the rest of the journey.

In some ways these guards were like the ones on the truck. They were just as carefree, even more so, and just as prone to use that certain "f… word." What was different was that the two accepted him from the beginning as if he was one of them.

They shared what food they had. He gave them some of his salami and chocolate in return for some of their biscuits. "Bloody crumpets," one guard said. Then everyone had one last quaff of wine from his canteen. "Bloody terrific," the other guard said. Finally they smoked Players. It was his first English cigarette. With each draw he held back the smoke as long as he could, savoring its mild and aromatic flavor. Upon exhaling he let the smoke curl out of his mouth and nostrils simultaneously, before the draft of the moving train was to blow it away.

The train was rolling westward. For the most part it was travelling on a single set of track. But at railway stations with two or more sets, it would usually be shunted to the side to let a train from the opposite direction pass. Such trains were invariably carrying American troops with their equipment. He had a feeling that there was a whole army on the move, an army that was bound to carry the war from North Africa to Europe.

Later in the day the train began to go through mountainous country. What he remembered from school was that the Atlas Mountains—if that was what they were—were extending across western North Africa for a distance of some two thousand kilometers, twice the distance of any in Germany. Now the train was going even slower. Sometimes it slowed to a crawl, especially when going around a curve or when following the course of a valley. Then it took on the appearance of a crawling caterpillar, at least as seen from the roof, with cars swaying and bumping sideways and up and down. And above the noise of screeching wheels and of creaking wood there would go off, from time to time, the thin whistle of the steam locomotive.

What mountains he had seen so far in his life were mountains back home in Silesia: once after biking to Dresden with the Hitler Youth, and another time after going with friends to the Altvater range by train. Coming from the flat country of industrial Upper Silesia, where height was a matter of the size of slagheaps, he had been greatly impressed by those real mountains in the other half of Silesia.

But here were the Atlas Mountains. Already at their easternmost reaches, somewhere in that vast no man's land between Tunisia and Algeria, the mountains were of unsurpassed grandeur. Summits under that dark blue sky were like sentries of bare rock to the gates of past ages with their titans and half-titans. He tried to recall the story of Atlas, the titan or half-titan of Greek mythology, who had given these mountains his name. But he was not sure anymore of the connection between the latter and the sky-bearing Atlas. He found himself wishing his mind would yield an answer. When none came he started to look for signs of human life in this wilderness of mountains and gorges. He saw none. He looked for animals. Again he saw none. If there were any they must have been forewarned by the train and had fled.

Then again the tracks would straighten out and the train would have a good run. The mountains would recede and the gorges would disappear, and soon the first vineyards and olive groves and the first squalid hovels of the natives would come into view, with barking dogs and with children whose playing the train must have interrupted.

Otherwise the farms and the occasional towns along the railroad looked more or less like farms and towns in southwestern France. The signs on platforms and on rail buildings were in French. The railroad equipment was French, from notices on the boxcars to the thin, high-pitched whistle of the locomotive. And at night, when the train stood on a siding before resuming the journey in the morning, he could sometimes hear French among workers in the yard. One night there was music coming from a radio through the open window of the station. Off and on a woman sang chansons.

His mind drifted back to Jonzac in France. It was there, only last fall, that in his search for something to eat he came across this bakery. Not that as a German soldier he went begging. It was just that he was hungry, as so often; and since bread and other foods were rationed in France, German soldiers, who had no ration cards, found it next to impossible to buy anything to eat in French stores. But on this day, his first day out in Jonzac, he came across this bakery. It was in a narrow street, just off the town square. With the smell of bread in the air, he could not but yearn for a piece of bread.

Mustering what he knew of the French language, recalling especially the phrases of polite requests, such as *"Veuillez etre si gentil…"* (Would you be so kind…) and *"Pourrais-je acheter…"* (Could I buy…) and seeing that no one, with the exception of the owners, was in the store, he entered. The doorbell went off sharply with a clangorous sound. Inside was an elderly couple. The man reminded him of his father, thus appearing larger for his size. There was also that gentle and kindly look in the man's face. It was a look that was not all that unusual in older men with soft blue eyes; and neither was, for that matter, the untrimmed mustache.

Before he had a chance to say any of the polite phrases, the doorbell went off again. In came an elderly woman, dressed in black, looking delicate and thin like a figure of porcelain. A black coat was part of the wardrobe of widowhood. So was the black hat. Its rim was pinned to curls of gray hair. As she entered he became aware of her perfume. It had the fragrance of roses. But also present was a slight odor of mothballs.

He said "*apres vous*." In return she gave him a smile, saying "*merci*." While being greeted by the man as "*Madame, la Professeur*," she placed with quick movements of her small hands several coins and a sheet of coupons on the counter. Soon she was engaged in a spirited chitchat with the couple, with smiles and nods and lively gestures on the part of all three. Eventually the man was to lift, rather carefully, a loaf of bread into her bag. It was a loaf of French bread, long and crusty and of golden brown color. Then the woman turned to leave. As he opened the door for her, rather mannerly, she smiled again and, said, "*Danke schoen*."

Taken aback by the German word, he was suddenly seized by the fear that he would be denied even a small piece of bread. He had no bread coupons, there was no way for him as a German soldier to have any, and that was the way it was. No coupons, no bread. He felt like leaving, like fleeing from this store with its loaves of French bread in two big baskets that stood on a wooden rack, and loaves of dark bread on the shelves. But the eyes of the couple were already on him, the man's soft blue eyes and the woman's lively dark ones, and it was the eyes that held him back. There was nothing for him to do now but… to utter…

However, they were to speak first by directing a flurry of words at him. Words that came so fast that he was at a loss understanding them. Words that dumbfounded him, what was he to make of them? What was the meaning of words that were being passed between the man and the woman as much as they were directed at him? Of words, that were, spoken in a kind of rapid singsong? Yet there was, after all, a friendly tone to them, and he could only guess that the words were not derogatory or offensive in any way. Moreover, the faces of the man and the woman had something whimsical about them, had a winsome smile. He felt that at worst there must be something odd about his appearance, something very unusual about his presence in the store to draw that kind of attention. He groped for an explanation… until at last, from the rush of words, he was able to single out the words "*grand filou*" and "*bebe*."

They kept repeating the words, the man the first and the woman the second. The man kept saying, with a bow and with a motion of his hand, "*apres vous*," and added, "*Madame, la Professeur*." Whereupon the two had a good-natured laugh. And finally he found himself laughing too. He did so in spite of the fact that he grasped only the "great dandy" but not the "baby" part of their conversation. He never did, at least not on that day. Then, in handing him a loaf of bread, the man said, "*Komm bald wieder, Du grand filou.*"

He came back as soon as he could, two days later, around closing time. Again he entered the store when no customers were inside. The man and the woman greeted him cordially, almost cheerfully, as if it was the most natural thing to do and, to his surprise, invited him to stay for supper. "*Pour fromage et jambon avec du pain,*" the woman said. Seeing him hesitate, the man added, "*Alor... iss* [sic] *schon gut.*"

At the table he found out that the man had been a prisoner of war in the previous war. In Germany. "*Mein Deutsch iss* [sic] *nicht gut,*" the man said somewhat apologetically, "*iss* [sic] *lange her.*" In turn, he found himself answering in French, or at least trying to, and he wished his own knowledge of French were as good.

He also found out that *Madame la Professeur* was teaching German at the local *Lycee* and that one of her students was the daughter of the couple. The girl was sitting across from him at the table. She was beautiful. The soft blue of her eyes, which she had inherited from her father, was alive with the quickness of her mother's eyes. There was a sensuous look in her face, with those high cheekbones and the full lips which, when parted, revealed a row of teeth as perfect as pearls. Her dark hair was combed back, falling in long waves on a flowery dress. The girl looked lovely, she looked lithesome and alluring. Perhaps the best way to describe her was that "*bebe*", as her mother called her, was coming into womanhood.

It was for the first time in months that he was sitting at a family table again, with an assortment of cheeses and smoked ham and with a bottle of red wine before him. And while the woman was urging him to eat more and to drink more, even reached over to put additional cheese and ham on his plate, the man asked him to tutor his daughter in German, if he could, since the *lycee* had closed temporarily. There was no mention of anything else, nothing about the fact that it was the battery that had forced the cancellation of school by moving into the building since the firebombing of its previous quarters by the French underground in nearby Mirambeau.

He would go there as often as he could, about every second day, for supper first and then for the German lesson with the girl, before he had to return, with leftover sandwiches, to his quarters, where Matthes and the others from the crew were waiting. Sometimes Papa and Mama would sit in on the lesson, reading and crocheting respectively. Sometimes he and Jeanette would be alone, at least for a while, and she would quickly turn on the radio so they could listen to music, to *chansons* in particular. And she insisted that he translate the words, words about love and longing and waiting and happiness, and she would repeat, in her lilting way, the German words, while he in turn was seized by a fierce desire for her.

Suddenly he became aware that the music had stopped. A man showed up momentarily in the window, closed it, and stepped back. Then the lights went out. And the railway station, whatever its name and wherever its location in Algeria, receded into the dark of the night. And with the lights and the music went the memories of the last time he had seen her: she stood on the viaduct above the Jonzac rail yard, where the battery, after receiving sudden marching orders, was loaded on a train. He dared not wave. He was in battle fatigues and he would never know whether she recognized him. When at noon the train pulled out, passing under the viaduct, he saw her first on one side and then on the other side of viaduct. And soon it was too late to wave.

Clearly, the two English guards did not like Americans. In fact, they loathed them, detested them, and went on to say that the Germans and the English are fighting the wrong enemies. That the two should have gone together and fight these bloody spoilt and coddled Americans. For proof they pointed to American C rations, sealed in wax and luxuriously packaged, breakfast, lunch, and dinner each, which they had received at one stop. For additional proof they pointed to American military installations, from motor pools to laundries, all large.

Other than that they came from London, he never found out much about their background, as if they were reluctant to talk about it. Nor were they interested in his background. Most of the time they just sat there, on the roof, looked at the wild and inhospitable country, with its mountains and its gorges and canyons, and watched out for tunnels. The clearance between the ceiling and their bodies was mere inches. Just before entering a tunnel the locomotive would give two short blasts, whereupon it was time to take a deep breath, hold it for the thunderous ride through the smoke-filled tunnel, take if necessary additional short breaths of air through cupped hands, and at last fill the lungs with sweet fresh air again as soon as the train was out of the tunnel.

If he had one fear about tunnels, it was not the obvious one of being knocked down during one of the rides through a tunnel. For one thing, the brakeman's cabins on several of the boxcars were in fact higher than their prone bodies on the roof. For another thing, he would never, while sitting, miss the approach to a tunnel. For that he was too cautious, too alert. Besides, the three on that roof were looking out for each other in several ways, from fetching water and tea and crumpets at stops to calling warnings at the approach of a tunnel. And making sure that in the hundred-fold clackety-clack of the train the warning did not go unheeded. His one fear about the tunnels was this: suddenly, just ahead of a tunnel, there would be electric wires, sweeping them off the roof and sending them to their death.

But that was not how death came to one of the prisoners. That prisoner suddenly appeared on the roof of one of the boxcars, about ten boxcars ahead, and, kneeling, he looked in their direction. For some reason he kept looking, with his back to the front of the train, in their direction as if waiting for a sign of approval from the guards. Ahead loomed a tunnel. They waved to warn of the danger ahead. And the more they waved the higher on his knees the prisoner rose, until the back of his head was hit by the stone arch of the tunnel. There was a terribly sounding thud, amidst the sharp clackety-clack of the train. Once out of the tunnel, there was no sight of that prisoner anywhere.

Ahead lay the city of Oran. The guards had told him that much. Until then, as the train rumbled on, his eyes were taking their fill of so many sights along the track: of rock-strewn wasteland, of mountain ranges, of green valleys, of stately farms with miles of vineyards and olive orchards, of stretches of highway with star-emblemed military vehicles, of Arabs riding donkeys. He dreamed of times after the war when food would be no longer rationed, when city lights would blaze again, when there would be dancing in village inns and city cafes, when back in the village they would fly the racing homers again from Emmerich in Holland and from a place on the coast at Dover.

He was not at all sure anymore whether Germany would win the war. Not after seeing American Liberators bomb the port of Naples, with impunity and in broad daylight; not after seeing a few days later the same bombers fly over Capri, where near the marina the big barrels of an Italian antiaircraft battery would follow the planes in the sky, without ever firing a shot; it was the same day after day; not after seeing what happened last April 20, when their battery was part of a force that launched an offensive as a "birthday present for the *Führer*" to "chase the Americans into the sea." At Casablanca of all places, which must be at the end of this line. Instead of the Allies running, it was the Germans who ran for their lives that day. But then Captain Schmittz had never said anything about that. He thought of the ordeal of the last few days, with their false hopes and empty expectations. And now there were all those trains full of troops and equipment.

The guards kept telling him that at Oran all prisoners would be turned over to the Americans. At one stop, in fact, they suggested he get away. "Just get behind those bushes there, take a piss, squat down and pretend you are in the middle of a shit, and forget to come back."

Oran's rail depot with several platforms was a cavernous glass hall. As the train came to a stop, on a track with a platform on either side, his fears of captivity revived sharply. There stood the Americans: in two rows, one row on each side of the train, soldier after soldier, with guns at the ready, with shiny steel helmets, snugly fitting khaki uniforms, with pressed shirts and ties, with pressed trousers and polished half boots, wearing blue armbands with the letters MP in white. The same letters were also on the front of their shiny helmets. He had no idea what the letters meant. He only knew that these soldiers, in two rows of over one hundred each, looked stern, grim, unflinching, forbidding.

As he climbed down the ladder he heard one of the guards say, "Bloody stiffs." But to himself he kept saying, "My God, they must be the American SS."

11

ACROSS THE ATLANTIC

No sooner had the train left the station, with the English guards on top, when the prisoners were marched to an open square. To get there they had to cross the tracks first. Escorting them, with their guns still at the ready, were the American guards who looked like men on a hunt; like men expecting wild game to flush from cover at any moment. Meanwhile guards and prisoners were marching down a narrow street.

At the square the prisoners came to stand at its center. There they were now surrounded not only by the guards but by French gendarmes as well. It was then that it occurred to him that there might be another victory parade. But the gendarmes had sealed off the streets leading into the square and in effect were keeping the crowds away. And without crowds a victory parade would be like a circus without spectators.

Again and again he looked at the guards. In their rigid bearing they had reminded him at first, back at the station, of the German *SS*; to be reminded of the *SS* was about the last thing one could expect in this corner of the world. In fact, no unit of Himmler's dreaded *SS* had ever served in the Africa Corps. With the reminder came the remembrance that when he himself was faced with the choice, as a volunteer about a year ago, between the *Waffen-SS* and the *Hermann Goering* Division, he had not hesitated one moment. He had chosen the *Hermann Goering* Division. It was that simple. Without ever saying so, he had never wanted to be part of the *SS* with its reputation, even among Germans, of ruthlessness and fanaticism.

The association of these guards with the *SS* had stirred up memories. All of a sudden he remembered again the incident in the store of the haberdasher in Jonzac, not far from the bakery, where he had gone to try to buy a handkerchief. Right behind him an *SS* trooper had come in, promptly went over to the corner of the counter where the haberdasher was at that moment, and facing down the old man, pulled his pistol. Then, icily, the *SS* trooper began to point at several items on the shelves, and with each pointed move the haberdasher put item after item on the counter. After one final motion with the pistol the haberdasher stuffed everything into a paper bag. Now the *SS* trooper took the bag, put the pistol back into the holster and left. At this moment there were only the haberdasher and he in the store, whereupon he, unable to endure the questioning and frightened look of the man any longer, also left. Out in the street he hastened away in the opposite direction the *SS* trooper had taken.

And he also remembered that the *SS* were guarding the *Konzentrationslager*. He also knew that when Johann, his much older pigeon fancier friend, was taken away at night by the *GESTAPO*, several years ago, there were *SS* men on the scene.

And with Nazi power and with Nazi policies came the jokes. Jokes like the one that asked for the looks of an Aryan type: the answer was... as tall as Goebbels (who was barely five foot tall), as slim as Goering (who weighed a ton), and as blonde as Hitler (who was dark-haired).

Among the jokes was the one that told of Hitler and his entourage going for a ride in the big black Mercedes, out into the countryside, where they end up running over a dog. Hitler insists that an apology be made to the farmer. But neither the propaganda skills of Goebbels, nor the joviality of Goering, nor the dark insinuations of Himmler are of avail. The farmer remains adamant over the loss of the dog. Finally the *Führer* sends the driver into the house to talk to the farmer. When the driver eventually returns he carries loads of wartime goodies, from *Speck* to *Schinken* to whole rings of *Wurst*. "What did you do," the four ask in disbelief? "All I did," the driver says, "is say '*Heil Hitler*' and 'the dog is dead.'"

But he also remembered the most morbid of jokes that had made the rounds in Germany. It was about the poor quality of wartime soap, being scratchy and devoid of foam. Why that? the joke wanted to know. And the answer was that unfortunately they had allowed the Jews to become too emaciated to render any good soap any more.

And then there had been rumors. After the war had started there was the persistent rumor in the village that at the rail yards at Hindenburg, among the freight trains, cries for water had been heard from time to time. Always at night. The cries were coming from people who were clinging to the iron grates in the boxcars of trains that were heading in the direction of what had once been Poland. And each train was guarded by *SS*. At hearing such a rumor, he had never failed to wonder what had become of the Jewish students in class, of his friend Pinschover in particular, who had not come back to the *Horst Wessel Realgymnasium* in Beuthen after the *Kristallnacht*. All he was able to find out, whenever he went past the store of Pinschover's father, was that the store had changed names, that it had been "aryanized."

With these American guards here, for all their height, for the stern expression in their faces, for the fixed gaze in their eyes, he sensed, nevertheless, that there was something that was different. What set them apart, certainly, from the black uniforms of the *SS* were the sharp creases in khaki uniforms, the civilian-looking collared shirts with ties, the polished boots with brown spats. Spats that were going up half-way to their knees. Somehow these tall, clean-looking, stern-faced, mostly young soldiers stood in this open square like extras on a stage. Like extras in a school play. The more he thought about it, the less sinister they looked. Meanwhile, on command, the soldiers had shouldered their guns.

A short time later trucks drove into the square. Unlike the English lorries, these trucks had canvasses on, which he took as a further sign that there would be no victory parade. In fact, the Americans wasted no time in getting the prisoners on the trucks. Thirty to a truck. The instructions in flawless German were shouted through a megaphone by a uniformed man who was without an MP armband and who wore an officer's cap. The booming voice said that the faster they moved, the sooner they would be in the camp... where a hot meal was awaiting them. From then on everything went fast. Truck after truck came up to the head of the column, got a load of prisoners, and drove a short distance down the square into a street where they stopped to form a convoy. Soon, with the guards riding in jeeps, the convoy was headed for the camp.

Under the canvas there was no telling which way the trucks were going and, in the absence of signs, how long of a ride it was going to be. But with the promise of a hot meal, it should not take too long. *"Im Lager erwartet Euch warmes Essen,"* the megaphone voice had shouted. But what, he asked himself, if the promise of a warm meal was just a lure to get them on the trucks quickly? What if it was just a hoax? What if the camp to which they were going was no better than the first? Was worse? He found himself wavering between hope and despair. In the meantime, under that truck canvas, his thoughts went back to the last warm meal he had had.

It was on the night of the bombardment. The soup had been brought up to the front from the supply base, under the cover of darkness. It was the same kind of soup that they had been having for days, with that same flotsam of some kind of legumes in it, together with something that at first had looked like pieces of gristle. The gristle, however, had turned out to be maggots. First to float to the top, they were the first to go down, unless they were removed. Otherwise the soup was more or less just plain gruel, looking grayish and tasting stale. As for the maggots, he had tried to float them unto the spoon and toss them away. But it meant losing some of the broth and, moreover, it meant delay and his hunger could not stand such delays for long. Hunger drove him to slurp down the slop regardless.

Besides, it was always dark anyway. That way the maggots went down unseen. And that night, after they had eaten and had settled down in the tent to play blackjack, under the light of a candle, the guns had opened up.

The prisoners arrived at the camp sooner than expected. Camp Chancy was a tent city, with hundreds of tents, regular American army tents with eight cots to a tent. Moreover, each cot came with two blankets and a pillow, all of which was simply too good to be true. With the exception of the bunk bed during basic training in Utrecht, which had a jute bag stuffed with straw for a mattress, and the hospital bed in Bagnoli, and except for the bed in the convalescent villa on Capri, he had slept on nothing else but on bare or on straw-covered floors, often dirt floors, in such buildings as hangars, barns, farm-sheds, in the school at Jonzac, and in the empty barracks at Caserta. A cot was a luxury.

But it was the food at Chancy, which, for variety and goodness, went beyond anything he had ever had in the German Army. For that first meal in this POW camp they had ham, mashed potatoes with gravy, green peas, fruit salad, coffee and two slices of white bread with butter. After devouring the food he could have eaten more, had there not been lines of other prisoners. Besides, the mess kit had to be returned. [See Appendix 2, Article 2.]

An American mess kit was as different from the German mess kit as a tray from a pot. While the American was shallow and was divided into several spaces for different foods, the German mess kit was something of a pot with a lid, shaped more or less oval and holding, when full, close to half a gallon. Into that pot, then, there would go day after day the mainstay of German army food, a ladle or two of *Eintopf,* the name for a 'one pot' meal. On the best of days it could be *Gulasch* (beef stew), on a good day either bean soup or potato soup; but on bad days—and there were many—they most likely got a gruel said to have been made of ground fishbone. Finally, during the waning days of the war in Tunisia, they had not had much more to eat than the *Eintopf* full of maggots.

As for other meals at Camp Chancy during the one week he was there, they had scrambled eggs with bacon or ham for breakfast, in addition to boxes of so-called cornflakes, which was totally new for the prisoners, plus bread, butter and jelly, and plenty of real coffee and milk. For lunch there would be slices of sausage and cheese, again with bread, butter, and coffee. And while mashed potatoes and vegetables and bread came with the main meals, the meat dish would vary from the aforementioned ham to meat loaf, to a kind of pressed poultry.

He had never eaten better food and certainly not any more varied food in his life, not even at home. As such, US Army food had so far been the greatest surprise of captivity, especially after the Spartan diet in the German Army and after the English crumpet-and-tea provisions on the train. Nevertheless, he was leery. For all the plentifulness and deliciousness of the food, he was worried that it would not last. That the *Füllhorn* (cornucopia) would soon become empty.

There were even times when, however furtively, the idea took hold of him that everything was but part of the proverbial last meal of condemned men, of men condemned to hard labor or some such thing. What he did not know was that, as a result of American adherence to the Geneva Convention, the abundance, as it happened, was in accord with the letter of the Convention: POW's were to receive the same rations as the soldiers of the country holding them captive.

Accordingly, German prisoners got US Army rations and American prisoners got German Army rations. The difference was like the proverbial difference between day and night. For on the German side, in addition to the *Eintopf,* the daily ration consisted of no more than a fourth of a loaf of stone-hard *Kommisbrot,* a slice of sausage or of cheese, a dab of margarine and a dab of marmalade, and a ladle of coffee of roasted barley, even under the best of conditions. Moreover, part of the bread ration was to be saved for the next day. But as long as he could remember, he had never been able to save any of the bread for the next day. He was always too hungry. He had always eaten all of the ration. For him, each day had started with gnawing hunger.

When it happened, after one week in the camp, the selection was done at random: tent by tent, 8 prisoners at a time, until about 300 prisoners with their belongings were assembled on the camp street. He was one of them. It happened from one moment to the next. They were not told why they were chosen, neither were they given any clues where they would be taken. In short order they were marched off to the gate, where a convoy of trucks was waiting for them. One truck for every thirty prisoners. Within minutes they were on the road to Oran.

After one week of eating good food and plenty of food, and after sleeping on a cot, his worst fears were over. He still had no real answer for the generous and humane treatment they were receiving from the Americans, the same Americans *Herr Hauptmann* Schmittz had called "gangsters from across the Atlantic," or at times "gutless wonders." All he could do was to wait and see. In the meantime the trucks had reached Oran. Eventually their truck stopped. The tailgate was opened. They got off. They found themselves next to a gangway leading to the deck of a ship. On that gangway they went up. The ship had a coat of fresh gray paint and looked like new. Once on deck they were immediately sent down some iron stairs into the hold of the ship.

If there was one certainty in the life of a prisoner of war, it was uncertainty. The prisoner could never be certain whether, or when, he would be moved, and if he was moved, to what camp.

In this hold, which was a huge cubicle of steel, he could only guess that their destination was either England or America. He felt England was the more likely choice, since it was not as far away as America. But then the ship was American... and one never knew.

The ship sailed sometime after midnight. The steel floor on which the prisoners had spread their blankets came to life with the vibrations of the engines. So did, with the movement of the ship, the steel cubicle. Garbage cans, though chained to an iron post, gave off a hollow rattle whenever the ship lurched. From his place near the stairs he could see the outline of the hatch. Its two doors were barely visible in the light of a lamp that had been left burning all night. Lying awake most of the night, he kept wondering how soon they would see daylight again.

Some time later the hatch was opened. Sunlight streamed into the hold. On the floor it formed a square of bright, blinding light, lying there motionless. Only sometimes did it creep this way and sometimes that way, and then there were times when it edged away diagonally, up to a point. Otherwise the sunlight on the floor was about as inert as a square of white paint. If the ship was in open waters—and from all indications it was—it was holding steady course. Roll it certainly did not. .

In the open hatch they could see the sky. It was intensely blue and glaring. While gazing at the sky, they made no attempt to go up the stairs. Instead they crowded at the base of the stairs, staring at the sky. There, in that square piece of sky, they would see sea gulls from time to time, hovering or gliding across the sky, across that bulkhead-size piece of a sky, and sometimes, with screams of hunger, they saw the birds hurtling down in a flash of white— and out of sight.

There were now voices on deck. Occasionally sailors could be seen passing by the hatch. He was tempted to go up, perhaps as close to the hatch as possible, in order to take a look at the outside. But he hesitated. Everything in this captivity was again different, as different as the change from the roof on the boxcar to a cot in a tent at Camp Chancy. Now it was the steel floor in this hold of a ship. And while the change from the easy-going English to the disciplined American guards was extreme enough, here, on this ship, one was not even sure of the guards. Would they be sailors? Or would they again be soldiers with the MP armbands? Whoever they were, would the guards let them out on deck? It was that last question that had worried him all night. Just then three sailors, carrying boxes, came down the stairs. The prisoners stepped back. After putting the boxes down, one of the sailors held up a package, the size of a brick, from each carton, pointing at the men. Another motion, this time with both hands, was directed at the garbage cans. It was clear: each prisoner was to get one package out of each box—and as for the garbage, it was to be discarded into the cans.

The boxes contained so-called C-rations, with packages marked either as breakfast, as lunch, or as supper. At one stop during the train ride, the prisoners had already received such a C-ration. He had marvelled then about the ration and he was marvelling now: each package of dark brown cardboard was sealed in wax, containing cans and tubes of food, like an egg dish for breakfast, a ham dish for lunch, hash for supper, a can of fruit compote (so-called fruit cocktail), plus a tube of cheese—and each one of the packages came with crackers, with cocoa, lemon, and coffee respectively, all powdered, with a plastic spoon and fork, and, wonder of wonders, with a pack of five cigarettes. As he opened first one, then another package, he felt like a child opening presents at Christmas.

Both the breakfast and the lunch he ate at once. It was all so unique, the way the food in these rations was canned, was kept in tubes, was wrapped in cellophane. He ate the food with relish: fork after fork of the egg dish and the ham spread, spoons full of canned fruit, and crackers with cheese. It was all very tasty, very rich..., very satisfying. Then he smoked his first American cigarette. It was a Chesterfield. It sent him groping for the rail of the stairs, so powerful, so heavily perfumed and so dizzying was that first American cigarette. It took several breaths of fresh air to clear his head; then, inhaling the smoke more carefully and less deeply, he finished the Chesterfield.

For the powdered coffee they got water—in a fashion. Again it was the sailor with the sign language who, standing in the hatch, motioned with a pack of powdered coffee to come up. Once there, the prisoners fell (from years of drill) into line—and were each given a plastic cup of cold water. And into his cup of water the sailor emptied the powdered coffee. They did the same. He saw that the powder dissolved quite readily. Unlike the German *Ersatz* coffee, this was real *Bohnenkaffee;* it was strong, tasty, and, even though cold, this coffee felt good.

Ropes marked off the area on deck where the prisoners were allowed to move. From morning till night, as it turned out. At dusk they always had to go below deck, back into the steel cubicle of a hold, and stay there until dawn. As long as they were on deck, in that roped-off area from each side of the hatch to the railing, they were guarded by two sailors who always sat in the same spot, on a lower portion of the ship's superstructure next to the hatch. They sat there with their guns on their laps. The guards took their turns. All wore frayed-looking shirts and frayed-looking trousers of some rather coarse material, from light to dark blue in color. Covering their heads were white caps, with the rim turned up all around.

The sailors were the most unsoldierly looking and acting men he had ever seen. If there were any officers on the ship, he never saw any evidence. At least he never saw any men in a regular, well-cut uniform, nor did the sailors ever act differently whenever more than the two guards were on deck. They never came to attention, never acted snappily, never even did so much as standing up when doing guard duty. These American sailors on this ship were about as relaxed as the American soldiers with the MP armbands were rigid. He felt reassured. And when one of the sailors pointed at his *Hermann Goering* Division band, which was attached to the left sleeve, he used the sailor's knife to cut the yarn and handed him the band. To his surprise the sailor gave him a carton of cigarettes. Camel cigarettes. Other prisoners, prompted by the offer of cigarettes from about a dozen sailors, cut off their stripes designating rank, from *Gefreiter* to *Obergefreiter.* The latter were the only German soldiers on the ship with a rank higher than the lowest ranking *Soldat* or *Kanonier* (private or gunner). There were no *Unteroffiziere* (corporals) or *Feldwebel* (sergeants) on board.

But aside from the immediate impressions on deck—the roped off area on part of the afterdeck, the low structure with the guards on top, the real superstructure with the bridge, the masts and the open turret with a gun that looked like an 88—it was the sea that was spellbinding. The sea with its gentle breeze and the blue waters and the azure sky. It was the sea at its best.

Altogether there were five merchant ships, two tankers and two destroyers in the flotilla. With the coast on the left and the open sea to the right, the ships were sailing westward. The tankers and two other ships were keeping on the inside, thus closest to the shore, and the other ships were steaming on the side of the sea; and crisscrossing the waters farther out, trailing black smoke, were the destroyers. Off and on he had thought of submarines. But as he looked at the ships and at the sea and as his eyes, guided by the coast on the left, swept ahead of the ships in search of more land, Gibraltar came to mind.

Gibraltar and Cannae were *Oberstudienrat* Scholtze's favorite topics. Close seconds were Marathon and one or two battles of the Seven Years' War, in which *Friedrich der Grosse,* with his oblique battle line, was "laying the foundation for Prussia's greatness." At Marathon it was the sagging center of the Athenians that was to draw the Persians into near fatal encirclement. But for verve and vivacity, Scholtze's stories of Gibraltar and of Cannae were in a class by themselves.

Scholtze told these stories to the class more than once. What happened was that the class, at the end of each term in geography and history, was invited by the *Oberstudienrat* to voice its choice of favorite stories. Gibraltar and Cannae were invariably chosen.

To relate how at Gibraltar the waters of the Atlantic Ocean are actually rushing into the Mediterranean, because of the difference in sea levels, and how at Cannae the Romans suffered their worst defeat, because of the genius of Hannibal, never failed to send the *Oberstudienrat* into something like paroxysms of the most fervid storytelling.

Arms flailing (as when the Romans advanced into the dust and the rising sun at Cannae), arms going in half circles (as when Hannibal sent his cavalry crashing into the Roman flanks), the right fist knocking the palm of the left hand, (as when the faltering Romans were hit by the onrushing Carthaginians)... the right arm zigzagging from left to right, (where the waters of the Atlantic drop off into the basin of the Mediterranean), arms going round and round (as when the colder waters of the Atlantic mingle with the warmer waters of the Mediterranean to create, in the Straits of Gibraltar, some of the most turbulent waters on the face of the earth). In fact, he remembered Scholtze's remark that, because of the strong current, no man had ever been able to swim across the narrow straits, and no man, the stentorian voice of the portly *Oberstudienrat* had proclaimed, ever will. And last night, when in the semi-darkness of the hold some words about escape and Gibraltar and Spain went around, like words groping for an answer, he spoke up and mentioned that fact. There was no response. There was only silence.

Standing at the railing and looking at the waters that were gliding in small bubbles and rivulets along the hull of the ship before disappearing around the curve of the stern of the hull to be churned up by the ship's propeller, his mind was to embrace other details of his teacher's Odyssean ruminations. It marked the first time since leaving school that he thought with fondness of one of his teachers. How Scholtze at the end of each class, his dark suit dusted and smudged with chalk, stood there breathing heavily while cleaning his wire-framed glasses. And in that connection he recalled Scholtze's remarks that, compared with the waters of the Atlantic Ocean, the waters of the Mediterranean have less salt, are warmer, are less affected by tides. Finally, he remembered how the Mediterranean without the waters from the Atlantic would dwindle to about one fourth of its size, down to the size of at least two large interior lakes, given the factors of condensation and the few large rivers that empty into its basin.

He knew from his teacher's penchant for the history and the geography of the ancient world, a penchant that went hand in hand with maps and battle-plans and time-lines that were drawn on the blackboard, that Gibraltar could not be all that far away. For that matter the ships had begun their maneuvers—slowly and almost imperceptibly in that flotilla of vessels—and now the ships on the lee were moving ahead and their ship was falling behind. Eventually it was the last in line. By now Gibraltar had begun to appear on the horizon, like a raised fist, and soon the lands of Africa and Europe were converging to where the Rock was.

Gibraltar turned out to be true to its name. The Rock itself rises dramatically from the soft greens of the coast and soars all the way to the crag-like summit. And its rise is steep and, in turn, the face of massive rock on the eastern side plunges straight into the sea.

That afternoon the coasts of Africa and of Europe seemed so close in the placid waters of the Straits that, with the ships in the middle, the two continents seemed to be linked with each other. From Scholtze's excited remarks about the Straits he had expected the waters to be much more agitated in their rush from the Atlantic into the Mediterranean. But on that afternoon, under the sunny sky, the waters were altogether gentle, were almost placid. For a moment he was afraid that anyone of the fellow-prisoners would remind him of his dire warning last night. But no one did.

As the ships were passing through the Straits, with one destroyer out ahead and the other bringing up the rear, and as the terraces of houses on both coasts faded into the distance, he knew that soon, perhaps even before sunset, their destination would be decided. If the ships were to steer to the right, it would be England. If they kept steering ahead, the destination was most likely America. As it were, by the time the sun was setting behind the ships and as the sailors with the guns kept gesturing at the prisoners to clear the deck and return to the hold, the ships had begun to steer to the left. He was the last one to go down the stairs. Behind him was the sailor with whom he had traded the armband for a carton of Camels. On the stairs, before the sailor had time to close the two doors of the hatch, he asked, "To America?" And the sailor replied, "You bet," which he took to mean that they were indeed headed for America.

That night, off and on, he thought of America. He thought of all the things and events related to America that had come into his life. It had started with those *Amerikaner,* a piece of round, flat cake, about the size of a small saucer, with one half covered with a glaze of sugar and the other half with a glaze of chocolate. These *Amerikaner* were his favorites; at least on those rare occasions when, catching his mother at a weak moment, she would let him have the 5 *Pfennig* for one such *Amerikaner* — and he would run to the bakery, with the jovial *Herr* Wlochowitz or the motherly *Frau* Wlochowitz behind the counter and, by now out of breath, he would gasp: *"Ein Amerikaner, bitte."*

Next, in this train of recollections, he remembered mother's rejoinder to his complaints about a coat she had made for him: *"Aber Rudele, das ist doch ein Opossum aus Amerika."* But on that occasion, neither the endearing diminutive form of his name nor the strange-sounding animal, to say nothing of America, was of much help. The coat with the scratchy and itchy possum collar was to become the bane of his life, for one winter to be exact. A year later, having outgrown the coat, mother took it apart and made a jacket out of it, without the opossum collar.

So far, as far as the boy was concerned, the score on America was even. One for *Amerika* and one against *Amerika.* What really was to tip the scales in America's favor were the boy's hero Tom Mix, his favorite comedians *Pat und Patachon* (Laurel and Hardy) and that wonder of beasts, King Kong. And in between it was Charles Lindbergh flying across the Atlantic to be feted in Nazi Germany eventually, and Jesse Owens at the Berlin Olympic Games, where the German film showed him sprint to victory a record four or five times. And he remembered only too vividly those Sunday afternoons when, after earning 10 *Pfennig* for doing all sorts of extra chores around the house all week long, he would run as fast as he could to the movie theater in the neighboring town—to be among the first in the throng of children to be let into the theater for the Sunday matinee. There then, in the semi-darkness of the theater, he would wait with mounting excitement for his favorites to flicker on the screen, punctually at 2, either Tom Mix on his white horse in America's Wild West, or *Pat und Patachon* in the gorges and canyons of New York, or King Kong terrorizing New York and snatching a beautiful woman out of the Empire State Building. And the children in the theater would cheer and applaud and moan each turn in the fortunes of their heroes, and sometimes there would even be sobs. Amidst such recollections, in the dark hold of the ship, which was not all that different from the movie theater in Klausberg, he began to look forward to America, the land of his childhood heroes.

Next morning, as their ship was cruising at a reduced speed in a westerly direction, he saw other ships coming out of a harbor on the African coast. The houses, a thin line of them, were white, and Casablanca came to mind. By mid-morning they were on their way: a huge convoy of ships, freighters on the outside, tankers on the inside, and far out on the horizon an aircraft carrier. In between were several men-of-war.

The convoy itself looked like something of a cross between a behemoth and a leviathan, with the ships standing out on that vast surface of the ocean like fins and dorsals of such a sea monster. And that monster was moving from one end of the horizon to the other. Except for occasional light signals, when the ships from a point onward would make a turn, something like a quarter turn, sometimes to the left and sometimes to the right, the convoy just sailed on and on, always the same ships sailing in the same pattern and at the same distance from each other. Only the position of the men-of-war changed. On some days, for a while at least, the aircraft carrier stood out far on the right of the convoy. Then, after being gone for a day or two, it would reappear. As for the destroyers, they were likely to show up anywhere.

He had no idea how fast they were going. He only knew, from war talk among the veterans of the last war, that a convoy sails only as fast as the top speed of the slowest ship. Whenever he looked from the railing at the waters that were gliding past the light gray hull of the ship, he sensed that they were not going all that fast. Or at least it seemed that way, in waters that were dark blue and were quite often as still and as smooth as a mirror. Standing at the railing, he watched the sea for every change of color, for every ripple on its smooth surface as flying fish, fins whirring, were darting about. And he watched whole schools of dolphins swim close to the ship, their faces smiling, while doing leaps and dives, in perfect harmony.

By now there were times when he felt happy. He was alive. He had survived. Captivity, so far at least, had turned out to be humane and generous beyond expectations. His dreams for a world beyond the smoke-filled skies of Upper Silesia were in a sense coming true, if only on a ship carrying POWs. Be that as it may, the sea and the sky were vast and they were beautiful, and ahead lay America.

What was he to make of America? By and large the school had been silent about America. From the movies he knew America as the land of skyscrapers, of lasso-swinging cowboys, of pert and cute girls like Shirley Temple. Then there were the books of Karl May with their Winnetous and Old Shatterhands, brave Indians all. And he remembered the night of Schmeling's debacle against Joe Louis, when for millions of German listeners, who had stayed up half the night, the fight was over before a snag in the radio transmission was cleared. He and his father were among the millions who had lost several hours of sleep that night. And he remembered his father's consoling words afterwards: "*Einer von zwei muss ja verlieren.*" (In a fight there has to be a loser.)

Then there was the news (but no pictures) of the fiery crash of the Hindenburg at Lakehurst, New Jersey, for which the Jews, in a kind of whispering campaign, were suspected of sabotage.

And finally there was the war. If the war had done little to diminish the image of the English as fair and tough in the German mind, the Americans had fared less well. In fact, the string of Japanese victories throughout 1942 and the smashing success of the German submarine war were generally taken as proof that America was on the ropes, that one knockout punch was all that was needed. In fact, the Germans were quite willing to believe, in return for an early end of the war, that Americans simply lacked the guts to stand up and fight. And even though his battery had never faced the Americans, he had seen their Liberators bomb Naples and their Flying Fortresses bomb Tunis, to say nothing of the intrepid Mitchells and Marauders that had been making the lives of the German troops at the front miserable; and finally there had been the daredevil Lightnings. And what was even more alarming was that these American fliers did their bombing and strafing in broad daylight and not, as Nazi propaganda had so often stated, sneakily under cover of night, gangsters and cowards that they were.

Moreover, he had heard that in America everything was possible: fabulous wealth and grinding poverty... spoilt children and kidnapped children... diamond-dripping women and women wrestling in mud... huge advertising billboards and men carrying placards seeking work. And had he not heard his own grandfather say, in an aside during a game of cards one Sunday afternoon, that in America the women dominate the men and the children dominate everybody?

And had not the German UfA shown in the weekly *Wochenendschau* murder and mayhem and strife in America? And then there was the fact that one of his uncles had been murdered in America, if only because of mistaken identity. And now he kept going over his own week-long experiences: the riches of food, the extremes between the soldiers and the sailors, the practical side of such things as mess kits, army cots and tents, the light and yet warm blankets, the pillows.

And in yet another twist of recollections he pictured America as the land where immigrants could become millionaires… gangsters were known to roam the streets... Negroes lived in shanties… excelled in athletics. In his musing he saw America as the land of skyscrapers… of big cars… of stunt men… and then he remembered the hot summer day when, after school, he had an ice-cold, bubbly Coca Cola in the Woolworth store in Beuthen. The picture he had of America was all very confusing, was enough to render one, as German high school students said, *meschuge* (crazy).

As for the war, now that it was over for him, it had lost its grip on him. In fact, in this situation he hoped for nothing so much as that the submarines would either not find the convoy, or would stay clear because of the German prisoners on board some of the ships, or that the torpedoes in case of an attack would miss their target, at least miss the ship he was on. It was the first time that he hoped German arms would fail. Now that the war had shown him the precarious nature of human life, where death came with the speed of a bullet, with the split-second force of an exploding shell or bomb, there was nothing he wanted more than to stay alive.

The convoy, changing course from time to time, was sailing in the smooth waters of the Atlantic as if stories and reports of stormy seas and packs of lurking submarines had been mere figments of imagination. Only once, down in their hold for the night, had they heard so much as a detonation, dull and distant. They thought of submarines and they listened into the night. But all they felt, more than ever, were the steady vibrations of the steel floor under them. That night no one said a word.

They were a curious lot. He was not sure whether any of the men had known each other before they got on the ship. If two or three were from the same unit, they did not show it. Most of the time the men were either silent or, down in the hold, were staring at the ceiling. Thus they never talked of home, they never talked of the war. And if they had any doubts about the outcome of the war, they did not express them. Neither did he. All that mattered were C-rations, cigarettes, and lice.

There were no showers. Nor were there toilets in any other sense than a kind of an outhouse, made of wood and canvas, which was fastened to the railing and, for obvious reasons, protruded over the side of the ship. He saw that he was crawling with lice. By now the lice were not only in his trousers, especially in the crotch, but in his tunic as well. And even after he had traded a pack of Camels for undershorts, the latter too became infested in no time. All that anybody could do was to spend hours each day in the sun and pick lice... by squashing the lice and the nits between the thumbnails. Water to wash the clothes the prisoners had none, not even seawater. Their cup of drinking water with each meal was all the water they got each day. It seemed there was no escape from the tormentors.

If he had one wish it was for warm water, both to drink and to wash in. On that day both wishes came true, at least in part. He was no sooner on deck when he saw, at the far end of the deck, hot water dripping from a pipe... a drop at a time... in a puff of steam... until a puddle of water had formed on the steel floor. There was precious warm water. Wasted. After all these days on the ship with nothing but cold food and cold water, he yearned for hot water, if only for a sip. But the place where the water leaked out of the pipe was beyond the rope. It was near the superstructure with the bridge on top. To get to it, to catch it, he would have to ask the guard.

First he went down into the hold to get his cup. Then he went up again on deck. He was nervous. He must not fail. What he was going to do was to ask the guard to place the cup under the pipe with the leak. He knew what to say to the guard, a young sailor with an open and friendly face that was slightly marked by acne. He said: "Would you please be so kind and put the can under the water." The guard did not seem to understand. Repeating what he had said, he pointed in the direction of the dripping water. At that the guard came down and, seeing the leak, took the cup, placed it under the leak and went back to his post. And he? He watched the water drip into the can, drop by drop, making sharp little sounds. Then he heard the guard say, "Tell me when it's ready." He nodded. He had understood. He was happy. He was happy over the prospect of having warm water and over his successful encounter with the English language. And when he saw after a while that the water had stopped dripping, he called out to the guard that the cup was ready. The guard came down, got the cup, and gave it to him. He drank the water ever so slowly and he relished every drop of it. He relished it more than anything he had ever had to drink.

Later that day, the crew uncoiled a fire-hose on deck and turned on the water. The water apparently was pumped up directly from the sea and, as it gushed from the hose, the prisoners were frolicking under the water like vacationers on a cruise ship. "*Wie auf einem KdF Schif*," somebody exclaimed. With a thin film of salt on their bodies, they found later that night that the lice were less of a torment.

By now he was without any sense of time. The days on that ship, whose name he did not know, were going by as if time had become an abstraction of itself, as if time had turned upon itself. Each morning he found the ship sailing on the lee of the convoy, with a white and black tanker to the right, and another ship that looked like theirs to the right of the tanker. And ahead and behind were ships as far as the eyes could see, all on the same straight course, unless there was a change of course. Then, with lights blinking and with horns giving off short dark blasts, the convoy sailed for a while in the shape of a crescent before straightening out again.

He kept wondering about the mirror-like stillness of the sea. Was the convoy near the horse latitudes? Was it perhaps in the same waters where the sailing vessels of the early sailors to the New World would sometimes be left dead in the water for lack of wind? When the horses, to save water, were the first to go over board?

He had questions about the huge beds of seaweed that swayed in the waves of the ship. Questions about the lone flight of a clumsy-looking, heavy-winged bird. Questions about whether the appearance of a flying boat one day meant that land was near. What he also did was to have all kinds of objects and images that were near him go through his mind, in a kind of exercise, first in German and then in English. And he wished he had a dictionary.

One day, long after he had lost count of the days, he saw the first sea gull again. It sailed for a while in the draft of the ship. Now he knew that land was not far away. Soon there were whole flocks of sea gulls and, moreover, the ships had begun to maneuver. And by the time some ships had formed a line and others had veered away, mostly to the right, he caught the first glimpse of land: a thin, low line of land looking sandy, especially along the horizon, and green. He was filled with excitement.

What also happened was that the guards pointed their guns at the hatch. For the prisoners it was the sign to go below deck. From now on, for about two hours, they listened to every change in vibration, to every noise, like that distant metallic rumble that came from the direction of the bow. And then there were but the sounds of foghorns and the cries of sea gulls, sounding muffled and abstract. Then, in that semi-dark hull of the ship, they felt a bump. A short time later the hatch was opened and a voice was shouting in English to come up. Instinctively they grabbed their belongings and went up the stairs. The deck was awash in the glare of the setting sun.

Next to their ship, tied to it in fact, lay another ship. It was much smaller, but it had the same gray color. He couldn't believe his eyes: strung around the ship was barbed wire, all the way from bow to stern and all across. The weave of the wire so narrow that not even a bird, like one of the sea gulls, could have gotten through. At first he did not connect the ship with their captivity. Escape was the last thing on their mind. But then he saw soldiers on the ship with MP armbands, soldiers with guns at the ready, and he knew that they were going to be taken somewhere - and they were.

While they were taken across the open part of the harbor he saw on a warehouse or two the name of the harbor. It was Norfolk. He had no idea where Norfolk was. He could only guess that it was somewhere on the east coast of the USA. Within minutes they disembarked on a pier; from there they were marched to a hall with railroad tracks on one side and a long building on the other. There they were assembled. All 300 of them. Surrounding them were the guards with the MP armbands, tall and stern-faced, holding their guns at the ready. His eyes went around: in front were the tracks with the darkening waters of the port... in back was the building with rows of well-lit windows... also in back was a wide door with a hallway beyond... at the far end of the hallway appeared to be a large room.

Into that room their group of about fifty was led. There they were handed a piece of paper. It said in German that they were going to be deloused. The paper also instructed them, by word and by picture, to place all clothes into the left satchel and all valuables into the right satchel. After undressing and after leaving their clothes and what valuables they had behind, they were on their way to yet another room, its white walls glaring in the white light. There they were made to stand in line, one after another. Eventually the line advanced. Ahead of him he saw a black soldier whose white uniform contrasted sharply with his black skin. The soldier had something like a pump in his
hand. It was bigger than a bicycle pump. Every time the soldier pumped, a cloud of powder shot out of its nozzle. The powder had the smell of a chemical. When it was his turn, he stepped with raised arms in front of the black soldier, whereupon the soldier pumped a spray of powder into each of his armpits. Then, lowering the gun, the black soldier pumped two sprays at his genitalia, one from the front and one from the back.

After that the group assembled in a room where each prisoner was given a bar of soap, the size of a German matchbox, and a towel. The towel was soft and fluffy. The soap had the feel and the fragrance of peacetime soap. It was not at all like German wartime soap.

And then they stepped into a large room for their showers. The showerheads were in the ceiling. There was no sign of water anywhere. Their group was the first. He looked at the ceiling. It was white. So were the walls. The whiteness, in the harsh light of the room, was almost blinding. There were rows of showerheads in the ceiling. They were round and each one of them had rings of small holes, pointing straight down. Soap in hand he stood under one of the showerheads, waiting for the water. He looked up and he waited. He looked at the shower head with the ring of small holes, as he waited for the first warm water in months, for the first real soap lather in years, for the water to come down like balm on the hundreds of sores from the bites of lice covering his body.

As he looked at the showerheads he was suddenly jarred... from deep within he was suddenly jolted by a terrifying thought: WHAT IF GAS...

At that moment water came out of the showerheads. It was warm and it came in gentle profusion and the lather of the soap was like a caress. He stood under that shower and it was bliss.

12
ON THE TRAIN

They never knew their destination, nor did they have any idea how long it would take to wherever they were going. All they knew was that they had boarded the train at Norfolk and that, since then, the train was heading westward: as when on three successive evenings it had a good run in the direction of the setting sun; or when, with less drama, it had the rising sun at its back. In the end, they were to be on that train for three days and three nights.

They were German prisoners of war and they were now in *Amerika.* It was at Norfolk, after crossing the Atlantic in ships that had sailed in a convoy from North Africa, that they had been deloused and had been *processed.* *Processing* was the name for having their identities recorded by German-speaking interrogators and for having been fingerprinted. After that they were lined up on the platform of a railway station, where the sea was just beyond the tracks; and while waiting for whatever was going to happen next, some of the prisoners talked about the *crime* of having been fingerprinted like ordinary *gangsters.*

It never occurred to them that the train that backed into the station was for them. For one thing, it had the looks of an express: the coaches had wide windows and behind the windows were plush-looking, upholstered seats; also, in keeping with fast trains, this one appeared to be a *D-Zug,* or vestibule-train, on which passage from one end to the other was possible. Even after coming to a stop, directly in front of the prisoners, and even after the guards had divided the latter in groups of twenty or thirty, or whatever, the prisoners still had no idea that the train was for them. To them travelling by train meant boxcars. It meant 40 soldiers to a boxcar, just as it was spelled out on every German boxcar: *40 Personen—8 Pferde* (horses).

The prisoners just stood there. It was as if they were under a spell of aversion to everything that went on around them. Meanwhile the guards tried, in their way, to tell the prisoners to get on the train, by gesturing, by stepping on and off, by shouting *OK.* At last the prisoners understood and got on. As soon as they had settled down in the coaches, one prisoner for every two seats, they felt at once relieved and suspicious. Relieved, that they did not have to endure the hard knocks and bumps of a boxcar, to say nothing of the stench and the slosh of human waste in buckets; and suspicious, because they could not help thinking that, in this first class setting, the Americans were up to new tricks.

For the moment he had only one fear. He feared that the ride on that train would not last all that long. Perhaps only minutes, at best an hour, before they would be at a camp somewhere outside Norfolk. So he gave himself to the luxury of reflection that *so far* in this war he had survived, that *so far* captivity had been surprisingly humane, that *so far,* from the meals at Camp Chancy in North Africa to the rations on the Liberty Ship, food had come to the German prisoners of war in a cornucopia of plenty.

There was no whistle, no command, no last-second shouting as the train moved out of the station. There was nothing even remotely similar to the drama and drill with which passenger trains were dispatched in Germany. As a commuting student he had ridden them every day. This train just started out, gained speed and, once in open country, was going at full throttle. His first reaction was to open the window, to lean out and savor the sensations of speed and steam and smoke. But he found that the window was partially blocked and that it could only be opened to about the width of a hand. Still, he could feel the pull of the locomotive, he could hear the hiss of steam, the rush of smoke, and he was aware of the big wheels stomping and clanking on the tracks. He was keenly aware of all that.

Meanwhile, the guards had taken their stations: one at each end of the coach. Like the guards at Oran in North Africa, they wore blue armbands with the letters MP in white. Their uniforms were pressed and looked starched, and their boots and helmets were shiny. But whereas the guards at Oran in their ramrod bearing had reminded him of the German SS, these guards here were the picture of casualness, smoking cigarettes, talking to each other, chewing gum; they did all that while standing guard. The prisoners were more like an afterthought. In fact, the only time the guards paid any attention to them was when one of them raised a hand.

He had to go to the toilet and so he raised his hand. After food and after sleep, there is nothing more crucial to a prisoner than being able to relieve himself, especially during a transport. Then he finds himself more than ever at the mercy of the guards. And so as soon as he saw that the guard waved back at him, he went down the aisle and stepped into the toilet. He was alone. It was the first time in a long time that he was alone, if only for a few minutes, alone with the need of moving his bowels, alone in the privacy of a toilet with such luxuries as toilet paper and paper towels and running water, alone with a mirror. He had not seen his face since his capture and what he saw pleased him. He had grown a beard which was strictly *verboten* in the German army, and his hair had outgrown the army's standard, which, for the low ranks, was the length of a matchstick.

Back in his seat another surprise awaited him. As it was, on this day he had already had his share of surprises and, yes, fears: like when they were taken off the ships and were herded on a tugboat under a cocoon of barbed wire for the short trip to the shore facilities; or when a short time later each prisoner was given a bar of soap and a thick towel for the showers; and when, during the final seconds before hot water gushed out of the nozzle, he was suddenly seized by the most terrible of all fears ... that the showers were just a disguise for gas. And now there was this surprise: there were these black soldiers in white uniforms who came down the aisle pushing serving carts and stopping before every prisoner to serve food; food that was warm and steaming, food that came in courses of meat and potatoes and green beans, and in servings of canned fruit and fresh green salad; and then there was bread and butter and coffee; and for dessert the prisoners were served vanilla ice cream with a topping of chocolate sauce. Here were blacks serving whites... as if the latter as German soldiers had never tasted defeat, had never been part of the surrender of Rommel's *Afrika Corps* a mere two months or so ago. On this train, then, the reversal of roles between members of the two armies was to go on for three days, or every time that breakfast, or lunch, or dinner was served.

It never occurred to him that just because America was Germany's enemy everything that was American was loathsome and hence had to be criticized and derided. He for one was free of such inclinations, perhaps because of his four years of high school English, perhaps because of the live-and-let-live attitude of his parents, perhaps because of his natural curiosity for the strange in this world. Thus, he felt free to enjoy this American train with its speed and its sounds and its amenities. Above all he felt free to observe America with undiminished and unabashed curiosity as it flashed by the window.

By now it was obvious that they would be on this train at least through the night. And night was not far away. In the coaches the lights had come on. Their reflections were like a game of hopscotch between the train on one side and the river on the other, as the train kept running along the riverbank for some time, at a good speed. It only slowed down as it passed through a small town. There, at a two-track station, it stopped and came to stand alongside another train, a regular passenger train. And in the window, directly across from the window of the two prisoners, there was this little boy, standing on his father's lap, the face beaming with excitement. The little boy waved and waved, first with one hand and then with both hands; and just as the one prisoner was about to wave back, there was the voice of the other prisoner: "You *Scheissamerikaner*, quit beating the air with your *Scheiss* arms."

It was that remark that kept him from waving back. Besides, at that moment the train started to move and the little boy was out of sight almost at once. And now there was nothing he could do but feel the shame of having let the little boy down, feel the anger of having let himself be browbeaten by the snarl of a Nazi. And in order to assuage his shame and in order to control his anger he made up his mind that next time, should another child be waving at him, he would wave back.

During the night, when not asleep, he was aware of nothing so much as... the blurred reflections of the windows running in a wild scramble along the tracks... the star-like quality of solitary lights in the darkness... the long-drawn haunting wail of the train whistle... the furious staccato of warning bells at crossings... the thunderous rides over bridges... the suck of air in a tunnel... the languor of a town at night... the languor of a rail yard at night.

But however much he saw, by day and by night, he was never sure where they were. One reason was that his knowledge of the United States was rather scant. Another reason was that the train, with one exception, would not stop in the railway stations of major towns, but in the yards. And once in a yard, the train was in no hurry to move on. And so it was only by a kind of reverse deduction that he knew where they were not: they were not in cities he would have recognized from pictures had the train passed through them, through cities like New York and San Francisco; neither had they passed through Chicago and Boston, since the latter were located on the waters of a lake and the ocean respectively. And after Norfolk they had not been near open waters again. There had only been land and nothing but land. And, finally, about St. Louis he knew that the city had given its name to Lindbergh's plane and that St. Louis was located on the banks of the Mississippi. But then he had not seen a river the size of the Mississippi. Or so he thought. And of Los Angeles he only knew that Hollywood was there.

Moreover, the train had not gone through the Rocky Mountains. Nor had it been anywhere near the so-called *Wild West,* to judge from Karl May's books he had read and the Tom Mix movies he had seen. There remained then, at least for direction, the sun. From its position he could tell that for the most part they were heading in a westerly direction. In fact they were passing through a countryside that did not look all that different from Germany. Exceptions were the ubiquitous automobile and the large number of churches and gas stations. What was also different was that most of the houses were of wood and stood in yards that had no fences. Finally, for the country's greatest difference with Germany, there was its size. This country was so vast and so immense that Germany, by comparison, was more like a dwarf.

Suddenly he was seized by a feeling of foreboding. Suddenly he knew that for Germany the war was lost: that the surrender of the Africa Corps was but the beginning of the end for Germany; that, to speak with a German proverb, *many dogs are the hare's death;* that in the United States and in the Soviet Union, Germany was faced with formidable foes. Finally, there was the newspaper.

What happened was that for once, on the second day of their journey, the train stopped in the station of a town by the name of *Springfield.* The name meant nothing to him. All he knew was that the name stood (in black letters on a white background) on the side of the red brick building that faced the platforms—platforms with shed-like roofs and with tracks in between. And on the platform where they had stopped there were American passengers who were waiting for the arrival of their train. Among them was a man in a business suit, reading a newspaper. The man looked up and, as his interest in the train with the guards and the prisoners quickened, their eyes met: the eyes of the American in the business suit and the eyes of the German prisoner who, because of the heat, sat shirtless behind the window. Presently the prisoner pointed at the man's newspaper, whereupon the man folded it and, after a word with the guard, came over to hand it through the small opening in the window. It all happened as if it were the most natural thing to do, this handing of a thick, large-sized American newspaper by an American to a news-starved German prisoner. It was the prisoner's first American newspaper. It was the *Chicago Tribune*. And for starters the headline read: "Senate considers Beer Bill Favorably."

He had been without news since May 11, the day he was taken prisoner. And now it was a day in July. Which day in July, other than perhaps a day in late July, he did not know. The weeks on the ship in the convoy had completely blurred his sense of time. What the voyage had not blurred, though, was a haunting sense that the war was not going well for Germany. Thus he kept asking himself: whether the Russians, after Stalingrad, were still on the move... whether the Allies had landed on Sicily, now that the war in North Africa was over... or whether they had skipped the island and had already landed in Italy... whether Allied bombers were continuing to rake German cities with bombs... what new dangers the German submarines were facing in the Atlantic. And in asking himself these questions he remembered, among other things, how the convoy, with its aircraft carrier and the destroyers and the flying boats, had sailed across the Atlantic without so much as a single submarine alarm... how war-weary and defeatist and anti-German the Italians had become... how the Allied war machine had worn down and had finally crushed the *Afrika Corps*... how the veterans of the Russian campaign would speak with undisguised terror of Stalin's rockets and Stalin's tanks...

And now, at last, he had a chance to find out how the war was going, if only from an enemy newspaper. But before he could make an attempt to read and to understand, there was the voice of the prisoner again who sat across from him. It was the voice of the boy-bashing Nazi: "You won't be reading this?!" The voice had trailed off, as if the words were to settle down on their own for a final meaning. Still, the voice had that sharp-edged, gruff pitch of a man who was used to giving orders in the army. As a corporal? As a sergeant? It was a question of rank. And the reason why rank was a question was because so many of the corporals and sergeants of Rommel's *Afrika Corps* had removed all piping and insignia from their uniforms since their capture. To confuse the enemy? To avoid being singled out for harsh treatment? It was never clear.

"Soldier, you have heard me?!" There, trailing off, was the voice again. Only this time it had changed to the formal address, to the *Sie* instead of the *Du* in German. This time the voice left no doubt that it was speaking to a subordinate.

He gave no answer. He felt only anger. It was the kind of anger which, after smoldering for some time, was ready to burst into flame.

At the same time there was something inside him that told him to be careful and ignore the Nazi, who most likely belonged to a type in Nazi Germany that had risen, like scum in a cesspool, to the top. Had risen to dominance. To bellowing, bullying, bawling dominance.

We should know that no German who grew up in the Third *Reich* and who served in Hitler's army ever escaped being shouted at, being screamed at, being subjected to inanities and indignities. And if that German was not careful and did not keep his mouth shut, there was always that chance of a fate far worse.

And so he had kept his mouth shut, although there had been times, especially in boot camp, when he wanted nothing so much as to scream contempt and to hurl defiance at these drill-sergeants. At the tormentors. At the sadists. At the whole lot of practitioners of hell.

But there was the voice again: "This is an order: You will hand over at once this bunch of enemy propaganda."

The words only exacerbated the worst of his memories. He remembered the times when as recruits, after having been kept on the run all day, they had to report for special duty in the evening: To be drilled again to the point of collapse. To scrub the *toilettes* with a toothbrush. To do push-ups in front of an iron stove in which a roaring fire was burning. To turn the rounds in ankle-deep sand of the exercise-grounds. To go through the paces of the goose-step. To don the gas mask for a running attack. To be sent scrambling to the top of their lockers. To frog-jump with arms extended. To frog-jump with arms holding the rifle. To crawl in seal fashion. To crawl through the muck. To stand inspection.

"For the last time, I command that you..." At that moment the voice faltered, cracked. Swallowing hard, the Nazi never did regain his voice. Clearly, the Nazi was overtaken by a failure to assert his authority. The only other time he had seen a similar failure was back in boot camp. It happened on the exercise-grounds of the *Hermann Goering* Division in Utrecht, on a day of blistering sunshine and high humidity, when the drill-sergeants, standing in the center, sent the company of recruits around the exercise-grounds, in round after round of running. Running in battle-dress, in their hob-nailed boots, in their steel-helmet. Running with rifle in hand. The marathon took its toll: after God only knows how many rounds, most of the recruits had collapsed. Left running were no more than a handful, the ones with the greatest endurance and perseverance. He was among them. By now they were running like robots. By now there was nothing—no commands, no shouting, no screaming by the drill-sergeants—that would cause them to run faster. It was at that moment that Chin-Willi, the most brutal and sadistic of the drill-sergeants, decided to set the pace by darting in front of the men. The marathon turned into a duel. Into a duel to the finish. Between Chin-Willi and him. Stride for stride. Round after round. Until Chin-Willi crumpled to the ground.

The train started up with a sudden movement. He looked at the man who had given him the paper. And as their eyes met, they both raised their arms—for a wave.

Springfield was like a point of no return. To him it was. They were all prisoners of war now. The world of rank, of unchecked authority, of rampant viciousness, of boot camp mentality was over. At this moment he knew that he would never submit again with cadaver-like obedience to the whole lot of drill-sergeants and arrogant officers and snarling Nazis. Not as long as he was a prisoner of war. He returned the Nazi's angry stare. Then he turned to the newspaper.

He had no difficulty grasping the news: *Italy is making peace bid... Mussolini is reported to have been seized... Badoglio is the new ruler of Italy... anti-fascist demonstrations in many Italian cities... Yankees drive for Messina... five-sixths of Sicily now in Allied hands... US Forces make second heavy raid on Hamburg... attack three other German cities in daylight raids... down 50 German planes... 23 bombers lost... American Flying Fortresses raid port of Trondheim in Norway... hit Nazi submarine and another warship... Yankees gain in Munda drive...*

The news was shattering. What had happened during the last two months was worse than he had expected. The war no doubt was going badly for Germany. For the German people the war had become a matter of life and death.

That night he thought of his mother. He worried about his father. His father was serving at the Russian front where the Russians were getting ready for a new offensive.

That night and the next day the train seemed to be in a hurry. Finally it came to a stop. There was no telling where they were. There was no name anywhere. There was only a siding... and not far from it there was a convoy of trucks waiting to take them away.

13

CAMP HUNTSVILLE

Unlike the camps in North Africa, with their bare grounds and makeshift fences, this camp had real barracks and double fences of barbed wire; and as for the watchtowers, they were sky-high by comparison. Moreover, Camp Huntsville was new. It was so new that, by the time the prisoners were arriving, the smell of new lumber, of fresh paint and of fresh tar was still in the air. And on the prison fences, on that maze of barbed wire that went round and round the camp seemingly forever, the sheen of new metal was still in place—so much so that at night, under a flood of lights, the sheen looked like hoarfrost.

The camp must have come up like mushrooms; all on the east side of a highway in the southeastern corner of Texas, down in a hollow, a few miles to the north of Huntsville; hence the name.

The prisoners who were headed for Camp Huntsville had been part of the Africa Corps. Earlier, in May of 1943, the year the tide of war was to turn against Nazi Germany, they had come under heavy Allied attacks; and in less than a week they had suffered defeat, retreat, and surrender. For Rommel's soldiers it was captivity from then on: first in makeshift camps in Tunisia; then in camps near Algerian ports; and after that on ships bound for the USA.

From the first day of captivity, the men were without their officers. Sending the latter to different camps was one of the provisions of the Geneva Convention. It was to remain in effect until the end of the war and beyond.

Rudolf visits Camp Huntsville in the summer of 1993.

And so the men were left to fend for themselves. And fend they did, if only in ways that for the uniform-minded and rank-conscious German soldiers were as unexpected as they were unusual.

What some of the men did was to get rid of their insignia. Insignia of rank and branch of service. Some even let go of their medals. All for a smoke. All for a few cigarettes, for a pinch of tobacco, at best for a pack of cigarettes. It was that kind of a swap between nicotine-starved prisoners and souvenir-hungry guards.

For the sergeants and for the corporals, for these German *Feldwebel* with their *Ober-* and *Unter-* and *Haupt-* and *Stabs-*prefixes of rank and for the *Unteroffiziere*, the swap for the time being underscored both the loss of rank and the loss of command. Instead, what was holding sway—on the bare grounds of makeshift camps, in windswept tents, in jam-packed boxcars, in the hulls of ships—was khaki brown uniformity and rankless indistinction.

It was in early July that the first POW transport arrived at Camp Huntsville. Here the prisoners were moved into Compound A. Other prisoners, coming a week or two later, were moved into Compound B. And then, near the end of the month, there arrived the transport that had sailed in a convoy directly from Oran to Norfolk, and from there it had come by train. At the gate leading into Compound C, the prisoners of that transport, numbering about a thousand, were divided into groups of forty. Forty to a barrack. All at random.

But random assignment and khaki brown uniformity were no match for fanaticism. Not when among the latest arrivals there were, as it went, a hard core of fanatical Nazis on one side and a few die-hard Communists on the other. To these we must add a handful of other anti-Nazis. The rest, in fact the great majority of the prisoners were more or less Nazi followers and as such kept clinging to the conviction that Germany was going to win the war, that Germany's cause was a just cause, and that survival under the Nazi regime was simply a matter of knowing when to shout *Heil* and when to keep your mouth shut. It was against that background of drifting expediency and rabid fanaticism that at Camp Huntsville, half a world away from Hitlerite Germany, the storms of strife were about to break, in the heat of that Texas summer.

The anti-Nazis were known from the start. There were twelve of them. It was as if they had been branded. In fact, it was a tattoo—the tattoo of a number—that branded them. And the number, which was several digits long and pale blue in color, ran down the length of their forearm. As such the tattoo identified the twelve as former inmates of a concentration camp, of camps like Buchenwald, Dachau, Sachsenhausen. It meant that the men were *KZ'ler* (*Kaah-Tset'ler*), and *KZ'ler* was the most dreaded of terms in the language of the Third *Reich*. It stood, like a modern-day *Apocalypse*, for wanton arrest, for incarceration without trial, and often for violent death. And it was only after the Nazi war machine was starting to run low on manpower, sometime during the third year of the war, that some of the *KZ'ler* were given a chance to exchange the striped prison garb for the field-gray of the military. To serve as cannon fodder.

Before long the men ended up in a probation unit. A more fitting name would have been damnation unit. What happened was that the unit, finding itself at the front in Tunisia, was damned if it fought and damned if it didn't. It was that kind of a dilemma. With Allied guns in front and with German guns in the immediate rear, with guns that were fired to inflict defeat and with guns that were fired to prevent defection, death was never far away. What saved these men in the end was the surrender of the Africa Corps in general.

The twelve had managed to stay together in several makeshift camps in North Africa and in transports halfway around the world. And as luck would have it, at Camp Huntsville finally, they ended up in Compound C in one and the same barrack; and so now, after surviving both the hell of Nazi terror and the hell of war, they wanted nothing so much as to tell of their ordeal and reveal the savage nature of Nazism.

But Camp Huntsville was no place for that. Not when Nazi fanatics and the most bullish among the sergeants and corporals, sensing American innocence and ineptitude in such matters, were returning to their old ways of drill and intimidation with a vengeance.

It started with the daily roll call. For the *Appell*, as it was called in German, the prisoners were ordered by the respective *Feldwebel* to line up in formation, barrack by barrack, in the open square. It was in that square that the parade ground stirred to life again: with a flurry of sharp commands, with the clicking of heels, with ramrod bearing, with unblinking eyes. All because the American officer, accompanied by the ranking *Feldwebel* and by two armed guards, would walk past the front row of each formation and do the count with a short downbeat of his right arm for every file of three men and with a stop between formations for the tally. And it was not until after the last formation was counted and the American officer had departed, that the command for dismissal was given, one for each formation by *Feldwebel* after *Feldwebel*.

Rank, command, and swagger were back. And it should not come as a surprise that the Nazis and the noncomissioned officers were back in their element. Moreover, as if to make up for the defeat they had suffered and since feeling emboldened by the American attitude of letting the prisoners handle their own affairs, the Nazis and thenoncommissioned officers in no time got to be bristling with fanaticism and bullishness. In fact, every one of them was as much Nazi as he wasnoncommissioned officers. If there was a difference, it was that there was no way telling where the Nazi in such a type started and thenoncommissioned officers ended, and vice versa. The exceptions were the Nazis who were notnoncomissioned officers and the noncommissioned officers who were not Nazis, at least not fanatical Nazis. But they were few. And as for the rest of the men, all these privates and Pfc's, they obeyed their former superiors once more as if they had never left the parade ground, and had never been to war, and had never been taken prisoner.

Rudolf reviews view from inside barrack in Camp Huntsville

Within a day or two, it was on to *Körperertüchtigung*. For the daily gymnastics, then, the sergeants and the corporals whistled and shouted the men out of their cots at the crack of dawn, just like in boot camp. What followed was a half hour of physical exercise, from knee-bends to push-ups, from jumping on-the-spot to body-twisting, from flailing arms to rolling the heads while standing still—while on the watchtowers the guards looked on. And it was because of the guards that the prisoners, under the barking commands of their superiors, did not continue with marching drills and with some basic infantry exercises.

But in still another return to garrison life, the *Feldwebel* and the *Unteroffiziere* moved into their own quarters, into two barracks that had to be vacated by the lower ranks. All with the *OK* of the *Amis* over at headquarters, which was somewhere outside the fence. That's what the sergeants and the corporals said. They also said, in an announcement from their new quarters, that the lower ranks were once more under orders to salute the higher ranks.

Meanwhile, the camp was settling down to routines: on the watchtowers the soldiers changed guard every two hours; the kitchens—there was one in each compound—served three meals a day, meals that were the most plentiful and the most varied the men had ever eaten in their lives, in and out of uniform; then there was the PX, with shelves that were bursting with cigarettes, tobacco, candy bars, cookies, toiletries, and so on; and what with ice-cold soft drinks and with JAX Beer: all at rock-bottom prices, all for coupons amounting to $3 a month a prisoner, which, unless one had a job and earned an additional $20, put a damper on wants and desires.

But there were no jobs. At least not for the latest arrivals in Compound C. What jobs there were had already been taken. Jobs like kitchen jobs and office jobs. Even jobs like driving one of the mule teams, teams that were carrying supplies from the quartermaster depot into the camp, had been taken.

What was left was nothing but time. But even here the routines caught on, if only as pastimes. For some prisoners it was round after round of card games. For others it was checkers. For a few it was chess. Then there were those who, while stretched out on their cots, did nothing but stare at the ceiling for hours.

For a new game, horseshoe pitching caught on at once. When it did, though, there was no way of knowing that the steel rods, in the hands of the Nazis, would become murderous weapons. And then there was ping-pong in the so-called dayroom.

It was this room that looked like a lounge. It was panelled and it had a few easy chairs and, in addition to a radio that played music all day, it had all kinds of magazines, *Life, Look,* and the *Saturday Evening Post* among them; it also had a newspaper. But since most prisoners had no knowledge of English and since the specter of pandering to enemy propaganda was certain to be raised by the newly emboldened Nazis, the paper was pretty much ignored. The same cannot be said of the magazines. They were the first to go. Or to be exact, the pages with the pictures of beautiful women were the first to go: as pinups on barrack walls.

Other favorites, albeit of a different kind, were rumors. They were always in the air. Most of them had to do with the final German victory, a victory that would come after a final battle. And that battle of all battles was either shaping up to be fought at the Russian front or was being fought at the Russian front at this very moment. For it was there that the German armies, by moving back, had supposedly set a huge trap for the hordes of the East. And if after that *Kesselschlacht*, if after that mass slaughter the *Amis* and the English should still have a hankering for doing battle with the Germans, then the newly built *Westwall* along the Atlantic coast would teach the invaders a lesson they would never forget.

Furthermore, there were hints of miracle weapons, of *Wunderwaffen,* bound to finish off the enemy. And it was in that triangle of *Kesselschlacht* and *Westwall* and *Wunderwaffen* that assertion after assertion about the *Final Victory* was being made — together with the ultimate assertion that in the end the genius of the *Führer* would always prevail.

There was one more rumor. This one was different. It was part rumor and part intimidation. It claimed that the camp had established contact with Germany, in a way or in ways that were never explained, in order to report all cases of insubordination: for immediate court martial upon return. And it was even rumored with darker and more ominous undertones that, for traitors, punishment would be on the spot.

He was in a quandary. For he had already been called a "traitor." It had happened at the day room where he had gone to read the paper, his only link with the outside world. Suddenly, close to him, there had been this voice: "Quit what you are doing!" It was the voice of the sergeant, the same sergeant who once before (on the train during a stop at the Springfield depot) had ordered him to quit reading an American newspaper. And he had defied the sergeant then and he was defying the sergeant now, by staring back at him. Only this time the sergeant's eyes were holding steady and the voice was keeping firm. This time, through clenched teeth, the sergeant so much as hissed at him, "*Sie Scheisskerl Sie!*...You are a traitor... a goddamn traitor of the fatherland... and you will find out...what happens to traitors."

Actually he did not fear for his life. At least not right away. Not with guards on the towers and with camp lights turning night into day. It was more that he was in a quandary about his parents. If word should get back to Germany alleging that he was a so-called "traitor," how would his parents react? Would they understand? Would his father, who was an officer in the army, would he understand? Would his mother, who had joined the Nazi Organization for Women, would she understand?

And as he was asking himself these questions, his apprehension grew and became nagging and double-edged. For if his parents understood, or at least if they sensed that whatever he had done was nothing more than doing what was right, in the moral sense of the word, then they themselves were in danger. Thus he feared for his father, who, after a run-in with a Nazi, had only been able to save himself by going into the army. And he feared for his mother, who, in order to placate the Nazis, had only grudgingly and reluctantly sought membership in the Nazi Organization for Women.

Suddenly he remembered those tense, dark days of that summer, back in 1938, when much of what had passed between his parents had been in whispers, in halftones, in mother's anxious questions to his father: "Alfons, will they come and get you?" Or: "Alfons, when will they come and get you?" To which his father invariably replied: "Martha, I don't know." And with the use of first names, instead of the affectionate Mama and Papa, he knew that the questions were far from idle, not after his father, in a moment of extreme agitation, apparently had told an obnoxiously persistent and goading salesman of Hitler pictures that he would never hang such "trash" from his walls.

And now, five years later, the fears were back and they were, like a fever, at their worst at night: when the air in the barrack became stifling and spent; when powerful floodlights sent shafts of glare through the windows into the barrack; when men, given to snoring, hissed and gurgled and gasped for air; when the night was awash with the sounds of crickets and, farther away, with the screams of locusts; when it seemed that nothing in the heat and humidity of a malingering summer night would ever come to an end.

At such moments he had thoughts of making his peace with the Nazis, however much on their terms. It meant he would have to quit reading the newspaper... quit seeing the men with the tattoos... he would have to rely for news on the rumor mill... and pay lip-service to all kinds of Nazi inanities... and, finally, he would have to start clicking his heels again and stand ramrod at attention again and salute smartly the *Feldwebel* and the *Unteroffiziere* again... and in reply to whatever the latter were barking, or were ordering him to do, he would have to shout "Yes-Sir" again... while to himself, in seething silence, he would inveigh against the Nazis and the bullies with the words: "You can kiss my ass."

It was this kind of defiance that had brought him that far. In a life that had seen stalking and preying and seizing Nazis, bullying and screaming and swashbuckling drill sergeants, strutting and swaggering and blandly arrogant officers. And whenever the Winters and the Chin-Willies and the Schmittz's and all the rest had made him shout louder and louder *Heil Hitler*... had made him do push-ups before a roaring fire... had made him clean latrines with a toothbrush... had made him don the gas-mask to run the "rounds"... had made him clean the drill-*Kapos*' (sergeants') quarters on hands and knees... had made him climb on top of the locker and shout "I am an idiot"... in short, whenever the tormentors had pushed him to the limit of human endurance and had driven him to the brink of losing his self-respect, at such moments he had always taken recourse into that silent and unflinching act of defiance. It was all he could do to save himself from a fate far worse.

For without that balm for bruised feelings, without that *Ersatz* for battered self-respect, without that lightning rod for seething anger—he either would have gone berserk or he would have lashed out at his tormentors. And most likely it would have meant mental asylum, or military prison, or the firing squad. It was as simple as that. Hitler's Third *Reich* was not known to give second chances.

There had been a few times, though, when he had gone beyond mere defiance: when he had vandalized, in the middle of the night, the garden of the village Nazi bigwig after the latter had made him repeat the Nazi salute several times... or when, after the *GESTAPO* had taken his pigeon friend Johann away, he had made it a practice to go to Johann's house every day to feed and water the birds—until the day, a few weeks later, when Johann's wife got a letter from Himmler's office that her husband had had a heart attack and had died; on that day she asked him, with tears streaming down her face, to take Johann's feathered friends away... and finally when, drunk and reckless, he had called Captain Schmittz "crazy" for trying to stop him as he was taking a canister of red wine to another gun crew. Instead, he had brushed Schmittz aside and had stumbled on, right through a cactus grove, where the battery had gone into position, and nothing had ever come of the threats by the cowardly Schmittz to have him court-martialled.

The memories more than ever flashed through his mind at night, as he lay awake on his cot, brooding for an answer.

Then morning came and his fears dissipated and something like the resolve *to be his own man* came over him. It was part of what his father had told him. The other part was *to do right and to fear no one.* The words were spoken at the time his father was home on leave, once after the campaign in Poland and once after France, and they were repeated in a letter from the Russian front. But until now he had never been sure how to apply the words in real life, much less how to square them with mother's frequent warning, if a warning it was, about the so-called seriousness of life. Somehow the two sets of parental words had remained in a sort of flux. Until now, until after several nights of anxious brooding the words finally took on meaning: there was no going back.

After ten years of life under the *swastika*, there was for this nineteen-year-old no going back anymore... not after he had seen the Nazis burn books and synagogues... not after the Jewish students in high school had disappeared... not after he had seen the statuette-like Hitler in that big black touring car... not after what the Nazis had tried to do to his father—and had done to Johann... not after hearing them boast, in word and in song, about bashing in the heads of those who opposed them and of seeing to it that heads would roll... not after eight weeks of hell in boot camp... not after living with the lies of Nazi propaganda... not after defeat and capture... not after finding the captors surprisingly humane and generous and, dare he say it, liberating... not after hearing of the ordeal the tattooed men had endured.

It was like freeing himself from the past. Still, there was this question about the war. The question was whether it was possible to hope for the defeat of the Nazis, but not for the defeat of Germany. The question was on his mind like a canker. Like a canker that was sore and painful and feverish. Like a canker that needed to be lanced before it could drain and heal.

What made everything even more painful was the fact that the Allies were demanding Germany's unconditional surrender. To the ordinary German soldier it meant that there would be no quarter given and that, so went the sardonic joke among the soldiers, there would not be enough lampposts to go around to hang the Germans from.

Goebbels' propaganda had already been going full blast about the Allied demand. He had heard the fulminations himself, on the radio in the gun carrier before his capture, to the effect that the demand was part of the Jewish conspiracy to bring about the ruination of Germany. So much so that nothing German would ever survive. And then there had been rumors about the demand in the camp. And while he was tempted to dismiss the consequences of such a surrender as typical "atrocity" propaganda by Goebbels, there were certain things about the demand that did not sound all that unreal.

For one thing, Nazi propaganda had claimed that the demand had been accepted by the so-called "war criminals" at the recent Casablanca Conference. And apparently there had been such a conference last December. For another thing, it claimed that the instigators of the plan had been the Jews in the Roosevelt government. And at least half a dozen Jewish names, from Frankfurter to Schlesinger, had been mentioned in Nazi newscasts.

Loath as he had been about the drumfires of Nazi propaganda about the Jews, from the trumped-up notion that they were part of the "Bolshevik inspired world-wide conspiracy against the German people" to the fulminations that as "vermin they were out to suck the blood of the German people," this time he was left with the uneasy feeling that it would be understandable, after what had happened to the Jews in Germany, if the Jews in other parts of the world were indeed seeking revenge.

And his thoughts went back to the *Kristallnacht*, when in a few fury-driven hours Nazi stormtroopers laid waste to tens of thousands of Jewish shops and Jewish stores in Germany, and moreover set hundreds of synagogues on fire. And once more the picture of Pinschover, his classmate and friend, rose before his eyes: how Pinschover stood in that square in Beuthen, with several hundred other Jews, in front of the burning synagogue. It was the last time he was to see his friend.

And as for the demand of unconditional surrender and as for Goebbels' earlier proclamation of Total War, he had the dark foreboding that this war was going to be fought to the bitter end.

It was at that moment that the idea hit home that, unless the Nazis were

Water hydrant with date the camp was being built.

overthrown, he was left with no other choice but to hope for the defeat of his own country. That way Germany would be freed from the scourge of Nazism. It meant defeat for the country where he had been born and raised, where he had gone to school, had received his first communion, had played soccer for the village team, and had left his pigeons and his rabbits behind. It meant defeat for the country where his mother and his sister and his friends were still living. And the coal miners and their families. All in that two-bit Upper Silesian village, where on moonlit summer nights, under leafy bowers and in haystacks out in the fields, the young were never squeamish about the lure of love.

He had made his decision. And he felt as if a weight had been lifted off his shoulders. As if, after a long illness, he was whole again.

And for the first time, really, he felt free. Free to go over to the day-room whenever he wanted to and read the newspaper without looking over his shoulder. Free to go over to the tattooed men and hear them talk. Free from feeling even the slightest compulsion, other than showing up for the Appell, to execute the parade-ground orders of the noncomissioned officers, at least not by clicking his heels. Free from being cowed by fanatical Nazis. Free from kowtowing to rabid noncoms. Free at last to be himself.

He lost no time in doing just that. Like when between meal times and the Appell he went over to the day-room to read the newspaper. And even though, for lack of a dictionary, the pace of reading was often slow and his understanding was halting, there would come these wonderful moments when an unknown word, a difficult phrase, a whole sentence would suddenly fall into place and make sense.

Or he would join the tattooed men in the crawl space under the barrack where, at the far end, they had been digging a hole large enough for everybody. Into that hole they would crawl, usually in the afternoon, to find relief from the heat and to talk.

And talk the tattooed men did: about the concentration camps... about the notorious conditions in these camps... about being forced to stand in their thin pajama-like prison garb for hours out in the cold... about being denied the one warm gruel of a meal a day.

And talk they did: about being thrown into solitary confinement... about being starved half to death on bread and water... about being strapped on a special rack for rounds of flogging... about prisoners going berserk and flinging themselves into the electric fence.

But the tattooed men also talked about bluffing the SS into believing they were reformed enough to be trusted with arms and to be sent to the front in Tunisia, where as so-called leftists they were not expected to defect to the capitalist West.

And finally they said, again and again, that the Jews, contrary to Nazi claims of "resettlement" in Poland, were being sent to the gas chambers. Gas chambers that were camouflaged as showers.

He sensed that what these men were saying was true. And that as former *KZ'lers*, having languished inside the camps, they knew more than all those millions of ordinary Germans who lived outside the camps. Where for news there was nothing but Nazi propaganda and rumors and where, unless one risked draconian punishment for being caught listening to an enemy radio station, any search for truth was doomed from the start. With the *Kz'lers* it was different. With them it was a matter of being behind the same barbed wire with members of the resistance movement from all parts of Europe—and find out what was going on.

Thus some of the terrible rumors that had been making the rounds in wartime Germany were beginning to make terrible sense: when Jews, jam-packed in boxcars, were heard crying for water as the trains passed through the rail yards of Upper Silesian towns... when something like half rumor and half joke had it that the reason why German wartime soap was so abrasive and so without foam was because it was made from the bones of emaciated Jews... when it was rumored that smoke-stacks at a camp in Poland were belching smoke that smelled of burnt flesh... when starving Russian prisoners of war were said to have turned cannibal... when soldiers home on leave from Russia were hinting that Russian Jews were rounded up and massacred... when hungry Greek women were offering themselves to German soldiers for a loaf of bread... when Yugoslav women were giving themselves to German soldiers to cut off their penis... when it was said about the Russian partisans that they neither expected mercy nor gave mercy.

The twelve spoke about the Nazis in their own peculiar way. What they did, literally, was to spit out their names, from Nazi to *SS* to *GESTAPO*, as if the names were venom. For that matter, Hitler was never anything else than Hitler, with no first name, with no adjective, with not even so much as an invective. The hideousness of the name was enough.

There were two more words that were also spoken with something like spit and venom. But only by the communists. The words were *Kapitalist* and *Kapitalismus*. It was here that he discovered that the twelve had some differences of their own.

The differences were over politics all right. Over politics of the past. At least that's how it sounded to him, to judge from the flurry of names and words that passed between them. Names like Karl Marx and Ferdinand Lassalle and Wilhelm Liebknecht and Phillipp Scheidemann and others. And all he could possibly know was that the latter were all dead, that some were Jewish, that all were either Communists or Socialists, and that, according to Nazi propaganda, the latter had ceaselessly worked to plunge Germany into the abyss of her greatest misfortune.

Then came words like *dialectics* and *evolution* and *revolution*, in addition to words like *bourgeoisie* and *industrial proletariat* and *class struggle*; and, other than knowing that the twelve were contradicting each other over the use of these words in the so-called grand scheme of history, he was completely lost.

He was baffled. All he knew was that the Communists and the Socialists among the twelve did not see eye to eye at times and would argue with each other and that, for once, the one Centrist and the one Liberal in the group, were keeping out of the fray.

He felt helpless. Furthermore, he was dumbfounded by it all, besides being impressed by the swift exchange of the arguments, by the fluency of expression with which the arguments were presented, by the ease with which esoteric ideas were advanced. Not just on the part of the Socialist Leipheimer, who was a professor in real life, but also on the part of the Communist Martin Schneider, who, with his wire frame glasses and his gentle manners, looked and acted more like a professor than the metal worker that he was. That is until the Nazis seized him. A decade later, after Sachsenhausen and after Buchenwald, Schneider's will was still unbroken and his gentle manners were seemingly unaffected.

For the kind of fast and furious politicking among these men and for his own reaction he had only one explanation: the Nazis had kept him, as they had kept everybody else since 1933, from learning. From learning about the past and the present. From learning about anything that did not fit into the Nazi scheme of things. And there arose in him, virtually overnight, the urgent desire to learn as much as possible as soon as possible and to make up for missed opportunities.

Thus, if he was not in the crawl space under the barrack listening to the discourses and arguments among the twelve, he would most likely be at the dayroom reading; and if he was unable to sleep at night, because of the heat, he would once again be in the same room. There he sat all by himself in the darkness, in front of the radio with the dimly lit panel of station numbers, straining to hear what the outside world had to say. And in those short announcements and drawn-out newscasts, and in all the wordy banter there would come those precious moments when he would understand a word or two, a phrase, an entire sentence.

At other times he worked on a dictionary. First, he wrote down, in alphabetical order, all the English words that came to his mind. Then, into another notebook, he started to write down the kind of German words that, in spite of their frequency, had either escaped him in English or had never been part of his English vocabulary. This way there was at least a chance that some of the words might come back to him, before he would look them up in the dictionary. In the Webster Pocket Dictionary, which was the size of half the palm of his hand and which he hoped to buy at the PX from his next pay.

The two notebooks and the pencil he had already bought from his first pay, for exactly 35 cents worth of coupons. The rest went for a Gillette shaving kit and for a carton of cigarettes. The cigarettes would have to last him for a month. And for a treat, finally, he bought himself a bottle of JAX Beer for 10 cents and a chocolate bar for 5 cents. After that he still had 45 cents worth of coupons left, or a beer and a chocolate bar for every one of the following three weekends until next payday.

That Saturday of the first payday, after supper, he went over to the fence near the main gate to watch the sunset. The sky was like a catch-all of fading daylight and simmering heat and hothouse humidity. It was like so many grays on grays, or like so many permutations of that color. It was like a foil for the sun. And the sun was blood-red. And as the sun stood poised for the plunge below the horizon, at that moment there was stillness everywhere. Until the stillness was shattered by the sounds of iron hitting iron, as a game of horseshoe pitching got under way, back in the camp.

But there was more to the evening than sunset and stillness and horseshoe pitching. There was also the highway. What he knew about the highway was that to the right it was going to the depot where they had gotten off the train not long ago, while to the left it was probably going to the town after which the camp had been named. And even though the highway itself was not visible, at least not from where he stood, there was some traffic going back and forth. Some cars and an occasional small truck. As it was, he could actually see the upper parts of the cars and the trucks, the compartments and the cabs really, which was enough to see the drivers and an occasional passenger, or passengers. And this, in itself, was more than enough to stir his imagination into asking questions like: *Are they going home? Who will be waiting for them? Is home a house with a garden? A garden with rabbit hutches and a pigeon coop?*

But his imagination also left him with other kinds of questions. Questions like: *Are they going to a woman? To a wife? To a girlfriend? Are they going to spend the evening with a woman? Spend the night with a woman?*

By now darkness was closing in on the highway, except when the headlights of a passing vehicle cut the darkness in half. Otherwise there was nothing out there anymore to his imagination, except for one final dilatation of all questions. And that question was *whether some day, somewhere in America, he, too, would be heading home on a highway like this.*

The camp was ablaze with lights. Lights that were on top of poles that were higher than the guard towers. And the poles with the lights were standing around the four sides of this mile-long rectangle like sentinels, like so many suns, each with its own halo of swarming insects.

There was no escape from the lights. Unless one closed one's eyes. And kept them closed, which he did, for one of the great treats of prison life: to munch on a bar of chocolate and to drink beer and to inhale deeply the smoke from a cigarette. All more or less at the same time.

It was his first taste of chocolate since the day he had eaten part of his iron ration. On that day, back in May, after they had blown up the remaining guns and carriers with demolition charges, the survivors of the battery had been told to save themselves. *Rette sich wer kann*—the captain had shouted. And after the captain had left in a chauffeur-driven command-car, it was his turn to set out on his own, towards a stretch of coastline on the Tunisian Cape Bon peninsula, from where he hoped to reach Pantelleria. And no sooner had he left the survivors of the battery—and Matthes was among them—when he had to stop. When he could not go on. All he could do was to cower on the ground and fight the urge to go back. Eventually he made camp there and then he fell over the food of his iron ration. Bread, salami, and chunks of chocolate. It was the last time that he had seen Matthes, his friend and comrade. The battle-scarred and battle-savy Matthes. The street-wise taxi driver from Berlin. The busted sergeant. The best of friend and comrade. And it was only because of Matthes' fear of the water, that they had gone their own ways. Matthes to some imaginary airfield on this bleak peninsula. And he to some imaginary beach from where he hoped to reach Pantelleria somehow. But he was never to see Matthes again, nor any member of the battery. It was as if they had been swallowed by the earth.

And he had been inquiring after them and had left notes for them on special billboards. In all three compounds. To no avail. What he found instead, that evening, was a typewritten note in English, saying that the Quartermaster Depot was looking for an English-speaking person. His mind was made up at once. He would inquire with the guards at the main gate, first thing in the morning, in order to (what was the word again?) 'applicate' for the job. That's what he would do.

A job would mean that he would get an additional twenty dollars, that he would be able to apply and to improve his English, and that for the better part of the day he would be able to get away from the camp. Away from the hostility that was everywhere: in the barrack where nobody would speak to him; in the formation for the *Appell* where he was the only one not to click his heels; on the camp street where he did not salute the newly emboldened superiors; in the dayroom where he was the only one to read the newspaper and to listen to the news on the radio; in the fact, that for every blank stare there were looks that were seething with hatred.

There were, of course, the twelve friends. They were in the next barrack. And they had tried, and he had tried, to get someone in that barrack to change places with him. Without success. And even though he spent much of his time in the crawl space under the barrack with them, and ate all of the meals with them, and even though he found that they were steely-hearted in their opposition to the Nazis and in their contempt for the Nazis—there were times when he wished for nothing more than a word by Matthes. Matthes who had always had the right word for the posturing and prancing and punitive ways of Nazi militarism.

If there was someone who reminded him of Matthes, if only because of his obvious anti-Nazi stance, it was the East Prussian at the far end of the barrack. East Prussians were everything that the Berliners were not. They were heavy-hearted and obdurate and their German was top-heavy with consonantal sounds. What Gerhard, a stockily built young man from a farm in the Masurian

Lake region, did was to warn him, when no one was near, that… *they were up to something… that something was going to happen… That they have sworn to get even with all traitors of the fatherland.*

And then, one morning, just as he was getting ready to go to work, he was quickly handed a piece of paper by Gerhard. Scribbled on that piece of paper was the following message: *they beat two to death last night... in compound A and B... with clubs and with iron rods... after smothering them with blankets.*

That was several weeks after he had started to work at the Quartermaster Depot. It should be mentioned that, in order to get the job, he had walked up to the gate, first thing in the morning, just as he had envisioned it, whereupon he was taken by one of the guards to an office in the Quartermaster Depot, for an interview, and that the interview by a friendly man in uniform had lasted no more than a few minutes. And the job was his.

It was a desk job. It was his job to make out the daily food requisitions for both the POW companies and the GI guard companies, on the basis of their respective head-counts. Otherwise the key for the type of rations and the amount of rations and the variety of food items for breakfast, lunch, and supper were exactly the same, for both the Americans and the Germans.

He was the only POW in the office. Others in the office were two sergeants and several civilians. Most of the latter were elderly men. But there was also a young woman. He guessed her age to be close to his own. She had a name he had never heard before, rather lilting and endearing in a strange sort of way. Besides, she was a woman of great beauty. And since her desk stood at an angle from his own, slightly ahead and to the left, in front of a window, the light all but revealed the lovely shape of her body.

He was like one of them. Thus they insisted he join them for the coffee breaks and for lunch. And whether it was in the lounge or in the office, they never failed to act with something like good-natured equanimity toward him. In fact, he never felt that his presence put any strain on the way they talked to each other. And except that they never inquired about his own background and that at the end of the day he would have to go back to the camp, instead of driving out straight to the highway, like they did, he felt like one of them.

On that day, the day he had received Gerhard's note, he had no sooner got back to the barrack when two armed soldiers entered. On a piece of paper was his name. The soldiers told him to get his belongings and come with them.

They took him to the office. There his tattooed friends were already waiting. More soldiers arrived. Some with bayonets on their rifles. Outside a crowd gathered. Quickly. The soldiers had to clear the street first. Then, with drawn bayonets, the soldiers formed a cordon around the thirteen. And eventually the thirteen were marched down the main street, past a huge crowd of prisoners all along the street, by now a crowd from all three compounds—and the crowd howled and screamed and shouted every obscenity under the sun.

They were taken to the stockade. For their own safety, they were told by the commanding officer, an elderly major, after their names had appeared on a list of traitors. The stockade, with cells for each one of them, was to the left of the main gate, in a barbed wire enclosure of its own. From there they were marched every day for every meal to the kitchen in compound C. Always under protection. Always inside a cordon of soldiers with drawn bayonets. And always, to the very end, past a crowd of howling fanatics.

Until one day, when among the requisitions to be made out, there was an order on his desk to make out a special two-day requisition for thirteen prisoners. For travel on a train. For the following day. That was all he knew.

14

WHICH WAY?

For two days, as seen from a train window, the country was to change from jungle to desert. Or something close to that. And yet, when the journey was finally over, they were not anywhere near the destinations he had had in mind.

At first he had thought they were headed for Alaska. Alaska was all he could think of. It was way up north and as such it fitted into the scheme of distances a train was likely to travel in two days.

But one day into the train ride, with the winds blowing hot and with all that land turning bone-dry, he gave up on Alaska. At the same time he gave up on places anywhere near Alaska.

California was his next choice. It, too, faded quickly. Finally, near the end of the second day, all he could think of was of some place north of Texas. And with that his knowledge of American geography, scant as it was, went blank.

Such guesses and ruminations were only too natural for a prisoner who found himself on a train that was to take him to another camp; especially for a prisoner who had at least a smattering of knowledge of American geography. In his case it amounted to knowing the names of a few cities and states and what they stood for: from New York with its skyscrapers to Chicago with its slaughterhouses and its gangsters to San Francisco with its Golden Gate Bridge. And as for California, its fame, as he saw it, rested more or less on past gold rushes and on Hollywood's current glamour. Oklahoma was one more state he knew something about, if only because it had cowboys and dust storms.

He also had a pretty fair idea that the Great Lakes were to the north and the Gulf of Mexico was to the south and that in between there flowed the Mississippi. Then came the Rocky Mountains and somewhere after that the Wild West.

Limited though his knowledge was, it was of his own doing. German schools had been of no help. For them America did not exist, at least not as a subject worth teaching. In fact, there was not one school in Germany, on either the primary or the secondary level that would spend so much as one hour on American geography or history. Instead, German schoolmasters would rather drill into the heads of the young whole litanies of German rivers and German mountain ranges, with the help of the cane, than lift their gaze on the world beyond the fatherland. It was like an exercise in terms of either Germany or nothing. An exception were the names of those rivers and mountains where German armies or Germanic heroes at one time or another had engaged in battle or had died. From Roland over Theoderic the Great to Alaric the Goth, or from the Pyrenees over Ravenna to the Busento river, respectively. Or, for that matter, from Blücher at Waterloo over Hipper at Skagerrak to Lettow-Vorbeck in the former German colony of South-East Africa.

Still, America was in the air and the Germans had their own ideas about

America. Foremost among them was the belief that America was the land of unlimited opportunities. A close second, at least as of late, was the idea that everything was possible in America. For better or for worse. Even for the worst: such as American millionaires leaping out of their skyscraper offices to their death because of the Great Depression. Or millionaires standing in soup lines. Or millionaires, with a placard in hand, looking for work. That kind of picture was the latest the Germans had of depression-ravaged America.

Until then there had been in the air all these stories about Germans emigrating to America. In fact, so many had crossed the Atlantic that there was scarcely a family in Germany that did not have an *Amerika-Auswanderer* in its ranks. Their stories were legend. They were mostly stories of people whose lives in America had become part of the American success story. Like all those farm laborers and apprentices and journeymen and sales clerks and ordinary wage earners who had gone over and soon were owning farms and shops and businesses and even factories—sooner than they would ever have been able to buy a new Sunday suit had they stayed in Germany.

There were exceptions. His uncle, for one, had the misfortune, after one week in America, of being mistaken for someone else. It cost him his life. And all he had done, as a baker in a bread factory in Chicago, was to sleep in the bed of someone who happened to be away working the day shift. Enter a third man. Mistaking the sleeping man as the one who had taken his girlfriend, or wife, away, the jilted lover decided to settle scores on the spot—with a gun.

Then there were the movies. In the twenties they had gone from hand-cranked magic lanterns to sophisticated motor-driven projectors, or from the unsteady flicker of light to powerful beams of light. By the time sound was added and stories with real plots and sub-plots were acted out by real actors and actresses, movies had become the standard fare of entertainment, for adults and for children alike.

In fact, all that the children could see in Germany in the late twenties and for most of the thirties, even under the Nazis, were American movies. There were hardly any matinee-filling German substitutes. Was it any wonder, after all the Sunday matinees he had gone to in nearby Klausberg, that his own views about America had some of the flavor and some of the flair of those movies.

To which we must add reading. In the course of his reading about America he found himself with Huckleberry Finn on the Mississippi, with Old Shatterhand among the Indians, with Buffalo Bill on the range.

And how could he ever forget John Maynard of poetry's fame. John Maynard, hero and helmsman of a ship that plied the waters of Lake Erie—until the day the ship caught fire. And how in that gathering inferno of flames and smoke Maynard brought the ship safely to port — and all on board were saved. All but John Maynard.

There was more. There was the book of Thompson, a gift of his father, with the wonderful animal stories where the wolves and the grizzlies and the eagles were coming to life in that great American wilderness. And then there was Arno, the pigeon, flying in the canyons of New York.

Thus, the movies and the books were all part of his growing up in Germany during the thirties. The war ended it all. American movies and American authors, from Mark Twain to Jack London, became a thing of the past. Even the novels of Karl May, with Indians as heroes, became suspect. Moreover, America disappeared behind a veil of Nazi propaganda. And not even the news about the war itself, with maps of countries where German forces were engaged in *blitzkrieg,* was to bring America any closer. If only because there was never a time when a single German shell was ever fired on a target in America, or a single German bomb was ever dropped on an American city.

For two days, from a train window, he had been looking for signs that would tell him where they were going. Signs that would yield some clue, or clues, about their destination. Clues like the direction the train was travelling, the towns the train was going through, the type of country the train was leaving behind. It sounds simple enough.

And yet there were times when the train would change directions and when because of the speed of the train the names of stations came at him with a blur and the landscape on both sides of the track was nothing but a vast expanse of scrub and brush. At such times all signs became like pieces of a jigsaw puzzle in which the pieces did not seem to match the picture he had in mind.

The guesswork had started the moment he saw the requisition order, back at the Quartermaster Depot in Camp Huntsville. As with all such orders for both the prisoner of war companies and the guard-companies, it was his job in the office of the quartermaster depot to calculate the food for three meals a day for each one of the companies. What was so different about the last requisition order was that it called for the issuance of food for exactly thirteen prisoners: for two days of travel on a train. There was nothing else on that legal-size sheet of paper. Not even a hint who the prisoners were and where they were going. All the sheet contained were headings and sub-headings and single-line entries for various and sundry food items. And yet the requisition of food for thirteen prisoners left no doubt who the prisoners were: they were the thirteen anti-Nazis who were held in the stockade—and he was one of them. And as he filled out the order, at his desk, he knew that by tomorrow he would be on the train and that he would never be back.

As a rule, prisoners who were about to be sent to another camp were given only the shortest of notice. It was like calling their names one moment and having them file out with their belongings the next... usually to a convoy of waiting trucks. And as for the name and the location of the camp, and as to whether the new camp was a regular prisoner of war camp or merely a temporary one, about all those details the prisoners were kept in the dark. At least as long as the war was going on. And after that they were not always told the truth.

It was no different with the thirteen prisoners. Next morning, at daybreak, after the guards had called their names through the open doors of their cells, the prisoners were told to get their belongings and to report outside. There, in front of the stockade, a truck, accompanied by two jeeps with guards, was already waiting. Moments later the prisoners were told to get on the truck. And then they were driven off before the Nazis, on the other side of the fence, had a chance to start screaming their hate-filled invectives at them. A short time later the thirteen anti-Nazi prisoners arrived at the railroad station where only two months earlier, as part of a transport of several hundred prisoners, they had arrived.

Now the journey was to continue. In a single railroad car. In a coach with wide windows and with cushioned seats and with toilets at either end. Once again captivity treated the German prisoners to a kind of travel that could only be called, even by peacetime standards in Germany, luxurious. A short time later, as soon as the car had been hitched to a passenger train, they were off and the guessing about their destination began in earnest.

Where were they going? On the way to the toilet he would ask each guard that question as the latter were taking their turns at the end of the coach. In his best school English he would ask, "Sir, could you tell me, please, to what camp we are going?" And he got no answer. All he would get was a blank stare or a shrug of the shoulders. And so the real guesswork began.

At first the train was heading south. It could only mean two things. First, they would not be going back to Norfolk, out on the east coast, from where they had travelled to Huntsville only two months ago, for three days through much of America. Through how much of America he had no real way of knowing. And second, because he felt that the Gulf of Mexico was not all that far away, it was his guess that they would not be travelling in that direction for very long. And sure enough, it was in the railyard of a big city that their car was switched to another train. From then on, even though their car was to be switched two more times from one train to another, they travelled most of the time in a northwesterly direction.

It was like a race between his own imagination and the speed of the train. And feeding his imagination about where they could possibly be going was everything he had ever heard about America, had seen about America, had read about America.

He remembered locating Chicago on the map, if only because his uncle had been murdered there and the city had the reputation as the gangster capital; and he remembered locating New York City on the same map, for the sake of King Kong; and, because of Huck's adventures on the river, he had followed the meanderings of the Mississippi; likewise, because of John Maynard, he had taken measure, as it were, of Lake Erie.

Now, with the winds blowing hotter than ever—through windows that would open mere inches to prevent escape—and with the land outside turning more barren by the hour, all the destinations that he had conjured up in his mind had one by one fallen by the wayside. It was as if the train was going to no place in particular.

In the end, they were still in Texas. All that had changed was that they were in another part of Texas. They were in a small town by the name of Fabens. And all there was to Fabens was that it was located in the Rio Grande Valley, with houses running for a few blocks between a stretch of highway and a stretch of railroad tracks. And as for the POW camp, which was not much more than a converted cotton barn, it was right in the corner between the highway and the tracks, at the north end of town.

15

CAMP FABENS

Camp Fabens in Texas looked rather ramshackle and makeshift. For that matter, it had none of the drawing board qualities of a regular POW camp. Of a camp like Huntsville, where the barracks stood in line, the barbed wire fences went around the camp in a rectangle, and the guard towers hovered like forbidding sentinels above everything.

Camp Fabens had none of that. All it had was a barn-like building of corrugated metal and an ordinary chain link fence, both dating from before the war.

But for the thirteen anti-Nazi prisoners who had barely gotten out of Huntsville alive, it was haven. And haven meant that the camp was peaceful and quiet and that the thirteen anti-Nazi prisoners had nothing to fear, not even from other prisoners who were already there. It was almost too good to be true, too good to last. And last it did not. After three months the anti-Nazi prisoners were back to fearing once more for their lives in still another camp. In the meantime they picked cotton.

From early childhood on, back in Germany, he had no real idea what cotton looked like. Like Spanish moss on a tree? Like candles on a chestnut tree? All he knew, or thought he knew, was that if the word *Baumwolle,* which was the word for cotton in German, was taken literally, then cotton ought to look like a *tree* with *wool* on it.

As it turned out, there was more to *Baumwolle* than simple semantics. There was, for instance, the much-ballyhooed drive in the Third *Reich* to make the economy independent from such imports as crude oil and natural rubber and, yes, from *Baumwolle*. What was at stake was to replace these foreign raw materials with home-produced synthetic substitutes, commonly known as *Ersatz*. And the *Ersatz* for *Baumwolle* and for worsted wool, for that matter, was known as *Vistra*.

Vistra sounded like a cross between Latin and popular science. Whatever it was, it was rumored that as a fabric it was coarse and scratchy. Worse, that it was bound to shrink in the rain. And shrink it did. In this case it was mother's new *Vistra* costume that did the shrinking. In a sudden downpour. On Easter Sunday. While they were out in the fields for the traditional Easter Walk. And even though father held his jacket over mother, as best he could, to shield her and the *Vistra* costume against the rain, and even though mother kept tugging at the jacket and at the skirt, as best she could, to keep them from shrinking, it was of no use. The Easter dress kept getting tighter and tighter, so mother said under her breath; and then at home, after pinning the jacket and the skirt to a board, with needles and with a great deal of holding and stretching on the part of everybody, the costume never was the same again. All that remained were two shrivelled, shrunken, discolored pieces of Vistra fabric.

Otherwise it had been an Easter Sunday of picture postcard perfection:

with sunshine and balmy airs, with Easter lilies in church and willow catkins down at the creek. If there was one more memory to that Sunday, it was that it was destined to be the last Easter Sunday before the war.

And now, four years later, he found himself picking cotton at the other end of the world. To his surprise cotton was not even close to being a tree. It was plainly a bush, quite like a fledgling currant bush. But whereas currant bushes with their clusters of red berries had their place here and there in the gardens back home, here the cotton bushes, hanging thick with fiber, were growing in row after row on huge tracts of land. Land that looked as if fresh snow had fallen on it.

Here, then, between the Rio Grande River and the highway there were these tracts of cotton. And cutting like a branding iron into this expanse of whiteness were the canals and ditches of a vast irrigation system, for which the river apparently had supplied the water. Everything else was parched, bone-dry desert.

And now the prisoners were picking cotton. Six days a week, from mid-morning until late in the afternoon each day, unless a sandstorm brought everything to a standstill. And even though picking cotton had the reputation of numbing the mind and bending the back out of shape, he rather liked it.

It meant leaving the confinement of the camp for the open country and getting to see the town. To be sure, the prisoners were always under guard and the town's main street they saw only from the back of a truck. Still, seeing Fabens' town life twice, once in the morning when they were on their way out to the fields and once in the afternoon when they were coming back, was like a tonic for their prison-cramped minds. Seeing the town was a reminder that the sight of women shopping and of men going about their business and of children going to school was something like the quintessence of the good life.

And after that, once they got to the field, there was always the chance that they would not be quite so alone in all those tracts of cotton between the river and the highway; that they would share the field in which they were picking cotton with others. With wetbacks. That's what one of the guards had called them. And then the guard had added, matter-of-factly, that wetbacks were Mexicans who had come across the river.

Sometimes it would take more than a day before the two *sides* would even get close. But when they *did,* they would simply stop. First, they would unburden themselves of the bags. Then, with nothing between them but unpicked rows of cotton, they would look at each other—for the most part in silence: as if each side was waiting for the other to make a gesture or shout a word or make a move. And yet nothing ever happened. Finally, as the guard would leave the shade of the truck to saunter over, they shouldered once more their bags and went back to picking cotton. First the Mexicans and then, after the slender bodies of the dark-eyed Mexican girls were far down the rows of cotton, the Germans.

There was still more to picking cotton. For fifty pounds of cotton a day, the prisoner would get $20 worth of coupons a month, plus an additional $3 as a monthly allotment. At PX prices, $23 was a fortune. Especially when cigarettes and beer and candy bars took only about half that sum. For the other half the PX offered used paperbacks and books and a few copies of the Webster Pocket Dictionary and even a used radio.

The first thing he did, with coupons left over from Huntsville, was to buy a Webster Pocket Dictionary. Now he knew what to do. Each day he would peruse the dictionary, page for page, for words that were foreign to him and write them down. The daily quota was a list of twenty English words with their German meaning. To memorize the words he would take the list with him into the fields, and there, while he picked cotton with one hand he held up the list of words with the other. And so it went: cotton one moment and English vocabulary the next. At the end of the day, after breaks for water and a half-hour luncheon break, he could count on having picked the required minimum of fifty pounds of cotton, for close to $1 worth in coupons, and on having memorized twenty new English words.

And while he never found out what the Mexicans on their part were getting for a pound of cotton—and each one of them picked up to 500 pounds a day—he never ceased to marvel at the ease and the speed with which a pair of Mexican hands would pick two rows of cotton at one and the same time.

The radio he bought from his first earnings was a used Emerson. It was of wood and the dial had numbers instead of the names of cities as was the custom in Europe. Once on the air, the numbers became stations with call letters.

The Emerson was his pride and joy. It brought the outside world to him. He would spend hours listening to it, often late into the night, always intent to understand what was said. And understanding the spoken word, such as in newscasts, was his greatest challenge. And meeting the challenge was his greatest joy. Nothing could surpass it, not even the Hit Parade on Saturday nights. And, for a weekend treat, it came with JAX Beer and Butterfingers.

There was one more thing he owed to the Emerson. It was at that time that he discovered the world of jazz. And, through the likes of the Duke and Satchmo and Cab Calloway, fell in love with it.

Still, there were other pastimes. One was to go outside at night, go into the back-alley on the north of the building that served as the prison yard, and look at the stars. Looking at the stars always reminded him of home, always gave him the consolation that the stars he was seeing would also be seen by his parents.

Another pastime was to go to the far end of the yard and watch the trains go by. Some, like the freight trains, thundered by and were gone. Others, like the northbound passenger trains, would stop. What was more, during such stops the locomotives were always taking on water. And since the water tower stood just outside the fence at the far end, it meant that the locomotive came to stand so close to the prisoners that their faces soon were flushed from the heat.

But the greatest diversion was yet to come. It came when one Saturday night they were taken to the stadium to see a football game. They understood that, for the last game of the 1943 football season, Fabens High School was going to play another high school.

For the German prisoners it was the first time ever to see a game of American football. They had no idea what to expect, both in terms of the game itself and in the fact that it was played by two high school teams in a stadium at night.

The stadium was ablaze with lights. Circling the light-towers were swarms of insects. The crowd was abuzz. Vendors shouted. Money changed hands. Hands passed bags filled with popcorn. Soft drinks frothed in cups. Youths shouted for attention. A baby cried. Cheerleaders, taking practice leaps, were getting ready to perform. Both bands were getting ready to play. And the football teams were about to take to the field. All in all, it was the kind of a spectacle the prisoners had never seen before in their lives.

Sure, the prisoners were escorted by guards and in the crowd there was a stir of curiosity, especially among those who sat close to them—but after that the fifty prisoners were pretty much a part of the crowd: when the crowd rose to its feet at the playing of the National Anthem, the prisoners rose to their feet; when the crowd stood facing the American flag, the prisoners stood facing the American flag; when the crowd sang the National Anthem, the prisoners did their best to at least feign singing. Only at the end, when the crowd burst into applause and kept whistling, the prisoners, out of sheer ignorance, did not.

At once the loudspeaker voice took over to introduce the players. With bursts of music, with leaps by the cheerleaders, with a big cheer: for each player of the home team. It was all plenty of fanfare and plenty of flourish. And with that the game began.

As the prisoners saw it, the name of the game was a complete misnomer, except for the few times when the ball was kicked. What they saw in the game was that most of the time most of the wadded and padded bodies crashed into each other, or players collided head-on with each other, or several players were collapsing like a stack of wood on top of each other. All of that amidst a flurry of whistles and little yellow flags. And if a player on occasion should manage to avoid the melee, or get out from under the melee, then that player, with the ball under his arm, kept running as if he was running for his life.

There were a number of times when the ball was kicked. And each time he asked himself why the players kicked the ball with the top of the boot? And not, for better accuracy and distance, with the side of the boot? But otherwise he cheered when the crowd cheered, and groaned when the crowd groaned. In the end, Fabens lost the game.

Every morning he hoped for two things. He hoped that Marvin would be their guard, and that on the way to the fields they would see the town. Otherwise there was always a chance that the new guard would turn out to be altogether too taciturn. And that the new farmer had his fields in the opposite direction from town.

And while the prisoners never had any reason to fear any of the guards, there were about three or four out of six who refrained from talking to the prisoners, at least not more than was necessary. They were the taciturn ones. It must be added that they were never hostile, it was just that they did not want to talk. Least of all talk about the kind of questions he had.

He had all kinds of questions. Questions about how certain words were pronounced. Questions about how a democracy functioned. Questions about organic chemistry. They were all the result of his nightly studies: of combing the Webster (which had no pronunciatory guide) for twenty new words; of reading a book (which he had bought used in the PX) about the structure and the function of American democracy; of trying to make sense out of a course in organic chemistry (in which he had enrolled as an extension course of the University of Maryland, after most other courses were closed).

For the kinds of questions he had, Marvin was like a teacher. In fact, Marvin had been studying for a college career in English literature when the war interrupted his studies. And here now, except in organic chemistry, there was never a question that Marvin could not answer. And answer with the kind of eagerness that comes from a kind heart and a questing mind. For Marvin, home after a bout with malaria in the Pacific war, also had questions. Mainly about the German language, which he spoke with some fluency. And so, to find time for the exchange, Marvin would often be near him in the cotton field. There, between picking cotton and between doing guard duty, the two were answering each other's questions. Right up to the last days at Camp Fabens.

At no time were there at Camp Fabens the kind of divisions that had been so pronounced at Camp Huntsville. Divisions that pitted Nazis against anti-Nazis, the high-ranked against the low-ranked, the (coupon) rich against the (coupon) poor. At Camp Fabens no one ever needed to dread the nights. And not even the tattooed men felt the need to remind the untattooed men that they had been terribly wronged: not when the latter were too young to be denied innocence.

16
WHEN TRAINS CROSS RIVERS

His mind was made up. If the train should cross the Mississippi, he would spit into it—and make a wish. Making a wish from a train that was crossing a river was nothing new for him. He had done it before. In fact, over the years he had done it from any number of trains that had been crossing any number of rivers, both in Germany and other countries in Europe; and now he was about to make his first wish for the first time in America.

Nothing else had changed. Not the custom itself and faith in the custom. Not even the drift of mother's about spitting into a river and making a wish about something that he wanted very much had changed; not when her words were in response to his childhood wish to get to be an engineer on a steam-locomotive some day.

Anyway, even after he started riding a train to school every day, he would keep up with the custom and make wishes. On that train his wishes were largely those of a schoolboy. Actually, they were more like so many worries and fears about failing tests and flunking courses and about being held back in class. And even though the river in question was not much more than a sluggish, brackish-looking, nameless flow of water—that had to go round a huge heap of slag from a nearby blast furnace before getting to the bridge—for the worrisome wishes of a German high-school boy it was certainly big enough.

Later in life, it was also big enough for the kind of wishes that would come with adolescence. Like when he kept wishing that, in dance school, his hands would quit sweating while dancing with a girl; or that his feet would quit stepping on a girl's feet while trying to keep up with the vexing rhythm of the waltz; but when it came to the tango, there he wished for nothing so much as to be able to slow down his steps in such a way that the girl's body, to his great pleasure, was bound to come up rubbing and pressing against his own. Finally, there was the usual assortment of adolescent wishes, from growing a beard, to growing longer sideburns, to growing real hair on the chest.

Then there was the train that would take him to his grandparents each summer. For some real drama, there would come near the end of that journey the ride over Germany's Oder River, on a steel bridge that was all trusses and arches. And during the thunderous ride over that bridge he would wish for nothing so much than to be back on the same train again next summer, heading for still another vacation with *Oma* and *Opa*.

In time, however, the trains and their destinations changed. Thus, during the second half of 1942, he found himself on a number of military trains that were to take him from Germany into such occupied countries as Holland and France. And whenever these trains crossed a river—be it the Elbe, the Rhine, or the Seine—at such moments he had only one wish: that he come out of this war alive.

Finally, there was the train that was headed for Naples. From there the battery, in which he was serving as a gunner, was to be sent to North Africa. It was on that train that he added a prayer to his wish for survival. It happened on Christmas Eve, moments after the train had crossed the Tiber River and had come to a stop at a railroad station by the name of Ostia. And Ostia he knew, if only from history. What he knew was that in ancient times, as Rome's seaport, Ostia had been bustling with trade. Now it looked deserted. At least the station with its empty platforms and the forlorn looking red brick building, with the name Ostia on it, looked deserted. If nothing else, it looked as if all other trains on that day had come and had gone a long time ago. And daylight was fading fast.

Presently he thought of home again. And once again his memories of past Christmas Eves were so strong and his longings for home so implacable that his eyes filled with tears.

But back at Genoa, at least, there had been snow on the ground. And fresh snow on the morning of Christmas Eve was bound to bring back the memories and to stir the longings except that in this case the snow was to catch him by complete surprise, especially after yesterday's ride along the Riviera. During that slow and leisurely ride along the narrow band of land between the sea and the mountains, there had been nothing but sunshine and warm airs and gentle breezes. And on the beaches and on the boulevards and in the streets of the resorts along the Riviera there had been crowds of sunbathers and strollers and resort-town people. And as he was standing guard on a train that was taking him to war, he could not help but feel envious.

It was only later, sometime during the night, that he felt the cold. It made him crawl under the gun's tarpaulin, where, between fits of sleep, he spent the rest of the night trying to keep warm under the one blanket he had and under a pile of oil rags he had found on the gun. Still, he did not think of snow. Or of Christmas. Or of home. These thoughts only rushed in on him after he saw, in the first light of the day, the snow in Genoa. Snow in Genoa of all places. The snow was fresh and fluffy and it reached all the way from the shoreline along the harbor to the crest of the mountains, high above the city.

In looking back, he also remembered that at that moment he tried to think of something else, of something that would let him blink back the tears.

Not that the tears mattered. For he was alone. As a guard on a flatcar, on which the gun was mounted, he was all by himself. There was really no one closer to him than the next guard on one of the guns farther down the train. In fact, on this train of flatcars and ordinary third-class coaches, on which the battery was being transported from Jonzac in southern France to Naples in southern Italy for combat in North Africa there was no one really close enough to see the tears.

And as the train made its way out of Genoa and was picking up speed, he was overcome once more by a surge of memories and longings and tears. Only this time, to save face, he blamed the tears on the speeding train. So he stared straight ahead and let the winds and the drafts of the speeding train blow straight into his face—until the tears were streaming down his face. Meanwhile he kept saying to himself: Let the tears flow for as long as they want to.

The make-believe, or whatever it was, had enough of a calming effect on him to stop the tears and to free the thoughts. Now he could think of things that had more to do with the present and with the immediate future than with all those lingering memories of past Christmas Eves. And with the train heading south, along lonely stretches of coast along the Tyrrhenian Sea, it was to Rome that his thoughts turned.

Rome lay directly ahead. Also, after more than seven years of Latin in school he had a certain familiarity with Rome. It was that fact of getting close to Rome and of being familiar with Rome, familiar in a bookish sort of way, that caused him to ask himself questions like: How much of the ancient city was he going to see? How close to such ancient sites as the Forum and the Colosseum was the train going to take him? What chance was there that he would still be able to make out any of the Seven Hills on which the city had originally been built? And, for one final question, he asked himself what chance there was that he catch at least a glimpse of the dome of St. Peter?

The questions gave him, as it were, a sense of expectancy and relief. But then, after awhile, he was also asking himself, rather anxiously, whether the battery was going to get anything to eat in Rome, before going on to Naples? Whether they were going to get an extra portion of bread? A ladle of soup? A piece of salami? Perhaps even a piece of chocolate, however brittle and stale with age. And while thinking of food, it never occurred to him that the train might not stop in Rome.

In the end, as we have seen, the train did not stop in Rome. Instead, it went around the city by way of Ostia, where it came to a halt at the far end of the station, to wait for a signal to send it on. On into the night. On towards Naples. On towards the war in North Africa. And once again he felt the memories and the longings and the tears return, only more intensely and more implacably than before. And it was at that moment that he felt the need to turn to God with a prayer. But he had not prayed in years and so praying did not come easily to him; and just when it seemed that he was not going to able to say a prayer that would console him and strengthen him, there came to him a prayer out of his childhood. It was a simple prayer. It was the kind of a prayer that could only add to his earlier wish for survival, a few minutes ago, when the train crossed the Tiber River. And so he prayed: Darkness is coming... It will soon be night... I come to You... my Saviour... to ask You... that You watch over me... and keep me... for as long... as it is in Your will.

Over a year later, he found himself on still another train. Only this time he was a prisoner of war and the train was an American train. In fact, it was a regular US Army train and as such it was taking several hundred German POWs from a camp or two in Texas to some other camp somewhere. To which camp, no one knew. For that matter, POWs were never told the name and the location of the camp they were being taken to. All they ever knew, if they looked at the sun, was the direction the train was going. And this train was going east.

At first the train was traveling through Texas desert. In some ways it was as if it was travelling over some kind of primordial land: where the horizons stay distant and the skies remain high and where the land was covered by a carpet of spring flowers, pearly-looking and breathtakingly beautiful.

Otherwise everything was routine about the train: one prisoner to every two seats, or two prisoners to a compartment, giving every prisoner a window-seat. But the windows were partially blocked and could only be opened a few inches, or about the width of a hand.

Another routine about the train was that the guards were white MPs. Standing at the end of each one of the coaches, the MPs saw to it that the prisoners would remain in their seats at all times, to keep them from mingling. Also, the guards were making sure that only one prisoner at a time would come forward to use the toilet.

By contrast, the men who were responsible for the food were all black. Whether they were soldiers or hired civilians was not clear. Wearing white uniforms, they would come down the aisle three times a day to serve either breakfast, lunch, or supper; and each time they came down the aisle they would push a long line of carts, piled high with pots and pans and utensils, from which they would dish out meals that came complete with courses and with choices. For example, breakfast, the most American of meals, came with a choice of juice, cooked cereal, scrambled eggs with a choice of bacon or ham or sausages, fried potatoes, buttered toast with jam or marmalade, and milk and coffee.

At the end of the day, the train was still headed east and the land was still vast and open and in bloom. What changes there were, they were subtle ones: like hues of green here and there, or specks of different colors coming from cattle grazing in the distance, or an occasional barbed-wire fence running away from the tracks in a sharp, thin line, to say nothing of lone ranches standing like ramparts in this empty and lonely land. By now he was asking himself whether it was America's prairie that he was seeing?

But trying to figure out where they were going was like trying to put together the pieces of a puzzle. From start to finish. Or from El Paso, where it all started, to wherever the train was taking them. And white MP's and black KP's were no help. But since the train was going east and since he knew a thing or two about America's geography, he had a hunch that the train, if it only kept going, was bound to cross the Mississippi, giving him a chance to make a wish. His first in America. For that matter, it was going to be a wish that was just as special and just as close to his heart as any of the other wishes he had ever made.

Nine months earlier, when first arriving in America, he had not made any such wish. And it was not for any lack of rivers. On the contrary. On the train from Norfolk on the east coast to Camp Huntsville in Texas—and we should know that both the train and the prisoners were different—the train was to cross all kinds of rivers, the Mississippi included. Still, it never occurred to him to make a wish.

For an answer we must go back to the time when, as a German soldier, his fear of captivity was second only to his fear of death. That fear was so real that on the day Rommel's Africa Corps surrendered—on May 11, 1943—he was desperate enough to risk his life in order to avoid capture. He tried to escape. On a raft. Across the stormy seas of the Mediterranean to Pantelleria. Under the guns of the enemy. The attempt failed and he was captured. And one of the first things he discovered was that his fears of being shackled in irons and of being guarded by trigger-happy enemy soldiers and of being starved to death by the enemy were completely unfounded.

There was no holding back the memories now: not when they were taking him back to the first camp he was ever in. It was a camp in Tunisia somewhere, hastily put up by the English for thousands of German prisoners. All there was to the camp were open pits for latrines and rolls of barbed wire that formed a large square of bare ground. It was in that square that the prisoners, from the sergeants and corporals on down to the lowest among the recruits, were all down together on the same bare, sun-burnt ground, either sprawling or squatting or just standing around, as if waiting for something to happen.

For him it happened fast. After the storms of war and after his last-minute, desperate attempt to avoid capture by risking his life, it struck him like a miracle almost that he was still alive. And so for the first day or two in that camp in Tunisia somewhere he felt like shouting it out loud that his life had been spared.

Moreover, deep down, he was glad that the war in Africa was over and that he would no longer have to fear for his life. At the same time he was just as glad that he would not have to suffer any longer the kind of indignities that sadist sergeants and bully corporals would routinely inflict on raw recruits: such as cleaning latrines with a toothbrush and polishing the drill masters' boots with spit and shouting "*Ich bin ein Schwein*" while crawling through muck and mire. To say nothing of the kind of drill and regimentation that went on as sergeants and corporals would strut their stuff and would bark their orders that would send recruits into binges of heel-clicking, *Jawoll*-shouting, snappy saluting and all the rest. Unless they found themselves at the front.

Still, he was sure that this kind of German militarism, in this part of the world at least, was dead. That it was as dead as a cadaver; and that there was no reason, then, to make anything like a wish to the effect that it would not come back to life.

He was wrong. After an Odyssey halfway around the world, by train from Tunis to Oran and in a convoy across the Atlantic and again by train from America's east coast to Camp Huntsville in Texas, German militarism was coming back to life with a vengeance. Without the officers that is, who had been taken to other camps. But the sergeants and the corporals, for that matter, were back to strutting their stuff and were back to barking their order that sent the rest of the rank and file, this time as prisoners of war, into heel-clicking obedience and abject subordination. And like in the days before they ever came to power, back in 1933, the Nazis were back to bashing in heads.

It was as if everything in this twenty or thirty acre world of Camp Huntsville, complete with guard-towers, barbed wire, mess halls, barracks and three thousand prisoners was going topsy-turvy; as if the lines between captors and captives were being blurred; as if in this corner of Texas the war had produced no real winners and no real losers.

This was no time to let go of the memories. Not with the train going one way and the memories another. Not when the memories were taking him back to Hunstville, where it all began. First with a thought. Then with an idea. In the end with a full-grown wish. And so now, in order to get on with the wish, all that was needed was for the train to reach the Mississippi—and cross it.

And now, on this train out of El Paso, he was once again among the Nazis. Alone. What happened was that, after there was no more cotton to be picked around Fabens, they were taken to Fort Bliss in El Paso where they were joined by other prisoners from other camps. Here they were either put on the train or they stayed behind. All at random. It turned out that he would never see any of the twelve fellow-resisters again.

He was back among the Nazis. Their sneering disdain for everything American was ample proof. Their targets ranged from blacks who would always remain children to whites who were held together mostly by the starch in their uniforms; from black women who slept with white men to white women who slept with black men; from shack-like houses to oversized cars; from grinding poverty to glitzy riches. For these fanatics, with their barrack-voices, everything American was either bad or worse or worst. There was nothing else.

As soon as the lands along the tracks started to fill with water, with miles and miles of brown water as it turned out, he had a hunch that ahead flowed the Mississippi. He was right. From that moment on he kept his face pressed against the window, close to the opening, and by the time the train started to rumble across the steel bridge, ever so slowly, and by the time he saw the brown waters of the Mississippi directly below the bridge — he put his mouth squarely into the opening of the window and he did what he had done so many times before: he spat into the river and made a wish. This time it was his wish that one day he would return, that he would return to the banks of the river, that he would return to the banks of the river as a free man of this country. Minutes later, as the train rumbled through Memphis, he had the answer to where the train had crossed the Mississippi River and where he had made his wish.

17

CAMP FORREST AT LAST

After Memphis the train had one more good run, this time deeper into Tennessee. Finally, at a small station by the name of Tullahoma, the train was shunted for a mile or two into a camp, and the journey was over. For a name, Camp Forrest was fitting. Unlike the sun-scorched camps in Texas, this camp was green with trees. Tall pines with their umbrella-shaped crowns towered over two-story barracks and budding young firs gave the camp an arboreal presence from which no mazes of streets and mazes of barbed-wire fences could detract. In fact, for the two years he was to spend in Camp Forrest, the camp itself and the woods beyond seemed to be getting larger and more expansive than ever, at least in his imagination.

There was something else that was on his mind. What he had seen of Tennessee so far reminded him of the Sandwiesen Woods back home: with their left-over pines and budding firs to say nothing of sylvan retreats and sandy beaches, perfect for revelers and lovers. But the creation of this great outdoors is a story in itself. Here we must go back to a time, several decades ago, when coal mining in Upper Silesia began in earnest. When over large tracts of forest in this Sandwiesen hinterland trees were cut and sand was dredged to shore up and to fill up depleted shafts and seams in coal mines. And in order to get the masses of timber and sand from the Sandwiesen hinterland to the heartland of Upper Silesian coal mines, the industry went so far as to build a special network of freight trains for the hauling. While he thought of Sandwiesen, war was also on his mind, war against Norway and France that for an opening round was over before the second summer had begun in earnest. It was *Blitzkrieg* that had done it.

For most of the people in the village, war at this point was too far away to be of more than secondary concern. For that, life in the village had to meet ever-pressing needs of survival: from having coal in the bin, to having food in the larder, to having potatoes in the root cellar... before anyone could even think of cooking a meal. But for extras, especially during the summer, there were herbs to be picked for tea, apples to be gathered from trees along the *Chaussee*. and blueberries to be picked in the Sandwiesen Woods. And talk in the village had it that this was the summer for blueberries.

It was a *Kriegerwitwe* (warrior widow) who talked him into going with her to Sandwiesen. Here we should know that in a deadly change of meaning the pun of *Kriegerwitwe* became *Kriegswitwe* (war widow) once war with Russia had started. But for now she was still a warrior widow and once they were outside the village they went to Sandwiesen together, on bikes, to pick blueberries. Her dress got windblown, and he thought he saw that underneath she was naked. Before long they were in the woods, and they ended up in a patch full of blueberries. They were alone. Picking blueberries back in those days meant that they had to be close to the ground because the berry bushes grew close to the ground. They had to stoop and crawl to get anywhere near to the berries for the picking.

Soon they were close to each other, at arm's length, and he saw that under the dress she was indeed naked. She made no attempt to hide her nakedness. By now it was only a question of who would make the first move. Then it happened: she let herself down, backwards, ever so gently, and as she reached out for him, she pulled him down to her, while fondling him free from his pants for a close embrace. It was the closest he had ever come with a woman. And then they made love.

Here in Camp Forrest, one year had passed since his arrival, and the Nazis and the non-coms had never got around to military discipline and strutting. At least not during the day since everybody had to work. Work by weaving nets. It meant standing at a loom all day and going through the motions of weaving by knotting strands of jute into a loose netlike fabric. Were the nets for fishing as the Americans claimed? Or were the nets for camouflage as the Germans insisted? Regardless of the flap between the two sides, the numbing boredom of the work never ceased.

But luck would have it that he got a job at headquarters as an interpreter and translator. His reception there, on the day he reported for work, was a bristling accusation by one of the sergeants: "You Nazi son-of-a-bitch, you killed my kid brother" and then he added, "in Sicily." And it was only after the accused told the sergeant that he had never been to Sicily, and that he was sorry for the loss of his brother, that calm returned. In the end, there came a time when the sergeant would do anything for the prisoner.

In the camp there were still the Nazis. Camp Forrest was large and sprawling and there was no way for all the several thousand prisoners to keep the scourge of Nazism and the cadaver obedience of militarism at bay. There were the rumors of visits with blankets at night, even of killings at night, hints of an anti-Nazi compound, always under four eyes. Once more he had reason to fear for his life, especially after he had started to work for the Americans at headquarters. Lastly there was the rumor that the Americans reported the killings as suicides to the International Red Cross. But that rumor together with the exact location of the anti-Nazi compound was to remain a mystery. It was the sergeant who in a first show of support told him that that compound was outside the main camp, and that a request for transfer had to be in writing.

Waiting began. After two weeks he still had no answer. Explanations had it that the soldier handling such transfers was on leave. That's when he took matter into his own hands. When on that day he marched out with the detail of net-working prisoners to the gate, he refused to go through the gate, telling the guards that his life was in danger from the Nazis, and that he should be taken to the anti-Nazi compound. After a call or two by the guards, a jeep with guards drove up, and they took him to the barrack to get his belongings. After that they took him to the anti-Nazi compound.

There were about two hundred prisoners in that compound, evenly divided between Germans and Russians. These Russians had been captured by the

Germans and put into labor camps. They were forced to do labor for the Germans until those camps were taken by the Allies and the prisoners sent on to Camp Forrest. But while the Germans were from the first to the last anti-Nazis, as former inmates of concentration camps, or for having run afoul of the Nazis in POW camps, the Russians appeared to be rent by disagreements and tensions. For one thing they had all been serving in labor battalions under the Nazis and may have come away with varying reactions to these battalions, and for another they appeared to be having fallouts over such issues as Soviet Communism and border-state(s) nationalism.

Eventually, after the end of the war, there were news reports about numbers of Russian repatriates jumping ship in Seattle and committing suicide by drowning.

Among the anti-Nazis, it was with Heinz that he became the best of friends. Heinz had turned into an anti-Nazi after his capture in France in the summer of 1944. By then he had done garrison duty in Cherbourg for almost four years, and as a result spoke nearly perfect French. Moreover he had become a Francophile *par excellence*. As the son of an art dealer in Germany, Heinz was well-versed in art and art history. Thus it was natural for Heinz to lecture about these subjects and for him to listen. As a result art and their friendship became a gift for a lifetime.

At headquarters there were sometimes such cases as suspected sabotage. In all of his translations he never strayed far from the literal side of questions and answers. At stake in these confrontations were charges against prisoners of tearing up nets or of cutting into rolls of thread. And for an answer it was always a straight "*Nein*" or "*Ich habe keine Ahnung*." Thus a prisoner either denied or rejected a charge. And in no case was a prisoner ever handed over for court-martial.

In the meantime the war in Europe was coming to an end. And his mind was made up. He would try to escape. Not in order to get home, as had always been the reason for attempted escapes in the past, but in order to prevent repatriation. He would try to escape for only one reason: to stay in America. And now was the time to get ready. He would head for Tullahoma... pay his twenty dollars at the station... catch the train for Birmingham. Upon further reflection, he knew that it would be easy to get through the barbed-wire fence, since there were no guard towers on this side of the compound, and to run the one or two miles to the station. He also knew that at dawn next morning he would be in Birmingham, a good distance away from Camp Forrest.

For all that it took all kinds of preparations. He would have to convert a sizeable number of PX coupons into forty dollars of greenbacks. Here the sergeant was a great help. For clothes without PW markings he was able to finagle plain khakis and a trench coat from a fellow prisoner in the supply room in return for some PX coupons. And for a new name he decided on James Jarnigan. For the city of origin Boston was his choice. The two came closest to his English/Irish accent in his speech as some guards had told him casually. Finally there were two more obstacles left. One was to say goodbye to Heinz, and the other was how to eventually get a social security card. It was his understanding that without that card nobody could get a job in America except for picking cotton or cutting tobacco or bundling sugar cane.

As it turned out, he could have saved himself the trouble of preparing for the escape. For when he saw Heinz to say goodbye, their eyes went teary.

Christmas card sent by Rudolf to his parents in 1945

And with tears in his eyes there was no way he could ever leave.

By now he was more than ever worried about his parents, about his mother and his sister in the village and about his father at the front. Would they be able to escape the cauldron of the Russian armies? In fact, in the face of not having received a single letter from them for over three years in captivity, and even though he had sent the regular quota of POW letters to his mother, the most pressing question for him was whether they were still alive.

For by now Hitler's Thousand Year *Reich* lay in ruins after a lifetime of a little over twelve years. In the end the final cauldrons of war had been at their worst and at their most revealing when he heard the news and saw pictures of gassed and emaciated inmates in concentration camps, when he saw millions of Germans on the run, when he saw armies of refugees seeking escape from the Soviets, when he saw old men and boys of the Hitler youth being pressed into service to save the Third *Reich*, when he saw bombed out cities and a country that had been raked by war thoroughly, and when he witnessed a Germany plunging from such highs as *Deutschland über Alles* to a 'nadir' of nothingness.

For him, with Silesia in Russian (and eventually in Polish) hands there was no way to go back. There was only the choice of staying in America for as long as possible. Even if it meant going back to the Nazi compounds, since the anti-Nazis were about to be sent back to Germany. And after they were in fact sent back to Germany, within a week or two he did end up with the Nazis again while he kept his job at headquarters. But Nazism and militarism by now were dead in word and in deed.

In the meantime the rations of all prisoners had been reduced to 800 calories a day. Because American POWs were no longer in German hands, equal treatment was not an issue. Therefore it meant that day for day they got two slices of bread and a dab each of margarine and jam for breakfast, a herring and a red potato and a cut of lettuce with dressing for lunch, and two slices of bread with a slice each of cheese and baloney for supper. To this we should add one cup of coffee for each meal. Compared with the original rations of generous and sumptuous meals, the 800 calories by now per day were like a diet of starvation. Here again the sergeant looked after him. [See Appendix 2]

On top of it all, one day the sergeant asked him whether he was serious about staying in America. After he said so once more the sergeant told him that he would arrange for him to go to his sister who lived on a farm with her husband out in the East somewhere. There he would find a safe haven. It would only be the first step to making his home in America. The offer was tempting. But for a professional soldier with the rank of a sergeant, and for a fine American, he knew that he could never accept the offer. For it meant that such action could expose the sergeant to serious consequences. And he had no other choice but to say no.

In the meantime, though, he was given a chance to get ready for a job as translator of German documents. This time he waited for several months, or until the offer was withdrawn for lack of sufficient documents. By January of 1946 he was on his way to Camp Shanks near New York City, together with other prisoners, and after New York, on a ship across the Atlantic to Bremerhaven and by train to Marburg in the American Zone. And the destinations, each time, were spelled out for the first time in three years of captivity. So was the statement that in Marburg they would be released from captivity for repatriation.

18

SURVIVAL

By now he was numbed by a feeling of hopelessness. And that feeling after his disappointment over the chance to translate German war documents, which would have allowed him to stay in America longer, was bound to lead him to such questions as: Where will I go in Germany? What will I do in Germany? How will I find out where my parents are? Are they still alive? And what about my sister? Even among the relatives, there was no one who had ever lived outside Silesia. But Silesia was Polish by now, and millions of Silesians had fled the province.

On that train from Tullahoma to Camp Shanks the feeling of hopelessness never left him. Even the train seemed to be going through something of a vacuum. In fact, it was like a no-man's-land of sorts where nothing made much sense anymore: like when the names of stations and towns remained a dead letter, or when he was not tempted to spit into rivers anymore in hopes for a wish to come true, or when people looked like walk-ons on a stage for a bad play.

At Camp Shanks finally, the prisoners went through a process of identification again, even though their release from captivity was only days away. About that process he kept telling himself, in a play of words, that redundancy is the mother of bureaucracy. Meanwhile a fierce winter storm lashed out at New York City and its Port. The storm was at its worst later that day when the train backed into one of the quays and came to a halt across from a Liberty ship. Shimmering wet and gray in the semi-darkness, it looked like a troop ship. But now, as if coming from nowhere, there were MP's on the scene. In their ramrod bearing they reminded him of the *SS*, except that back then in North Africa, close to three years ago, the MP's were taking over a trainload of German prisoners from the British, while here in the port the MP's were taking over a similar trainload of German prisoners from ordinary American soldiers. Before long the MP's lined up along the train and began to gesture to the prisoners to come out. Others kept pointing to the gangway where the prisoners should assemble. And no sooner were the prisoners outside when a voice on a loudspeaker announced in perfect German that they should go up the gangway and board the ship. They ended in quarters down in the hull of the ship somewhere, where rows of bunk beds went as far as he could see, and beds going up to the ceiling were about four or five high. Quickly he made up his mind to climb to one of the uppermost beds, to the one with a grated opening in a ventilator that would allow him to breathe fresh air.

Before long the ship was on its way. By the time it reached the open sea it acted as if the storm was getting the better of it. Heaving from bow to stern and wallowing from side to side, the movement of the ship was tantamount to a mix for seasickness. Soon the prisoners did get sick. Among the hundreds of them the sickness came on in waves: from gagging sounds of nausea to gurgling noises of vomiting, and from throwing up fouled food to the stench of fouled food. All with a suddenness that left vomit everywhere: on beds, on the floor between beds and around garbage cans.

As soon as he started feeling sick, he pressed his face against the opening in the ventilator and inhaled fresh air with deep breaths. It seemed to help; and as he was getting over the spasms of gagging he knew that he would have to get away from the stench and the vomit. So he ran to the mess hall where the bell had just rung for supper. For the few who made it, there was plenty of food, just for the asking. In fact, the cornucopia lasted for three days. Most of the time during those three days he spent either in the mess hall or on deck. For the night, of course, he had to return to the sleeping quarters, and despite the stench from vomit and the sounds of vomiting he fell asleep.

With the ship reaching calmer seas the mess hall began to fill up with half-starved prisoners. Promptly they ate as much as they could get. Between meals he was still spending as much time as he could on deck. On the fifth day he began to look for the entrance to the English Channel: for the English coast on the left and for some of the French-Belgium coast on the right. That's how he remembered it from geography. But he saw no land. But on the sixth day it happened. Suddenly the engines cut back, and the ship slowed down. As he looked out for the Channel he still saw no land. Then he looked straight ahead, beyond the bow, and there he saw land in a thin line of coast, yellow along the bottom and green along the top. By now the deck was full of prisoners. Beyond them, with guns at the ready, stood the MP's. Suddenly the voice on the loudspeaker came on and announced in perfect German again that Bremerhaven was full and that therefore they would have to go to Le Havre. From there a train would take them to Marburg for their release from captivity. A short time later there was the voice again, telling the prisoners to get their belongings and make ready for disembarkation. In the end the ship went through some docking maneuvers and eventually lay still.

On the quay the train was already waiting. Boxcars for the prisoners and two coaches for the MP's. The latter were already standing at guard. Otherwise, except for some railway men, no Frenchmen could be seen on the quay. After coming off the ship, the prisoners were counted into platoons of forty and made to get into the boxcars. It reminded him of boxcars for the German army with the inscription of 8 horses or 40 men. They were no sooner in the boxcars when French railway men all along the train started to slide the doors shut and to slam the crossbars into lock.

During the ride he cowered on the floor, between the door and his duffel bag. It seemed to calm him. For by now he feared that they would be turned over to the French. He had that fear even though in the nine months since the end of the war he had never heard anything about such transfers of prisoners by the Americans to the French, or for that matter, to the Russians or the British. And thoughts of escape were on his mind, only this time to get back to Germany. After several hours of short runs and short stops, the train seemed to come to an end of the journey. Outside in the darkness, whenever he heard voices, they would always be in French; or sometimes he could hear heavy footsteps. And then, at first daylight, there was a clank and somebody on the outside rolled back the door. Down below stood two French soldiers with guns on the ready and with bayonets fixed on the muzzles. At first it looked like a stand-off between the French soldiers down below and the prisoners in the box-car. It was almost like a confrontation between the French and the Germans. In fact, after almost three years of captivity, he had never seen anything as hostile as that.

Suddenly, with shrill and cutting voices, French soldiers all along the train began to shout, "*Allez!*" And, getting his duffel bag, he waited for French soldiers down below to back away so he could jump. They did that, and he jumped, and the first thing that happened was that another French soldier took his duffel bag away from him. It turned out that in the end all of the German prisoners on the train lost their belongings to the French. This was Camp Compiegne.

He never saw the MP's again. Nor did he see the famous railroad car in which in WWI and WWII the French and the Germans signed a total of three armistices. Camp Compiegne was not even so much as a makeshift camp. There were no barracks, no tents, there were not even pieces of tar paper or pieces of cardboard for cover. The only likeness that Compiegne had with an ordinary POW camp were barbed-wire fences and guard towers. There were only guard towers with bare ground in between. And the bare ground was wet and dank from the weather. Into that ground the prisoners dug holes and trenches with bare hands. And into these holes and trenches the prisoners would crawl at night for some sleep, and by lying next to each other, for a shred of warmth. The other trench in the camp, only deeper, was a long hole with boards on top from which the prisoners could relieve themselves.

Within days the prisoners were starved from hunger. Their daily rations were two ladles of gruel that looked like it had been made from leftover fish and bits and pieces of vegetables and potatoes and sometimes a piece of stale bread. It did not take long for some of the prisoners to think of grass they could eat: grass that was growing in between the barbed-wire fences. But rumor had it that the French guards on the towers must be trigger-happy, because one or two prisoners from a previous transport had been shot while reaching for grass. But desperate with hunger he was willing to take his chances. He would walk over to the tower and look at the guard, and once he had his eye, point to the grass and then make motions of eating. He did all that, and then he said, in French: "*Puis je manger des herbes?*," while nodding to the guard. When the guard turned away, he reached through the fence and, grabbing a bunch of grass, tore it off. Then he backed away from the fence and walked to his hole to crawl into it. There he ate his grass.

But hunger, cold, sleepless nights and the stench of human waste was not the worst of the ordeal. What was worst was not knowing where they would be taken next. To ports along the Atlantic coast? To clear mines? To one of the battlefields of recent times again to clear mines? To French farmers to work? In fact, it was even rumored that they might be sent to French colonies in North Africa. But as rumors go, the most surprising was that the SS, of all German troops, would be sent back to Germany for refusing to work. That rumor came with a hint that until recently the SS had been shot by the French for the same refusal.

  He could not help but ask himself whether the world was going topsy-turvy: for such changes in destinations from Bremerhaven to Le Havre and from Marburg to Compiegne; or for such changes in food for the POWs in the States from plenty to sparse; or when his sense of justice was jarred when finding out that all Germans from innocent children to the old and infirm were subjected to the same meager rations as the rest of the Germans after VE-Day. His reaction to the latest surprise, the one with the SS, was that if he somehow could pierce the blood type-O into his underarm and pass as an SS he would not hesitate to do it. But there was no way to do that. Be that as it may, a few days later, the three platoons of SS marched through the gates for their return to Germany. So, at least, it was rumored.

  Nevertheless, his own luck would change. Sauntering one day near the gate he saw an announcement posted. It was in French. In that announcement they were looking for an interpreter. And he applied for the position on the spot and was taken by one of the soldiers to the office, where in halting French, he had a friendly talk with a lieutenant. And he got the job. Later in the day the prisoners in the camp were marched out through the gate for an unknown destination.

  Meanwhile, he was assigned to a barrack not far from the French quarters. In that barrack were several other German prisoners who worked in the kitchen or worked in the laundry; and a prisoner from that *blanchissage* offered to launder his clothes the same day. For the first time since Tullahoma and after his two months of living in nothing but bare ground, he had his first hot shower. And after the shower with his clean clothes on, and after a good meal, he felt like a newborn.

  His spirits revived. Since there were no prisoners in the camp anymore, he brushed up on his French by writing down, with the help of a dictionary, French words he did not know. Page after page, day after day, he did everything to commit these words to his memory. At times he tried his French on members of the staff, especially on the lieutenant, who was always open to such exchanges. He could not help but feel good about his progress.

  There were still no new prisoners in the camp with the bare grounds. One day, to his surprise, the lieutenant asked him whether he would like to go home on the 25th of the month. He only nodded. Also going home would be all the prisoners in the barrack. From that moment he began to count the days until that day in May.

On that day their boxcar was hitched to another train of German prisoners. He had no idea where they came from, but they seemed downtrodden. The ride to the German border was uneventful. But as soon as they crossed into Germany, the despair of German women especially was all apparent. For whenever the train slowed down (and it went mostly at slow speeds) or when it stopped, there were the women with their children. They came out running to the track or to the station and kept shouting the names of missing soldiers or held up posters with the names of missing soldiers. They came by the hundreds, came all together by the thousands, while the children in their innocent ways held out their hands begging for food. There was no food.

19
ANOTHER BEGINNING

At Marburg, where he was to be discharged, the first question he faced was where to go in Germany. He chose the American Zone. The British Zone was somewhat of a distant second, while the Russian and the French Zones of Occupation filled him with dread. But the American Zone came with a hitch. He would also have to name a place of destination in order to qualify for the rationing card and to receive the forty marks in severance pay. Forty marks were like a fraction of a penny per day for over three years of captivity, or buying 10 American cigarettes on the black market.

He had never even so much as set foot in any one place in that part of Germany. And he was in a quandary. All he could do was to ask some men who were standing in line with him to name the place of a small town nearby. Alsfeld was one of the answers. And Alsfeld he chose. With that he got his discharge papers. But at the same time another man behind the desk said: "*Ich glaube, das ist fuer Sie*," and handed him a piece of paper. Smaller than a postcard, it came with a Red Cross in the upper left hand corner. Before he could even read the note, he recognized the handwriting. It was his mother's. The note, which was addressed to him in Camp Huntsville, Texas, his first camp in America back in 1943, said: "Am barely alive in a camp in Austria. Margarete and Dad

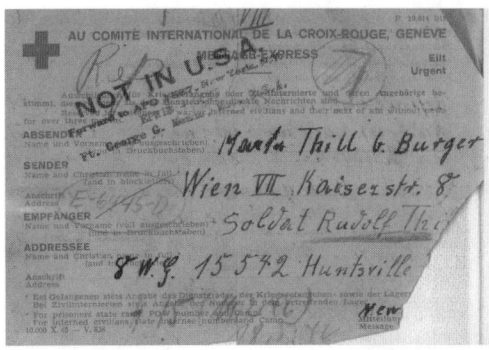

Martha Thill with Burger
Vienna VII, Kaiserstr. 8,
Soldier Rudolf Thi..,
8WG 15542 Huntsville...

Papa's and Margarete's whereabouts unknown. Gerda is in Zwickau, Saxony, Lothringer Str. 2. Am healthy and cling to life. 1000 kisses. Vienna, 2 Nov., 1945 Your Mother, Martha Thill, Vienna.

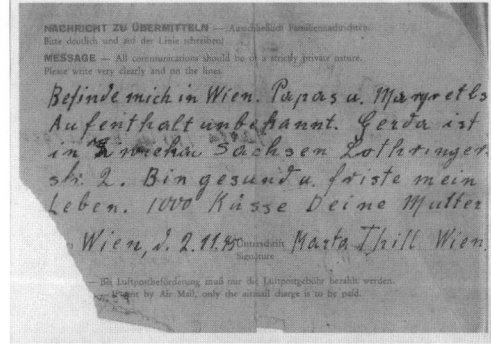

209

are missing. Hope you are well. Gerda's address is Zwickau, Lasalle Strasse" (the number was smudged out).

In spite of all the loose ends in that note: how Mother ended up in a camp in Austria, how his sister got lost, how Gerda, his favorite cousin, ended up in the Russian Zone, his reaction was to get to Alsfeld as soon as he could and get a room there for an address, and write to Gerda. And with that he left the camp and headed straight down the tracks for the station. At the station, though, he had to stay overnight to wait for the first train to Alsfeld, on a Sunday.

Alsfeld turned out to be a small town untouched by war. On that Sunday morning he saw people in their Sunday best and in their country costumes going to church. As if nothing had ever happened. For a moment he felt like joining them but then decided against it. Ultimately he felt as if they and he were from different worlds. So he went back to the station to see whether he could get something to eat. Perhaps in the restaurant adjacent to the waiting room. But he had no food stamps and could get nothing. That's when a man of his age, sitting at a nearby table, came to his rescue and ordered for him a meal of chicken soup and meatloaf and dumplings, in addition to cake for dessert. While eating they exchanged their stories. It turned out that Friedrich had been taken prisoner by the Russians, but had escaped. Now the former Berliner lived here. But dare to get discharge papers he did not for fear of extradition. Instead he lived off the black market. His favorite trade items with American soldiers were German cameras in exchange for cartons of American cigarettes or greenbacks.

One trouble for Friedrich was that he spoke hardly any English; and so the deal was struck between the two that he would move with him into his room and they would do the black-marketing together. An hour later they were on a train to a small station nearby where they got out and went into the station to take a flight of stairs to Friedrich's room. As *Landsers*, the popular expression for soldiers in Germany, the two hit it off right away.

They did their trade either at Marburg or in Giessen. Given his fluency in English and given the penchant of the GI's for German cameras, their trade proved to be a boon. They could easily live without any registrations on the money they made. In the meantime he had written to Gerda and was waiting for an answer. On Saturdays they would go to dances. In those villages, around Alsfeld at least, the young and the old would dance their hearts out, after years of Nazi-ordered prohibitions against dancing. Real dance bands played live dance music now. And on this Saturday, he had a date. Friedrich had arranged it. She was a teacher from a nearby village. With the invitation she had sent a red tie for him to wear. And he wore it on his black PW uniform. It turned out that in spite of the war years she had a quiet charm about herself and a kind of beauty that was not ostentatious. They danced dance after dance, and in between they talked about themselves. From the first they felt drawn to each other, in ways that made him look forward to walking her home. And indeed this night early in June was like a gem of stars and moonlight. In the end they walked through the fields on the way to her village.

Ahead of them they saw a hedge. They lay down so close to it as if they wanted to keep their presence a secret. Then they listened into the night. But there was nothing but silence. If there was anything else it was their awareness of their yearning for each other, together with the feeling that under this sky, with its stars and its moon, everything would turn out to be all right.

Suddenly there was the song of a nightingale in the air. He felt like reaching out for the bird. It was that close. But for all the temptation he resisted and instead listened. It was the first time ever (and the last time ever in his life) that he heard the song of a nightingale with its long runs on melodies, with its glorious trills and with its staccato-like twitters. Then the bird fell silent, only to start all over again. It was like a musical counterpoint to a great silence. They felt spellbound. But then the bird fell silent again, this time for good. And with all that new silence the village was on their mind again. When they got there, they kissed goodbye to each other. One week later he was on his way to see his mother.

He had finally heard from Gerda. Mother by now was living in a place by the name of Tittmoning, in Bavaria. It would take him two days to get there. The longest run of any of the trains would be from Frankfurt to Munich, where for the first time since coming back he would see some bombed-out and devastated cities. That train from Frankfurt to Munich was packed with people. Some were people whose travel luggage looked like the last belongings of refugees. Others looked like native Bavarians who spoke with a Bavarian dialect which he could barely understand. In fact, most of the Bavarians seemed to be at loose ends with the word "*Saupreiss*." And that word, whatever it meant, was beyond his understanding. Was it an expression for something in vogue right now, or was it a take-off on "*Preusse*" meaning Pig-Prussian, even though Prussia itself had ceased to be a part of Germany in 1918. As it turned out, the Bavarians were back to Prussian-baiting with a vengeance. Refugee-baiting would have been more fitting.

Munich was like a modern Pompeii. The inner city lay in ruins. But it turned out eventually that there was hope, for when the inner city was built in the eighteenth century it was built with massive walls of stone and brick. As a result the city did not suffer the kind of damage that other fire-bombed cities like Hamburg and Dresden had suffered. Here in Munich, at least, many of the bomb-damaged buildings remained structurally sound and could possibly be rebuilt.

In the meantime, he had decided to stay overnight in a park near the *Hauptbahnhof*. The night was unusually hot and humid; the blanket he had traded back in Alsfelt for a couple of packs of American cigarettes came now in good stead. He spread it on the ground and waited for the night to put him to sleep. But the night had different ideas. Before he knew it there were several women roaming around with the men in the park. One of them ended up with him. The idea that she was a prostitute entered his mind. She was very forward, and she seemed to know her trade. Suddenly, without any previous warning, such as distant thunder, a bolt of lightning crashed into the tree next to them. All he did was to grab his blanket to run to the station for cover.

The next day around noon he arrived in Tittmoning on the Salzach. To the locals the town was known as a marketplace, since most of the shops were around the square. One exception was the dairy shop. But before he knew that, and while he was still trying to find Klostergasse 3, where Mother was supposed to live, he was suddenly struck by the possibility that she may have entered a cloister. That she may be a nun by now. And he felt as if his last hold on life was going *kaputt*. He had that feeling until he discovered that Klostergasse 3 was no cloister. It had a dairy shop that was closed during the noon hour, but there was another door leading into the house. Once inside he found himself in a hallway, hearing voices at the end. He walked down there and knocked on the door. The room fell silent. Then somebody called "*herein*." After he entered he introduced himself, and added that he was looking for Frau Thill. No one said anything. There were several women sitting around a table eating lunch. He introduced himself again, and again he said he was looking for Frau Thill. Once more there was no answer. The women just sat there and stared at him. Is it not strange, he wondered, that no one gives an answer? But then, a woman rose from behind the table, came slowly around the table and walked towards him. Her hair was white, and she looked emaciated. And again it puzzled him why she did not say anything. But then he saw tears in her eyes, and only then did he recognize her. It was his mother. It was not her white hair or emaciated condition that had given her away. It was the tears.

They spent the afternoon together, up in her room, and were telling each other events about the last four years. Yes, Margarete got lost. By January of 1945, the Russian offensive against Germany sent millions of Germans fleeing toward the Oder River and beyond. Among these were his mother, Marta Thill, and sister, Margarete. Flight, in their case, was by train, at night, virtually at the last minute. After reaching the Oder the train stopped and could not continue because of a damaged bridge where it could not pass. It was still night and as the refugees, full of confusion and fear, got off the train to see whether they could walk across the bridge, his mother and his sister got separated. Despite shouting each other's names, they never got together again, at least not for the time being. Mother ended up in Austria and Margarete in a children's camp in Czechoslovakia. Eventually they were reunited late in 1946 in postwar Germany. But there was no word from Father. Yes, when she had to flee at the last possible moment, she asked a neighbor to look after his pigeons and his rabbits. And, yes, there was a lot that had happened during the four years they had not seen each other. And then they went for a walk around the marketplace, arm in arm, and she made sure to introduce him to everyone they met.

Life in Germany, he found out, was like going through a welter of requirements. First you had to report to the Police. Next you had to go to the *Wohnungsamt* to apply for a residence permit. After that, in order to fulfill the work requirement for all able-bodied men, you reported to the Labor Office in order to get a job. And only then, after presenting proof of having fulfilled all of these requirements, did you get your monthly food-rationing card. One exception in which you were on your own was big-time black marketing where you paid cash for everything. But, that was illegal. At the end of the day he was given a job as a farmhand just outside town.

The owner of that farm was a man in his fifties. It turned out that he was as depraved as they come. That man was a knave, a scoundrel, an egomaniac and a wife beater who could be very angry, very spiteful and very vicious. In fact, for his pleasure his life seemed to revolve mainly about stuffing himself with the best food the farm could produce, about meeting every second day or so a big black marketer who came to the farm in a big car, and to chain-smoke American cigarettes.

Within days he knew that he would not last long on that farm. For shelter he had a bed and a locker in a room in the barn. Sometimes, at night, he could hear cries of a woman, cries that were coming from the farmhouse next door, cries that came with clapping and slapping noises of a beating. And indeed, as it turned out after such nights, it was a case of wife beating. About the meals, he always ate with the woman and her four children, ranging in age from four to ten, while the man ate his meal all by himself in a separate room. For the six of them it was a fare of dumplings or potatoes in one big pot coming with sour cream or runny *Quark* in a smaller pot. In the morning they had bread with butter and malt-coffee, and in the evening they had buttered bread again and one or two slices of cheese and sausage. For the husband, however, in addition she always served him in her servile ways food with lots of meat or bacon or slices of hard sausage and cheese and fried eggs for breakfast. And coffee for him, to judge by the aroma, was regular American coffee that came already ground out of a can.

Eating with the children was a rather messy affair. With a spoon or with their hands they went into the big pot and came up with a piece of dumpling or a piece of potato which they dipped into the small pot of sour cream and runny *Quark*. Their father meanwhile was dining on scrumptious food in the next room, with the door open.

Back in the barn he had noticed that some hens were laying away. It meant that once the nest was full they would go broody and sit on the nest and eventually hatch a bunch of baby chicks. Driven by hunger, here is what he did. He took the last laid egg from the nest, making sure that when he shook each it would remain firm on the inside. These eggs he cracked open and sucked out the contents. The egg shells, then, in his defiant mood he threw behind the locker.

There were still the torments of doing labor on the farm. The day started with cutting grass for the cows. A whole wagon-full of grass that had to be cut with a scythe. Once or twice the farmer had shown him how to handle a scythe. And it should be said here that mowing with a scythe, because of the stance and because of the swing, was extremely difficult. After feeding the cows he had to go back again to mow half a wagon-full of oats for the pair of horses. The cut field was left in stubbles. And to make matters worse his only pair of shoes was in tatters by now. It meant that he had to stand and mow the oats with those stubbles bruising and cutting into his feet. Against the opposition of the farmer he went to Tittmoning to try to get a pair of work shoes. He went to the *Bûrgermeister's* Office in his bare feet to apply for a special stub for a pair of work shoes. That pair, as it turned out, was to last him for two years. The shoes had an all wooden footing with a fabric going up to the ankles for fastening. Before going back to the farm Mother washed his feet in a gentle solution of soap.

In time he became a good farmhand, doing practically all the work. Until one day, as he was coming up from the field, the farmer met him with a pitchfork and started screaming. What had happened was that the farmer had found a mass of discarded egg shells in his room. Now the farmer was going after him. He backed away, all the way back to the wagon where in a load of oats he had his own pitchfork. With the pitchfork in hand he now made his moves against the farmer, feigning thrusts and advancing toward him. In the end, the knave, the scoundrel, the wife beater turned and fled into the house. And as for him, he went to his room in the barn, got his few belongings and left.

20

POST-WAR YEARS AND BEYOND

He had decided to go to Munich. Since going to a university and studying for a profession was virtually impossible in war-torn Germany, especially for refugees, he had decided to become at least a skilled worker such as a journeyman bricklayer. He did not just want to become an *ungelernter Arbeiter* or unskilled laborer.

He headed for Munich on foot. That way, after one year in the army and after three years in captivity, he could at least walk the distance of some fifty miles at his leisure and for once be alone. Also that way he could see the countryside at his own pace and hopefully see the Alps in the distance. After two days he landed in a circus. In return for food and lodging (which was a bed in a crowded circus wagon) he would become a *Requisitenräumer*. He had no idea what it was. He had even less of an idea after he was fitted with a uniform, shabby as it was. As it turned out his job was to collect animal droppings after each act, from a few horses and a half-grown and half-starved elephant. For him there was nothing offensive about it. Had he not gone out for years to collect horse and cow manure on the highway and in the fields in a bucket? All for the garden. His father, who was always with him, would say that it's so much better than artificial fertilizer, to which his mother would add that it is also so much cheaper.

When after a few days the circus moved on, away from Munich, he resumed his walking. The city was full of surprises, both good and bad. One good thing was that at his age the duration of apprenticeship was shortened to two years. Another was that at Stoehr Construction lodging was provided at the Agfa plant where he was going to work, and that working as a bricklayer he would receive a ration card for heavy laborers, amounting to about 1,000 calories a day. The bad news was that Munich had suffered more extensive bomb damage than he had realized. It meant that in some parts of the city there was nothing left but the shells of bombed-out buildings. There were some other things that turned out badly, things like the heavy infestation of the concrete barrack with bed bugs, or like the constant hunger he suffered, or like the lack of basic items such as a toothbrush and paste or a nail on the wall on which to hang a few belongings.

As a smoker he had nothing to smoke. All he could do was get up early in the morning and hunt for cigarette butts American soldiers had thrown away. And trams, for that matter, did not run in the evening from downtown to the Agfa plant.

His first day at work looked as if it was going to be his last day. He had to climb ladder after ladder to the roof of an assembly workshop, and he was not certain whether he would ever be able to get down to the ground again. In fact, he spent the rest of the day just holding on to a wall while the rest of the crew was putting roof girders into place. He was in a state of vertigo. In the end, though, he did get down, ladder after ladder, by holding on for his life to the side pieces and cross pieces. Down on the ground it was the foreman's word, in his heavy Bavarian accent, that set him somewhat at ease for the next day. *Wirst scho schaffe morge.* (You'll get over it by tomorrow.) The foreman was right. Before long he had lost all fear of height and carried studs into position on the roof with ease.

For the bed bugs there was no cure. Perhaps because the barrack itself was built during the war out of concrete and had all the fissures and holes in the walls and the ceiling in which the bugs could hide. Back during the war that bunker-like barrack housed forced laborers. And even though the bed posts were standing in cans filled with oil, the bed bugs were still crawling up the walls and over on the ceiling to drop down on the victims. Proof of the torment was bodies full of bloody bites and bloody rashes. If there was one solution, it was to set beds and belongings in that hellhole of a bunker on fire.

Life went on. Whenever he could he would take the train and head out to Tittmoning to spend a weekend with his mother. These times were precious. Somehow she was always able to have food and cook meals on a spirit-stove— meals that reminded him of the good old times with Margarete and Papa at the table. However, there was still no word from them. After such a meal they would go out for a walk around the town square and out the gate on a highway to see the countryside. There in one of the fields they saw a tree, its branches full of golden apples. For apples it was a banner year. But not once did the whole apparatus of food rationing find ways to add at least a pound or two of apples to the meager rations. And while the native population had so-called "connections," the refugee population could only look at the abundance and go away empty-handed. Or as they would say, the Bavarians would rather feed apples to pigs than share them with fellow-Germans.

Later that evening they went out again and headed straight out to the potato field with the apple tree. While Mother felt her way among the bushes of potatoes in search of apples, he climbed into the tree and shook the branches. Suddenly he became aware of someone coming. He barely had time to whisper to Mother to take cover, and she threw herself on the ground to hide between the bushes of potatoes. By now three men stood under the tree arguing whether there was somebody around stealing. He clung to one of the branches. Suddenly they turned and walked away. Relieved, he climbed down and helped Mother to her feet. Then they filled a sack full of the precious apples. Suddenly Mother asked: "What would you have done if they had found me?" And he answered: "I would have jumped down and attacked them."

Later back at home, as they munched on apples, he asked her: "What would you have done if they had caught you?" "Mmm…" she said, "I would have waited for His Majesty to descend from His Throne… to liberate me." And at that they laughed heartily.

But not all Bavarians saw in refugees only Pig-Prussians. One exception was the owner of Klostergasse 3. Her husband was among the missing in Russia. She was really helpful when possible, like having Mother move into a room in the house when she arrived. The owner would also cook a meal at noon for the women who were knitting bags out of plastic string. And whenever he came for a weekend she would see to it that Mother had milk and cheese and bread, and one weekend she even had a pair of leather shoes for him. But that pair got him into trouble back at the barracks when it disappeared. His suspicion fell on one of the members of the construction crew. Enraged, he gave him a thorough beating. An hour later he was arrested by the police and spent the night in jail. But next morning the foreman appeared, after having fired the suspect, and got him released. But his pride and joy, the pair of leather shoes, he never saw again.

If he had another close call during his two years in Munich, it was with a Greek over a woman. Maria was a war widow with two children, and the Greek was her provider and lover. But whenever the Greek was out of town on black market business, which was usually on Fridays, she would burn a candle in the window for a sign that the coast was clear. Her weakness for him came with a bath, a meal and the luxury of a feather bed. However, on one of the coldest nights of the winter, the Greek was back with a knock at the door. Just as he was, with nothing on, he jumped out of the window and Maria threw his clothes after him, and, grabbing the clothes, he ran stark naked through the snows for cover.

But that wasn't the end of it, even though he had not seen Maria in the meantime. It happened a few weeks later on a quiet and dark street between downtown and the Afga plant when he saw three men coming towards him. They were about to pass him when one of them jumped him, and backed him against the wall while screaming and holding him around his girth. It was the Greek. The other two men began pummeling him with their fists. He knew that he was in a fight for his life. From that moment on it was all instinct. He jerked his right leg up and jammed his knee squarely into the Greek's face, who, still screaming, let go of him. And then it happened like in a flash. He saw knives, and driven by fear he lunged forward and crashed through the cordon of his attackers and ran for his life. He never saw Maria or the Greeks again.

The place to see the black market was down at the Isar River. There, in a street with the river on one side and rather majestic apartment houses on the other, was the usual black market activity. There was not one sign of illegality as American cigarettes and American coffee and American sweets were traded, usually for bundles of *Reichsmark*. Except when the German police and the MP raided the place. At that moment all streets leading to the market area were sealed off. From then on everybody had to pass inspection. It meant that all those with black market goods had to throw them away to escape jail. There you would see goods in the gutter, and anyone who dared to pick any of them up would also be punished. All he could do was to think back to the Crystal Night in Beuthen in 1938 when, with the SA standing in front of ransacked Jewish stores, he did not dare to pick up so much as a single orange.

There were other things happening in his life. His good friend, Heinz, from the POW days in Camp Forrest, had been writing letters in which Heinz urged him to come to Wetzlar or to Giesen to work for the Americans. But with his resolve to become at least a journeyman bricklayer there was no way he was going to leave.

Besides, they had changed his working place from the Agfa plant to the Evangelische Landesleitung in downtown Munich. The change came with a single room and a meal at noon, and for a construction site it was a much better place to improve his skills in laying bricks and to start getting the hand on plastering. The man he was working with was Gratza, formerly from the Sudetenland. Gratza was an expert journeyman bricklayer and plasterer, and the building which had been hit by a bomb or two was an excellent site for such work.

Plastering turned out to be much more difficult than meets the eye. In fact, plastering the ceiling was downright impossible at first try. It was not just a case of throwing mortar from the trowel to the ceiling and expecting it to stick. What would happen without the right action of the wrist and the right swing of the arm was that trowel after trowel full of mortar would come straight down on him. After a day of trying he looked like a mortar mummy. There was not one black spot on the black POW outfit. And Gratza, in his anger, went after him as if he were a fourteen-year-old apprentice. He let it happen. To tell the truth, he was furious with himself. From that day on he would always admit that mowing grass with a scythe and plastering a ceiling were the most demanding crafts he had ever encountered. Just as it was taking a certain swing with the scythe, so it took a snap with the wrist and a correct swing with the arm to make the flying mortar do nothing else but stick to the ceiling. And sure enough, with each day, he got better, until he had it completely *intus*, as a German expression has it.

But back in those days no improvement such as better quarters and a noontime meal came without a loss. What was lost was a sense of self-reliance of the most ordinary kind. Back at the Agfa plant, over an open fire outdoors, he would cook every so often a meal for himself. Its sole ingredient was a mix of water and crushed corn from America that was part of a special call-up on the ration card. For a pot he used a number 10 can. When done, he had his fill, and he dreamed about his years of captivity in America where he had developed a taste for corn.

On one of the weekends, he went to Tittmoning. And what a surprise awaited him there. His sister, Margarete, had returned. She had come out of a camp for lost German children in Czechoslovakia and had made it safely to Tittmoning. The camp itself seemed to have been run, or at least supported by Soviet troops who, as Margarete was telling it, were good to the children and brought them extra food whenever they came into the camp. Privately and out of earshot of Margarete, he and his mother worried that this young girl had been mistreated by the Russian soldiers. If the troops in charge of the orphanage were *Etappenhasen* (rear rabbits, soldiers far behind the front lines), that would have been all too possible. Those soldiers were pulled into service hastily and were looked down upon by the front line troops for being less disciplined, less educated, and less moral. But as they talked with Margarete it was obvious that the Russians in charge were of the elite, well mannered, well disciplined troops and their worries were laid aside. But about Father there still was no word from him or about him.

By now, in his second post-war year in Munich, life was like a mixed bag of hard work, of exhaustion, of trials and tribulations. He never had anything to eat in the morning before starting to work. The starvation rations of a thousand calories a day for *Schwerarbeiter* did not go that far. And laying bricks or doing plastering work on an empty stomach can only mean exhaustion. Moreover, he could only say that on many an evening, while attending classes in the School of Languages or while attending university sponsored classes in journalism, he could not help but fall asleep.

Or talk about other wants and other needs. To satisfy the basic need for paper to clean yourself after relieving nature, you had to get up before daybreak to stand in line for the only paper that was published in Munich at that time. It was *Die Neue Zeitung* which was a joint venture by the Germans and the Americans and which was a superb piece of journalism. Or say you needed a comb, or a toothbrush, or a pencil, or a pair of socks, or a bottle of aspirin, or a bottle of caster oil, or eating utensils, or a needle and thread to mend your clothes, or a pair of scissors to cut your nails, or a bottle of beer to drown your worries, or a candle, or a handkerchief, or a lamp to read by, or vaseline for the raw hands of a plasterer, or a pair of shoelaces, to say nothing of a pair of leather shoes... forget it. After total war and unconditional surrender Germany's economy had gone completely *kaputt*, or so at least it seemed.

And yet, there were times that some things in Germany were coming back to life. Thus he remembers that during the summer of 1947 he took the train to Augsburg to see *Salome* by Richard Strauss in the outdoor theatre. Or he took the train out to Bad Toelz to see the Alps. Or to go to the stadium near the Agfa plant to watch soccer games, especially when 1860 München played Bayern München. Or go to the Isar with Resi and join in the lovemaking that was going on in the open among dozens of couples. Or follow the invitation of Katharina for a cup of coffee and end up getting just a cup of coffee. Or join a former woman professor of English at a restaurant across from the Agfa plant and have great chitchats in English. Always on Sundays, if he was in town.

The next time when he went to Tittmoning he found that Mother and Margarete had moved into a new apartment. If Father should return now, the apartment was of the right size for a couple and a daughter. And the best feature about it was that it was overlooking the town square with its shops all around and with two running fountains in the center. By now Margarete was back in school and was doing well. And on Mother's new *Kachelofen*, instead of the spirit cooker, she cooked mouth-watering meals. And so for the first time after four turbulent years the three of them ate together around a table.

By the spring there was talk of an impending currency reform. The old, which by now was badly inflated, was to be replaced with a new currency. The demise of the *Reichsmark* meant for millions of Germans, especially for refugees, that their living conditions were going from bad to worse. Heinz had just written that at Military Government in Wetzlar they were looking for a translator and interpreter. The letter came at a time when he had finished his apprenticeship. He was now a journeyman bricklayer. There was no reason for him to continue a life of hard work, of constant hunger and of severe living conditions. The next day he was on his way to apply for the job.

He got to Wetzlar late in the afternoon and started to walk to Braunfels where Heinz lived. After about ten miles he came to the top of a hill, and there it was: Braunfels with a castle towering above it. It was late by now, and it was getting dark, and so he decided to spend the night in a hayfield to the left of the highway, and so he bedded himself down. What he saw was like a fantasia of old times. Before him was the sight of the castle with several towers and large inclined roofs and the sight of the town nestling below in a posture of deference. Meanwhile the lights had come on, a sprinkling of lights in town and a single

Braunfels Castle

light here and there in the castle. And with the lights there came questions of human existence. Questions like, what is life like up above in the castle, and what is life like down below in the town? Thus he would look at a solitary light in one of the towers and end up not knowing that a woman of nobility did wrestle at that moment with the German language to write poetry. Or he would look at the lights in the town and not know that a hundred years ago some of the townspeople had gone over to America to found a New Braunfels in Texas. And then there was something else stirring in his mind, something that seemed to have been lost in his own past. Suddenly he knew what it was. It was something of a two-liner that he had heard from Father. It went thus:

Amerika Du hast es besser,   America you have it better,
Du hast keine Schlöesser.   You have no Schlöesser(castles).

    He lay awake long into the night thinking about America, and wondering whether he would ever make it back across the Atlantic. In the morning, on that Saturday, he went looking for Heinz and his family and easily found the house. The reception by Heinz and his wife, Lieselotte, was like a homecoming.

    He had until Monday to get ready for the interview. His black outfit with white PW's on the pants and the jacket was near shreds, after three years of wear and work. So were the wooden shoes after two years of construction work. And again there were the rumors that the R*eichsmark* was about to be replaced by a new Mark. But until then shop owners hoarded everything away.

    Heinz and Lieselotte found answers for his clothing dilemma. Somehow they were able to get him a good-looking outfit, complete with a pair of leather shoes, and when on Monday he went for the interview, he got the job. One week later the R*eichsmark* was replaced by the *Deutschemark*, and Germany's economic miracle was on its way.

    The work at Military Government was mainly to protect the fledgling German democracy against its detractors, like old fanatical Nazis and new Communists, and, in addition, handle German-American relations. In local politics it was especially the KPD (The Communist Party of Germany) that received most of the attention. And here it was the so-called Five Percent Clause that drew attention. The Clause was designed to prevent too much fragmentation along party lines in a legislative body. If any one of the parties did not receive five percent of all the votes it missed representation. That the KPD would not last long could be seen from such election results on the local level, when it often received fewer votes than it had members in a given district. The bitter news coming out of the Soviet Zone of Occupation spelled an early end of the party. In matters of German-American relations it was requisitioned housing that was the bone of contention. It was a controversy between the German owners and the American occupants of these houses that simply would not go away. The second most controversial issue was the matter of illegitimate children. There was no way to force a GI to pay child support to the German mother. And marriage was not always possible. Finally, there was an assortment of complaints about unpaid bills and hunting violations and cases of violence.

In his translations he never aspired to play the judge by such linguistic devices as intemperate translations or by emphasizing or de-emphasizing stated facts. His translations were always straight to the point.

In the meantime he had heard from his mother. She did miss him, of course, she wrote, but she understood why he moved. He felt relieved. That same day he sent the first of many packages to her, with her favorite coffee and other goodies.

Rudolf working in Wetzlar, 1948

By 1949 changes were on the way. The old style of military government was replaced on the national level by the U. S. High Commission of Germany, a branch of the State Department. Its seat was in Berlin. On the local level the Military Government Offices were replaced by the Kreis Resident Offices. With the worst hunger and clothing problems overcome, it was time to do something for the German mind. Reorientation was the answer. Its aim was to awaken civic courage and to teach democracy on a local level.

It was a gargantuan undertaking, and the means for it were the so-called forums. They were local assemblies similar to town-hall meetings in America. Here in Germany centuries of political apathy had to be overcome. It was a case of awakening freedom and of arousing the courage of convictions in addition to keeping the Nazis and the Communists at bay. All together they started about sixty forums in a year's time. It meant that the American Kreis Resident Officer and he were out in the country almost every night giving speeches and talking about examples of citizen participation in village affairs, such as having a say in road repairs, in matters of schools, in public utilities and so on. Forum activities also laid the groundwork for engaging units of the U. S. Army in various civic projects. Foremost was the assistance given by engineer units to grade sports fields and playgrounds, to level bomb craters, to excavate building sites for refugee homes, for school additions, for gymnasiums and for churches.

Rudolf on the right

In two years some eight hundred thousand *Deutschemarks* were contributed in that fashion by the Americans. The forums and the engineering help represent one of the finest achievements of American and German cooperation.

But as the activities of the forums were gaining momentum, they stirred up a host of unlikely enemies, from old Nazis to new Communists and some local officials. Their main contention was that this *Ami* stuff was contrary to German traditions, and that it undermined communal life. In the end, the pro-

Germans and Americans work together

gram was called to a halt by higher U. S. authorities with the explanation that the program should run its own course. The effect was devastating. Without American help the forums withered away one by one, except for a few.

The news from Tittmoning was heartening. Mother wrote that she had received two notices in quick succession. The first one read only that an A. Thill was in Russian captivity. The second was even more hopeful inasmuch as it spelled out the A as Alfons. And sure enough, Father had returned in the meantime and looked forward to seeing him. He went to Tittmoning the following weekend for a joy-

Humanitarian projects such as school construction and houses for refugees.

ous reunion. Joyous especially that Father was in pretty good shape. The secret of his good health, as he explained it, was that he never ate fresh bread but kept it for a day to let it dry out. At night, to prevent theft, he kept that piece of bread under his rag of a pillow. Many a fellow-prisoners had died of diarrhea and dysentery. And the second reason for his relatively good health was that he always kept pieces of charcoal in his pocket. Charcoal, eaten under the circumstances, was the best remedy for diarrhea. Either you nip diarrhea in the bud, Father said, or that biggest killer will get you.

But then Father told them that at the end of the war he and other prisoners had been turned over by the Americans to the Russians. [See Appendix I article 77 of the Geneva Convention on rules of repatriation of prisoners.] A whole convoy of American trucks drove them over to the Russian side, and there Russian soldiers were already waiting for them in the ditches. Eventually they ended up deep in Russia in a POW camp. There Father worked as a digger of mass graves even though he was an officer. But officer or not, the Russians made all of them work except for ranking generals. Father's only plaintive note in this connection was not that he had to work, but that the death list of hundreds of German prisoners was taken away from him prior to his discharge. He had made the list himself from the dog tags of the dead and had kept it hidden. Even after spending four years in captivity he spoke movingly of Russian women and children, how they would come out to the camp and go over the prisoner garbage dump outside the barbed wire in hopes to find something useful or of finding something to eat. And he said: *"Ach, weisst du, die armen Menchen hatten noch weniger als wir."* "Ah, these poor people had even less than we." Father said that after spending four years on the Russian front in WWI, and four years at the Russian front in WWII, and four years of captivity in Russia, he could feel nothing but compassion for the Russian people. He was still the kind and gentle man he had always been even after so many years of oppression. Even after an unjust and illegal four year imprisonment.

Rudolf in Giessen, 1952

Something else happened that day. The mail delivered a package of letters and a wooden box. Both were from him. Both came via the International Red Cross. The letters that were sent by him from American POW camps to his parents in Upper Silesia, and not one of these letters had ever been delivered. (And as for the letters sent by his parents to him in America, none of those had ever reached him.) As for the box, it contained his Emerson radio and other memorabilia he had sent "on hold" because he did not know the whereabouts of his family. The radio, however, had all its wires torn out, and the cigarettes beneath the wires were gone. Fortunately some of the other items survived.

For three years there was not one piece of mail that reached the prisoner from his parents and neither did his parents receive any mail from him. But under the allotted number of letters he did not miss writing and sending a single letter. The complete shutdown of the mail, at least in their case, remained a mystery until recently. Now, however, it is known that German prisoners handled the mail for the POW camps in Texas. And the handlers, working in a camp in Texas, had lists of so-called pro-American prisoners whose mail was intercepted and never delivered. American authorities eventually relieved the German handlers of POW mail of these duties and replaced them with Italian POW's. But the delivery, at least in his case, did not improve.

[The camp in question was Camp Hearne, Texas, staffed by German non-commissioned officers. They were responsible for the distribution of all POW mail in the US. Source: Krammer, Arnold, Nazi Prisoners of War in America, New York: Stein and Day, 1979.]

In l952 the functions of the Kreis Resident Office were transferred to the army's S-5 Section, also known as the Civil Affairs Office. At the same time Wetzlar became part of the Giessen Office. The new Civil Affairs Officer was Capt. Ralph S. Cramer. What happened next was that one day before the Wetzlar Office was closed, it was announced that the captain would be coming over to grant interviews. He went to be interviewed, and they talked for about half an hour about all kinds of things over in the States, such as the camps he stayed in, and what he did in the camps, and that the Captain's hometown was Fort Madison, Iowa. In the end, to his surprise, the Captain asked him pointblank whether he wanted to be his assistant, and he answered, yes. It was the beginning of a wonderful relationship.

Translating for Col. Schindler, other American officers, the press, and a German *Bürgermeister.*

Shortly he moved to Wilhelmstrasse 20 in Giessen. Depending on the season he lived either in the gardenhouse, a kind of pavilion, or in a room in the main building. With Mrs. Cramer having come over, he was often invited to dinner, or to go for a ride with them or to go to the PX or the Commissary with them. The Cramers even invited his mother to spend some time with them, and all enjoyed being together.

The Civil Affairs Office was not supervisory anymore like the Military Government or the Kreis Residence Offices, but strictly functioned as a liaison between the U. S. and French military on one side and the German population on the

Translating for a Leica Camera representative.

other. In other words the primary function was one of trouble-shooting. Trouble-shooting about brawls, about taxi fares, about unpaid bills, and occasional fights over girls. And last, but not least, there were still the old problems of requisitioned housing and the issue of children fathered by American soldiers. By 1952 that number had gone into the tens of thousands in half of Hesse. Many of these children were to end up in orphanages or given up for adoption. At least until 1954, if not later, there was no legal way for these destitute mothers to file charges for child support against the fathers.

The matter of requisitioned housing was more troublesome than ever. By now the owners of these houses had organized in the Association of Occupation Sufferers, applying every means of pressure such as protest demonstrations, rallies, use of the press and the radio, and sporadic harassments of the French and American occupants of these houses. The frequency of these clashes may best be measured by the fact that the Giessen Office had at least one or more of these cases pulling at its sleeve every day. They were most difficult to handle, as they required a great deal of tact, diplomacy and firmness to be fair to all, which at times was impossible.

Nevertheless, the good will engendered by the Americans to help out on engineering projects and other gestures of understanding such as a helicopter-borne Santa Claus visiting German orphanages, or a folkfest at which both a German ump-pa-pa band and an American jazz band would play, continued. On all of these occasions the Captain or he arranged for speakers and provided the translations. One such case turned into a linguistic nightmare. At the Giessen German-American Friendship Day while serving as a translator he had a new experience. The speaker was a one-star general from the Frankfurt Area Command. He began with: "Ladies…" and fell silent. While he waited for the rest, the general looked down on him and said: "God-damn-it, translate!" From that moment on, for the next half an hour, in front of some three hundred Germans and Americans, the speaker would never say more than one or two words… and waited for the translation. He was in the worst possible fix between the two languages, given the differences in syntax. But he did the best he could by resorting to occasional omissions or additions of words.

Next it was the *Oberbürgermeister* of Giessen who gave his speech. Here it was not a case of paucity of words but of redundancy, so much so that the speech was delivered in nothing less than whole paragraphs. Let's just say that too little and too much were kindred in difficulty for opposite reasons.

On weekends he would still go to Wetzlar and to Braunfels from time to time to be with his friend, Knut, or with Heinz and his family. On Saturdays they would always go dancing, and his dates were women like Gisela and Hilde. Afterwards, in Wetzlar at least, he would go to a cemetery for a sexual fling, or he would go to the hay field where he had spent his first night in Braunfels.

A year later the Captain was being sent back to the U. S. To help out he took the Cramers' car to Bremerhaven for shipment back to the States. Then came the time to say goodbye. Ralph took him aside and asked whether he was serious about coming to America. He answered, yes. And then Ralph said that he was going to send him the necessary papers for an immigration visa. Within two months the papers arrived and he applied at the Frankfurt Consulate for a visa. Now the waiting began. At his next visit he told his parents what his plans were. His parents said nothing, but his mother turned her head away. He knew that he could never bring himself to say goodbye to them, and when the time came, he didn't. When he finally received an appointment for a visa at the Consulate, he booked a flight out of Frankfurt to America for the next day. On September 17, 1954, he was in a plane heading for America. With fifty dollars in his pocket and at age thirty he was ready to face the challenges of the New World.

EPILOGUE

Geraldine Schwarz

The author and gardener in front of the garden house he built using his bricklaying skills.

And so the former prisoner-of-war finishes his story. Now the retired professor of European History and German puts his pen down, leans back in his comfortable chair in front of the fireplace, and nods to his wife, Sigrid, across from him. But what has happened in those years after he left Germany? How did he eventually reach this home in the middle of Iowa?

At this point the narrator shifts from the author himself to one who has heard the story told in many settings and over a number of years. Trying to be faithful to the author's language and thoughts, this narrator will continue the story of Rudolf Thill as he traveled again to the United States, was able to receive an education and find a career as a college professor.

Arriving in Fort Madison, Iowa, in the fall of 1954 at the home of his sponsor, Captain Ralph S. Cramer and Dee, his wife, Rudolf searched for a job. The Cramers kept saying, "Now do you need any money?"

"Ralph had in mind, that once I came over he would get me a job at Sheaffer Pen. But Sheaffer Pen had (from the American viewpoint) some really unfortunate experiences with some German workers. They had hired some twenty or so German technicians. They were young men, they didn't speak very much English, but they wanted to have a little entertainment. And so they went into a tavern and they were coming out, walking the streets of Fort Madison singing German songs, which offended the townspeople and especially the families of soldiers. They ultimately got fired. And Ralph had a pretty good job. He was a manager at Sheaffer Pen and he sort of hinted to me, 'Right now there's no way to get another German in there.'"

Des Moines seemed to be a place that offered more possibilities than Fort Madison, so he looked for work in the capital city of Iowa. "I came to Des Moines sometime in September of 1954. I got out of the bus from Fort Madison to Des Moines and I had to have a place to stay overnight. I had only $5.00 in my pocket—$2.50 a night at the YMCA and then 20 or 25 cents for corn flakes.... And next day I had to have a job. I applied at the Savery Hotel.

"At the Savery itself there seemed to be no job. But I talked to the manager, Mr. Leftin, who was of German descent. We had a fine meeting and a fine conversation, half German, half English.

"He said, 'Well, there is one job, but I hate to offer it to you.'

"I said, "What is it?'

"'The only thing we have right now is as a portier.'

"'That's fine. I'll take it.' When the name 'porter' was mentioned, I thought I was going to be a *'portiere'* in a splendid uniform, opening up the door and so on, but after I got my so-called uniform I knew it was something else, and it was then just simply a clean-up man working on the night shift. I did a very good job at night because I had to work hard so I would not fall asleep. My mother had taught me that if you want to clean correctly, you had to get down on your knees and you had to get back into the corner—and I still do that to this day.

"I think I may have been the only white porter in the city of Des Moines, and I was earning about 52 or 53 cents an hour—but so what? I could live. And I would have to come in at 5:00 in the afternoon because there was a lot of business back in those days. People were asking, begging to get a room. It was not like today. So the room had to be cleaned up and made fresh for the next person in a matter of minutes.

And it was really the right kind of a job for me. I mean, I never drank on the job. I NEVER drank on the job. I was the last one to leave the second floor at the Savery. Only when everything was dark, and only when the porters—there were usually two night porters then—Freddy was one—only then would I leave. Not until everything was locked—lock, stock and barrel.

"I did also apply at one of the news agencies—which is defunct now—because I wrote pretty well. When I was working in the civil affairs office on German/American relations and events, I had to make these reports etc., etc., so I felt somewhat confident. And the person I talked to was interested in me and he said well, he would have to see about it and talk to somebody higher up and so on. 'But let me know where I can reach you.' I let him know that I was working at the Savery and there he could find out where I would be. I never expected to hear from him again.

"But then not very long after that, before Christmas at any rate, Mr. Leftin suddenly called over at the YMCA that he would like to see me. He said, 'Well I don't blame you. But I just got a call from so and so, from the news agency, and they want to see you. And I think you can get a job there. But before you go, I would have another job for you as assistant catering manager.' In other words, in the office. Well I had been there working several months, and I had gotten a little experience under me. I mean here at the hotel I knew I could survive. This business about the news thing, well after all, it was not my mother tongue. So I stayed at the Savery.

"Back in those days the Savery Hotel was a very, very, very busy hotel. You had to talk people out of beds because they were all filled. There were only three major hotels in all of the Des Moines area: the Fort Des Moines, the Kirkwood, and the Savery. And both the Fort Des Moines and the Savery were part of the Boss chain. The chain does not exist anymore. So I took the job as assistant catering manager, working on the evening shift or whenever I was needed.

"Then fate again sort of interfered. The Drake Athletic Club was always coming for their dinner meetings, and the man who would arrange that kept saying to me, when he was about to sign the check, 'You should go back to school.' School? I'm 31 years old! 'You should go to the University.' And finally he said, 'I'll bring you the papers.' Well, I didn't say no. Sure enough, he brought the papers. I signed them up. To my surprise, within a week or so I was then invited to take an admission test on a Monday morning at 8:00. The next surprise there in taking the admission exam was that I was subjected to a multiple choice test. I had NEVER seen such a thing. NEVER had seen such a thing! I had absolutely no idea what a multiple choice test was. I had not even spent the first ten or fifteen minutes when this woman—she was pretty uncouth, pretty unfriendly— came in and pulled that set of papers away from me. I said I had hardly started, and she said, 'That's it. You better get started.' I was convinced I had failed the test. I swore right then that if I should ever be in a similar position to ever test students, it would not, to the end of my teaching career, be multiple choice. And it never was. Whenever I run into students, the thing that they always remember is, 'Oh, you gave essay tests.'

And to my surprise—I passed the test! And had to see some dean there. The interview with the dean was also interesting because he wanted to determine what my major was. That dean, I mean he squirmed, he did! 'Why do you want to go back to school?'

"I said, 'To learn. For my stimulation.'

"He kept on hinting, 'But suppose you get through, what would you...?'

"Well, with my father being a teacher, I just simply said something about teaching. 'Ooooohh! We have it,' he shouted, relieved. The magic word.

I did actually get through the undergraduate thing there for the bachelor in about two and a half or three years. And so I ended up on the liberal arts side and was very successful and got—what is it called?—honorable mention or something like that.

"But I still worked then at the Savery at night. It was a wonderful arrangement. In other words, I could make money. The salary I made at the Savery Hotel was about $700-800. It meant I could pay tuition, but I could not take a taxi in order to ride back home. And I had moved to 38th Street, a distance from the Savery of about four or five miles. And for six or seven years I walked. I think I took about three times a taxi, come winter, come summer, or anything like that. I walked across that one cemetery there, coming from downtown (the gates were still open back in those days). At no time did I ever have any sense of danger or anything like that. With a job like I had, I mean it was not a fantastic salary but it was enough, as long as I didn't have a car and as long as I didn't get married. So those two things were out if I wanted to finish my studies.

"So it was a wonderful thing. And then I was getting through at Drake, so I stayed right on for my Master's Degree. I was still working. And I had already started to teach on a part-time basis. It happened this way. There was supposed to be a part-time job at Grand View College. And I thought that would be quite nice, something at least to test me mentally. The interview was with Dr. Nielsen, and we talked easily—Dr. Nielsen was a wonderful guy; he reminded me very much of my father—but at the end he had to confess that the job had been taken. Somebody with a PhD from Chicago had applied for the job and was going to teach German and history and so on. Well I understood that. But next day, all of a sudden, there was Dr. Nielsen calling back. He had then, especially for me, opened up two history courses, one I think was Ancient History and the other one was Western Civilization. That was 1960 or '61. And so I started to teach on a part-time basis at Grand View with the understanding that as soon as I got my Master's I would be employed full-time. So I was able to make a living because I was still working at the Savery. I could save a little money because I had these two part-time jobs and I wasn't married...."

At this point in the story, Sigrid, his wife, giggles and says, "He wasn't married, but that does not mean that he was celibate." This statement brings on much laughter and prompting for more details. A little reluctantly Rudi tells the story:

"After five years, you can get your citizenship. And sure enough, when I had been here four years I applied right away. In fact, on the very day that citizenship was being conferred on us and my name appeared in the paper—people could come to the ceremony who knew me of course, shaking hands and such a thing—all of a sudden about ten or fifteen minutes before I was supposed to go over to the Federal building, while I was still in the office at the hotel, working in the morning—there are two men coming in the door. One looks around. I think they are customers, but all of a sudden, somebody flashes an FBI badge. 'Are you Rudolf Thill?' and then he opens up, 'You have violated some law here.'

"Violated some law?

"In other words, I was visited by a lady and she visited me several times, and the FBI agent said, 'Have you ever heard of the Mann Act in America?' There was a federal law. If you as a man were caught, under the Mann Act, that is to say that you had sexual intercourse with a woman you were not married to, this was bad. It was of course never enforced. But I guess a foreigner like yours truly... Well the FBI agents said, shaking his finger at me, 'Rudi, we do not do that in this country.' I who work in a hotel? I'm supposed to believe that *we do not do that in this country?* But instead I said, 'I'm awfully sorry. I didn't know anything about the law. I was carried away.'

"I intended to leave for the citizenship ceremony within ten minutes. I was ready to go, but those two guys stopped me. If I would have gotten away, I don't know whether they would have stopped the proceedings. And then once they would have conferred citizenship on me, there was not very much they really could have done about it. Most people of course laughed about this damn Mann Act anyway.

"So everybody at the college was waiting, they were having a big party at Grand View for my citizenship ceremony. They didn't know that I hadn't received it though. I went through with the party and didn't say anything about the FBI and all that. And then I had to wait four more years and go to these classes, I think about once every month. And the only thing that saved me was that I had to then take an attorney, I had to fight it… but then I did become an American citizen.

"Meanwhile I was working on my next degree. And sure enough the day I got my Master's I was taken on a full-time basis at Grand View. During that time I was married and had a son, Stephen. I continued my studies toward a PhD at the University of Iowa, did all of my coursework, had to write my thesis. The thesis was going to be Communist Resistance in Nazi Germany for which I would have to go over to Germany. But then my divorce interfered, especially also the fact that I did get custody of the boy, and so I had to devote myself and my money to something other than research. So I just simply could not do it. I would have had to go back to Germany to do some research and writing there for easily about three-four-five-six months. And I simply could not do it. Just the other day I came across some remnants of my dissertation…."

The professor retired from full time teaching in 1987. This gave him an opportunity to work part time translating documents for clients and courts, and to work full time in his yard and garden. The Thills' home is tucked between a church and an elementary school near some of the busiest streets in Des Moines. But a visitor would not be aware of any of those surroundings. During the thirty-plus years of living in that place, Rudi planted dozens of trees (some planted themselves) which seclude the place and protect it from outside noise. This allowed him, in earlier years, to keep a nice flock of laying hens and a dovecot reminiscent of his dovecot in Upper Silesia. Now his only feathered flock is the assortment of wild birds at the feeders.

Using his bricklaying skills learned in post-war Germany, he built a summer garden house at the far-end of the yard, and he also brick-faced terraces for the vegetables, flowers, hostas and ferns. Because Sigrid, a retired librarian, and Rudi both love art and are avid collectors, many pieces of sculpture are carefully placed among the trees and flowers. Their house is filled with paintings, pottery, photography and sculpture. And books. A book is never far from either Sigrid's or Rudi's hand.

Reflectively he says, "But I loved to teach. It was of course a wonderful thing, a wonderful way to end— *Wer immer strebend sich bemüht, den könner wir erlösen.* Whoever continues to aspire to learn, only such a person can be saved."

Rudolf Thill looking over the mountains of epilogue toward the future of his writing.

APPENDIX 1

Stan Zegel

Upper Silesia—A province in the southeast corner of the easternmost part of Germany before 1945. It is called "upper" Silesia because it is along the upper banks of the Oder River, which flows down from the Sudeten Mountains heading north and west into the province of Lower Silesia on its way to the Baltic Sea. It was part of the Kingdom of Poland in olden times, was ceded to the Kingdom of Bohemia in 1327 and then inherited by the Habsburgs, who ruled from Vienna. King Frederick the Great of (German) Prussia took it from Austria by was in 1742. Containing a mixture of ethnic Germans and Poles, Upper Silesia remained part of Germany until the end of WWII, (although some parts of it were ceded to the new countries of Poland and Czechoslovakia at the end of WWI). The German province of *Oberschlesien* was occupied by Russian troops at the end of WWII. After WWII the German part was turned over to Poland and today's *Œl'skie* province is the most heavily industrialized part of Poland. Most ethnic Germans fled near the end of WWII to avoid living under Russian occupation, which is why the boy's family moved to Tittmoning.

> This area is a part of the great border belt between Germans and Slavs, more specifically a border corner where Germans, Poles, Czechs, and Slovaks meet and mix. Divided politically before the war among three empires: Germany, Austria-Hungary, and Russia, it is likewise divided now, but with different lines, between Germany, Poland, and Czecho-Slovakia. Although in many respects geographically united, the area has never had political unity within itself, but rather was always a peripheral zone subject to the political expansion of neighboring states. (p. 196)
> The political boundaries, representing diplomatic compromises, add to the confusion, geographically, by neglecting for the most part any one geographic boundary, and thereby developing a new one, and, in particular, by cutting through the very type of cultural landscape least suitable for boundary location. (p. 224)
> *Annals of the Association of American Geographers*, Vol. 23, No. 4 (Dec., 1933), 195-228.

Poland—A country erected after WWI out of parts of Austria-Hungary, Russia and Germany that had once been part of the Kingdom of Poland, before that country was abolished in 1795. Because Russia had required its Jews to live in its Polish province, the new country had a large contingent of that ethnicity. Border disputes between the aggressive new Poland and its new neighbors led to several armed battles, especially with the also newly invented Czechoslovakia. Thus in 1939 when Hitler accused Poland of invading part of Upper Silesia and seizing the radio station at Gleiwitz, the claim was quite plausible.

The Village—The Village in this book, (Pilzendorf "Mushroom Village", in German), is known today by that same name translated into Polish: Grzybowice and is in the northern part of the Polish city of Zabrze (Hindenburg, during German times). In Germany, but near both the Polish and Czech borders, it had about 2000 inhabitants, many of whom worked in the nearby coalmines. There was no church in Pilzendorf itself, which was part to the parish of St. ??? Church in Randsdorf. The Old Schoolhouse, in which the boy's family lived, remains today next to the 1904 Main School (still the most prominent building on the main street, now paved) and is again being used as a school. From his parents' bedroom window the boy could see the radio transmitter tower at Gleiwitz, site of the provocation staged by Hitler to justify (along with the Russians) the invasion of Poland in 1939. The bakery run by the Wlochowitz family was directly across the street form the old school.

Beuthen—The county seat of the *Kreis*, that included Pilzendorf, is about 10 miles east of it. It was here that the boy attended the *Realgymnasium* (high school). Because the western part of Upper Silesia was inhabited by ethnic Germans, and the eastern part by ethnic Poles, in 1921 the League of Nations sponsored a plebiscite, where the inhabitants could vote on whether their area was to become part of Germany or of Poland. As a result, when the areas east of it voted to join Poland, the 100,000-inhabitants of Beuthen suddenly went from being in the middle of its county to being a border town. Today it is known by its Polish name of Bytom.

Klausberg—The town of 20,000 inhabitants about 2 miles south of Pilzendorf and the site of the movie theater the boy visited when he could. On school days the boy walked to the train station in Klausberg (also interchangeably called by its Polish name of Mikulczyce during the boy's time) to commute to high school at the *Realgymnasium* in Beuthen. Today it is known only by its Polish name and now is part of the city of Zabrze.

Einhof—The fish pond at *Herr* Bernard's brickyard was located at this settlement. The owner's son Bubi was the boy's best friend. The brickyard was still functioning in 1986, using a steam engine from 1906 to power the process of mixing and cutting clay. Coal from the region's mines was used to fire the kilns.

Katscher—A German town of 9000 about 45 miles southwest of Pilzendorf where the boy's mother's family lived, and where the boy was born. The site of the wedding of *Onkel* Max and *Tante* Henny, it is today the Polish city of Kietrz

Gross Peterwitz—The town, about four miles east of Katscher, where one changed from the mainline train to the line going to Katscher. Today it is the Polish town of Pietrowice Wielkie.

Troppau—Formerly a city in Upper Silesia, but given to Czechoslovakia as part of the borders created after WWI. Troppau was about 50 miles southwest of Pilzendorf and had a population of 36,000 before WWII. It is about two miles across the border into the Czech Republic and a total of only 10 miles from Katscher. *Onkel* Max took the boy there for a visit and his first Coca Cola. It is now the Czech city of Opava.

Breslau—The capital of Lower Silesia, about 85 miles northwest of Pilzendorf. Breslau is the place where *Onkel* Max took the boy to see the *Führer* ride past. It was the University of Breslau that awarded Johannes Brahms an honorary doctorate in 1879, to which he responded by writing his famous "Academic Overture." Breslau is now the Polish city of Wroclaw.

Jonzac—A French village of less than 4,000, located near the Atlantic coast about halfway down the coast from the Peninsula of Brittany about 35 miles from Bordeaux. It was here that the boy, now a soldier, was declared a *grand filou*, and gave German lessons to the baker's daughter. It is south and a little inland of the wartime German submarine base at New Rochelle, and thus a part of Occupied France, because it was in a strategic zone.

Naples—A major Italian seaport. In response to the November landings of Allied troops in Algeria and Morocco, Germany sent troops to northern Tunisia, so the soldier took his life's first flight in an airplane, from Naples to the airport at Tunis.

Tunis—The capital of Tunisia. The soldier was landed as the airfield as being bombed by the Allies, with the plane barely stopping to allow its troops to jump out. He ran for cover, to open ground away from the terminal buildings because he knew that the buildings would be prime targets for the attackers.

Madjez-el-Bab—A Tunisian town about 40 miles west of Tunis. After the British victory over the Italians and Germans at El-Alamein, Egypt, on November 4, the remaining Axis forces had been withdrawing through Libya into Tunisia, pursued by the Allied Eighth Army. In December, at Madjez-el-Bab, the Germans were able to halt the Allied advance eastward. But by mid-April 1943 the Axis forces were hemmed into northeastern Tunisia, and the British began their final offensive, pushing the *Afrika Korps* up Cape Bon.

Cape Bon—A Peninsula in Tunisia jutting 50 miles out into the Mediterranean Sea toward Sicily. It forms the eastern edge of the Bay of Tunis. About 250,000 German and Italian soldiers on Cape Bon surrendered to the Allies in May, 1943.

Kelibia and Korbia—It was from between these two villages along the east coast of Cape Bon that Pantelleria could be seen, and the soldier's attempt to escape to it was made on the afternoon of May 11, 1943. He surrendered. Korbia is today named Menzel-Termime.

Pantelleria—An island about 40 miles east of Cape Bon. The Italian equivalent of Malta as a fortress in the sea, it was heavily bombed by the Allies the day after the soldier and his mates attempted to escape to it.

Oran— The Algerian port at Oran was captured from the French on November 10, 1942 by 39,000 US troops that landed by surprise from 105 Royal Navy ships in OPERATION TORCH. Oran—along with the ports of Algiers and Casablanca, Morocco—was a major Allied shipping base for supplies and troops.

Norfolk, VA—Located at the mouth of Chesapeake Bay, the extensive naval facilities there served as one of the two points of entry for POWs from Europe. The soldier's ship landed here and he was put aboard a train. He thought a mistake had been made and the train could not be for him because it had seats: in European armies only officers rode in such coaches; enlisted men like the soldier always rode in the boxcars.

Camp Huntsville—Located near Huntsville, Texas, north of Houston. As a concession to its former status as the state capital and the home of Sam Houston, a state penitentiary has been located at Huntsville since 1849, but the camp was not associated with it. The US Army selected the site of Camp Huntsville because it fulfilled the basic requirements for the establishment of a base camp and was accessible to major railroad lines and highways. The camp, about 12 miles northeast of Huntsville on State Highway 19, was constructed along the lines of military post and garrisoned by one or more army guard companies. It was completed by September 18, 1942, and consisted of approximately 400 buildings, four deepwater wells, a sewage disposal plant and an incinerator. The camp contained a laundry, bakery, clothing shop, postal exchange, barbershop, cafeteria, commissary, gymnasium, fire station, guardhouse and motor pool. Clubs for officers and noncommissioned officers and barracks for American personnel and prisoners of war were also erected. The hospital building was the largest and most expensive structure in the base camp. It consisted of seven wings for beds, one wing for a cafeteria, and one wing for dental work. With the exception of the hospital, the buildings were covered by heavy tar paper over wood frames. The camp was surrounded by two fences and 20 guard towers. Its grounds are now part of Sam Houston State University, including a golf course.

Camp Fabens—With so many US men in the armed forces, harvesting crops became a problem for area farmers. Agricultural officials worked with the office of the Army's Provost Marshal General (who administered all POW camps in the USA) to make prisoners available to help. The agreement was that the program was not to cost the government anything, and the farmer must pay out the prevailing wage in the area so that no local laborers would be put out of work. About half the wage for each POW went to the government to pay for administration of the program and the rest went to the POW. The community had to provide the camp at its own expense. Camp Fabens was such an arrangement, temporary in nature, located in Fabens, Texas, near the junction of the Texas, New Mexico and Mexico borders. It held about 200 prisoners, and was probably used as a CCC camp from 1936.

Camp Forrest—This camp was east of Tullahoma, Tennessee, midway along the state east-to-west and about 20 miles north of Tennessee's southern border. Named for Confederate General Nathan Bedford Forrest, it was one of the US Army's largest training bases during WWII. It was closed in 1946 and its site is today the US Air Force's Arnold Engineering Development Center.

Camp Shanks—This camp was along the west bank of the Hudson River at Orangeburg, NY, just north of the border with New Jersey. It and Norfolk, VA, were the only two points of embarkation or debarkation for POWs. Camp Shanks was built in 1942 as a military embarkation point through which 1.3 million US troops passed before taking ships to Europe. At the end of the war, 290,000 Axis prisoners of war passed through it on their way back to Europe. It was closed in 1946. Today it is suburban housing and parkland, with a small military warehouse and a museum to document its former uses. Camp Shanks was named for Maj. Gen. David Carey Shanks, who was commanding general of the New York Port of Embarkation during World War I.

Camp Compiegne—Located about 40 miles north of Paris, Compiegne is the site where Joan of Arc was captured and turned over to the English in 1430. Charlemagne's grandson Charles the Bald (843-877) built a royal palace here intending "Carlopolis"—as he was going to call the city—to be the capital of his planned empire and it was turned into a more elegant chateau over the centuries. In a railroad car stopped at the clearing named Rethondes in the forested park at Compiegne, Germany signed the armistice that ended the fighting of WW I (Nov. 11, 1918) . The same railroad car was used, at German insistence, when the French signed their armistice to Germany (June 22, 1940) in that same place.

The historic railroad car was then taken to Berlin, where it was destroyed during a bombing in 1942. Eventually the POW camp had 24 barracks, each 50 x 200 feet in size, inside a double fence.

Marburg—Located in the German state of Hesse about 12 miles north of Giessen, and about 40 miles from Frankfurt am Main. It is a college town with a 750 year-old castle. Hindenburg is buried in Marburg.

Tittmoning—Located on the German side of the river that separates Germany and Austria, Tittmoning was prominent enough by 1299 to be granted its own coat of arms. It is about 20 miles downriver from Salzburg, and was ruled by the Archbishop of Salzburg until 1816. It has about 6000 inhabitants. The soldier's mother first settled here.

Munich—Capital of the German state of Bavaria, Munich is 50 miles west of Tittmoning.

Wetzlar—Located in the German state of Hesse about 30 miles north of Frankfurt am Main, and about 6 miles west of Giessen.

Giessen—Located in the German state of Hesse about 30 miles north of Frankfurt am Main, and 250 miles northwest of Munich.

Frankfurt am Main—There are two Frankfurts in Germany: the Frankfurt on the Main River, and the Frankfurt on the Oder River. Frankfurt am Main, the country's financial center, is the one in this book, and it is the major transportation center for western Germany and thus the former soldier's departure point for the USA in 1954.

Ampermoching—Located about 10 miles north of Munich, this Bavarian town of about 2,000 is where the boy's sister moved when she married. Their parents followed and ended their days there.

APPENDIX 2

Geneva Convention
Relative to the Treatment of Prisoners of War
Geneva, 27 July 1929

Geneva Convention between the United States of America and other powers, relating to prisoners of war. Signed at Geneva, Switzerland, July 27, 1929; ratification advised by the United States Senate, January 7, 1932; ratified by the President of the United States of America, January 16, 1932, ratification of the United States of America deposited with the Government of Switzerland, February 4, 1932; proclaimed, August 4, 1932.

Recognizing that, in the extreme event of a war, it will be the duty of every Power, to mitigate as far as possible, the inevitable rigours thereof and to alleviate the condition of prisoners of war;
Being desirous of developing the principles which have inspired the international conventions of The Hague, in particular the Convention concerning the Laws and Customs of War and the Regulations thereunto annexed,
Have resolved to conclude a Convention for that purpose and have appointed as their Plenipotentiaries:

Chapter 2. Food and Clothing of Prisoners of War.

Article 11.

The food ration of prisoners of war shall be in quantity and quality to that of the depot troops.
Prisoners shall also be afforded the means of preparing for themselves such additional articles of food as they may possess.
Sufficient drinking water shall be supplied to them. The use of tobacco shall be authorized. Prisoners may be employed in the kitchens.
All collective disciplinary measures affecting the food are prohibited.

Article 75.

When belligerents conclude an armistice convention, they shall normally cause to be included therein provisions concerning the repatriation of prisoners of war. If it has not been possible to insert in that convention such stipulations, the belligerents shall, nevertheless, enter into communication with each other on the question as soon as possible. In any case, the repatriation of prisoners shall be effected as soon as possible after the conclusion of peace.
Prisoners of war who are subject to criminal proceedings for a crime or offence at common law may, however, be detained until the end of the proceedings, and, if need be, until the expiration of the sentence. The same applies to prison-

ers convicted for a crime or offence at common law.

By agreement between the belligerents, commissions may be instituted for the purpose of searching for scattered prisoners and ensuring their repatriation.

THE U.S. POW EXPERIENCE SINCE WORLD WAR II
By
William H. Forman, Jr.

I. Introduction

A Russian general asked General of the Army Dwight D. Eisenhower why German prisoners of war were treated so well by Allied forces during World War II. General Eisenhower replied that "in the first place my country was required to do so by the terms of the Geneva Convention. In the second place, the Germans had some thousands of American and British prisoners and I did not want to give Hitler the excuse or justification for treating our prisoners more harshly than he was already doing."

Reciprocity is an underlying principle in the enforcement of POW treatment standards. A government's violation of such standards destroys its moral position in demanding humane treatment for the members of its own armed forces who are captured during hostilities. In other words, a government's deliberate violations of POW treatment standards put its own soldiers, sailors, and airmen in danger. General Eisenhower obviously understood the principle of reciprocity.

Following the war in a report to Congress, General Eisenhower stated that the promise of treatment in accordance with the Geneva Convention Relative to the Treatment of Prisoners of War of 1929 caused a considerable number of Germans to surrender. If the Germans had continued to fight, a much greater number of American soldiers would have been killed. The promise to provide POW treatment in accordance with the Geneva POW Convention of 1929 was, therefore, and indirect means of force protection. (page 1)

III. World War II: 1941-1945

The Geneva Convention Relative to the Treatment of Prisoners of War of 1929 was in effect during World War II. Article 2 of the 1929 Geneva POW Convention restated the historic customary rule as to the treatment of war prisoners: "they shall at all times be humanely treated and protected, particularly against acts of violence, from insults, and from public curiosity. Measures of reprisal against them are forbidden." Article 3 added that prisoners of war are entitled to respect for their persons and honor. Women shall be treated with all consideration due to their sex."

A representative of the United States signed the Convention on July 27, 1929. Congress ratified the treaty on February 4, 1932. (page 4)

APPENDIX 3

Maps

Mary Skopec, PhD.

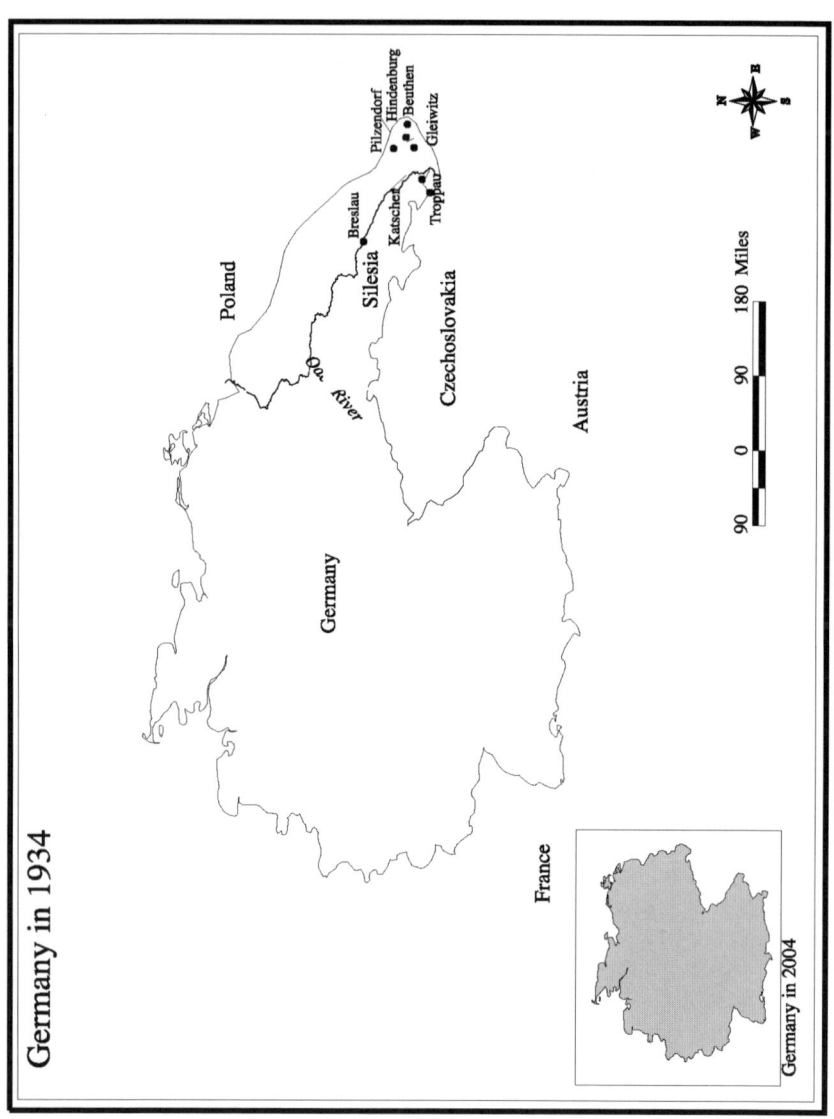

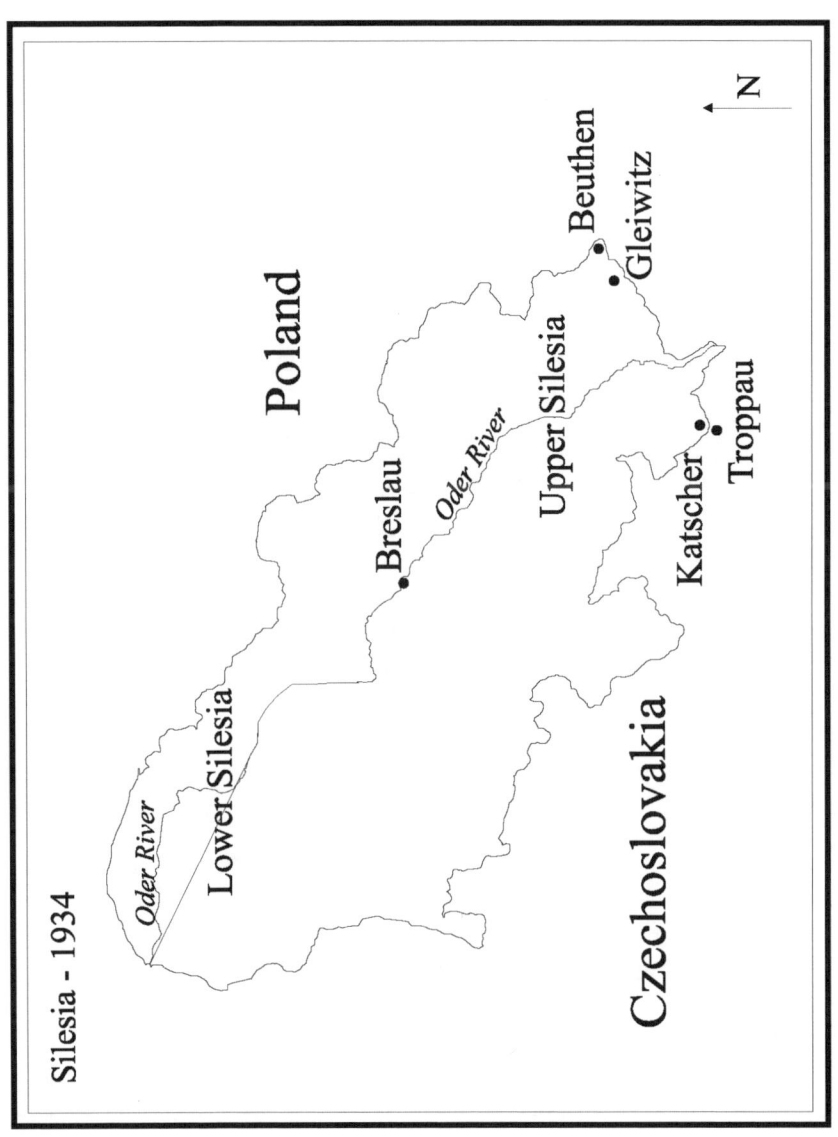

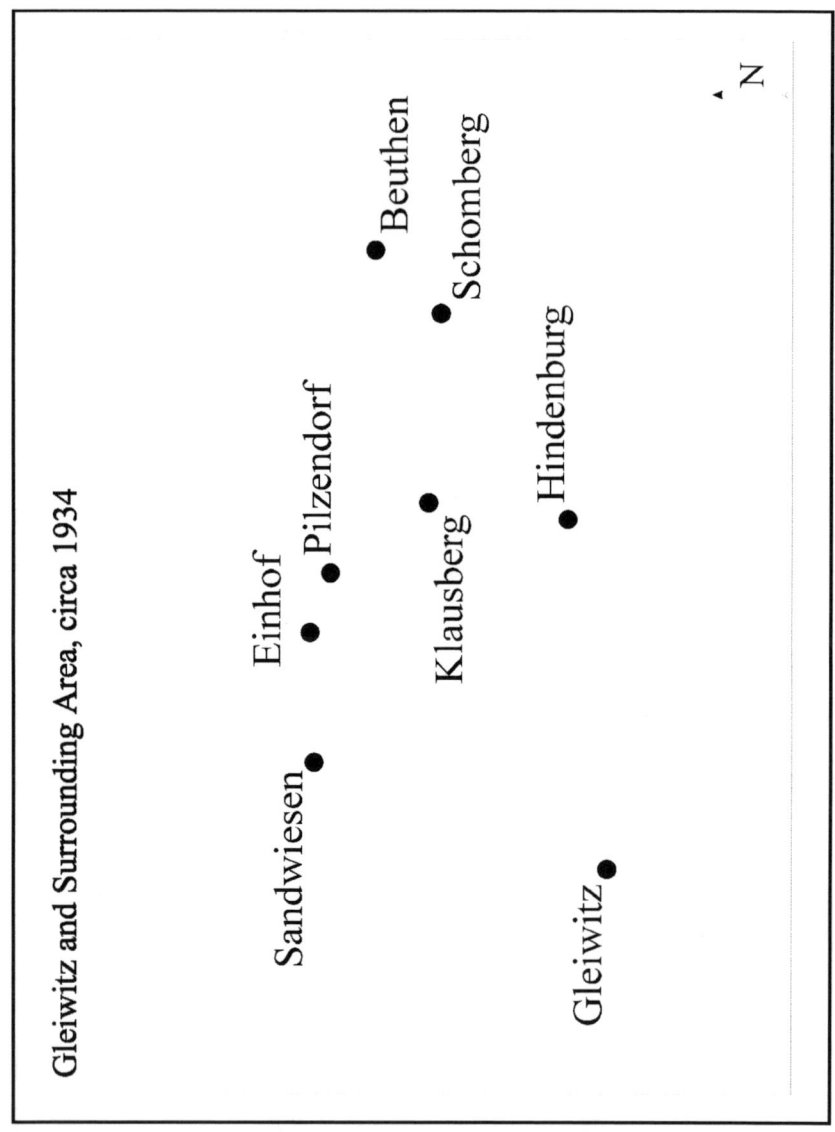

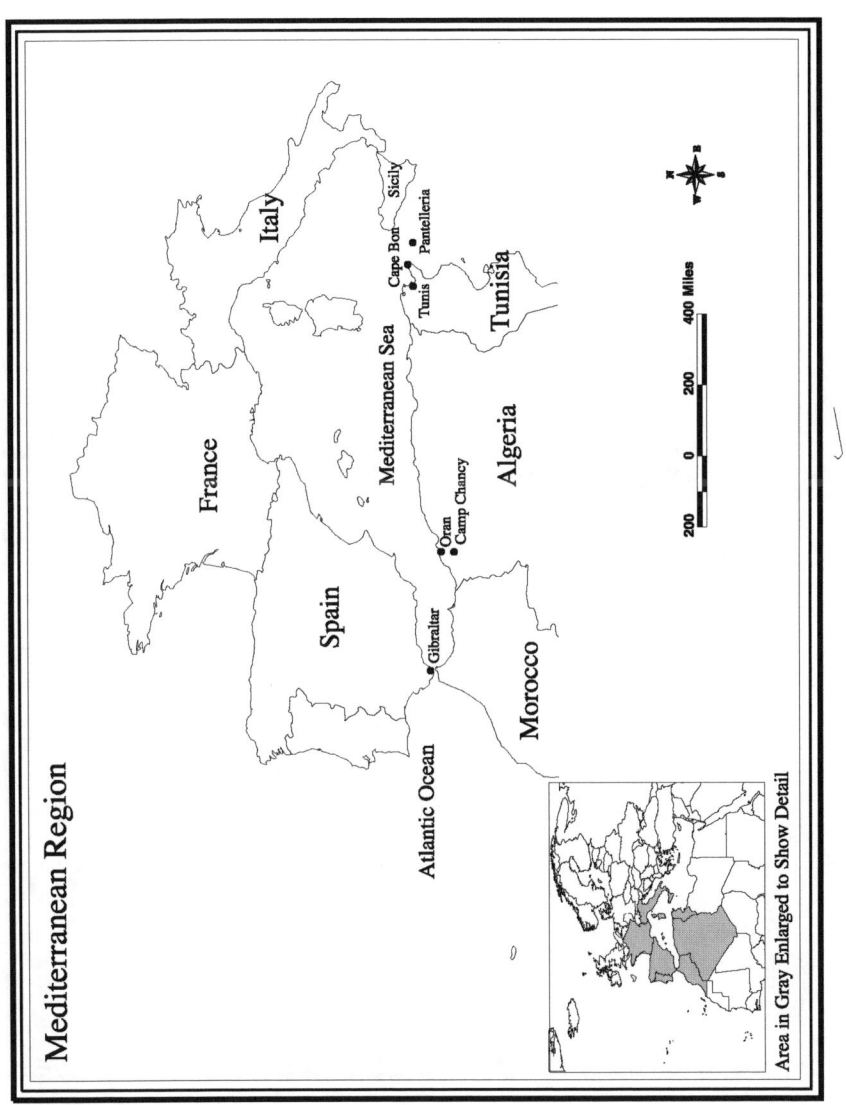

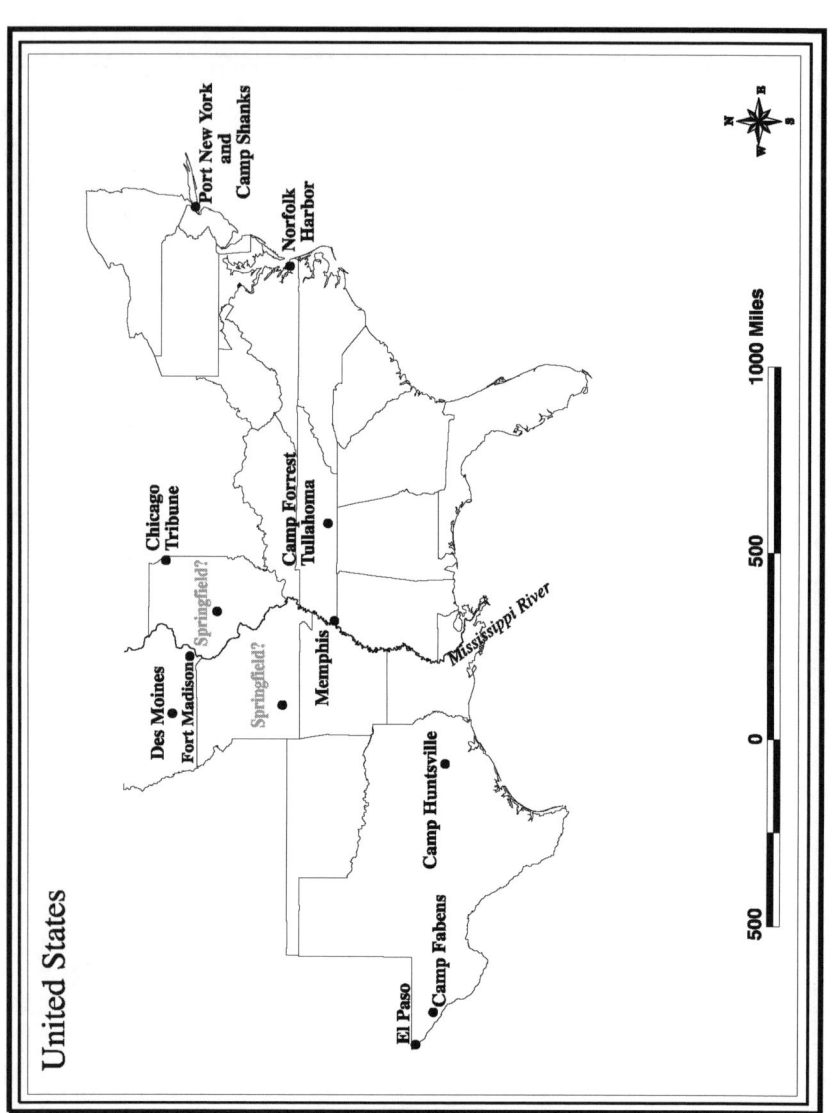

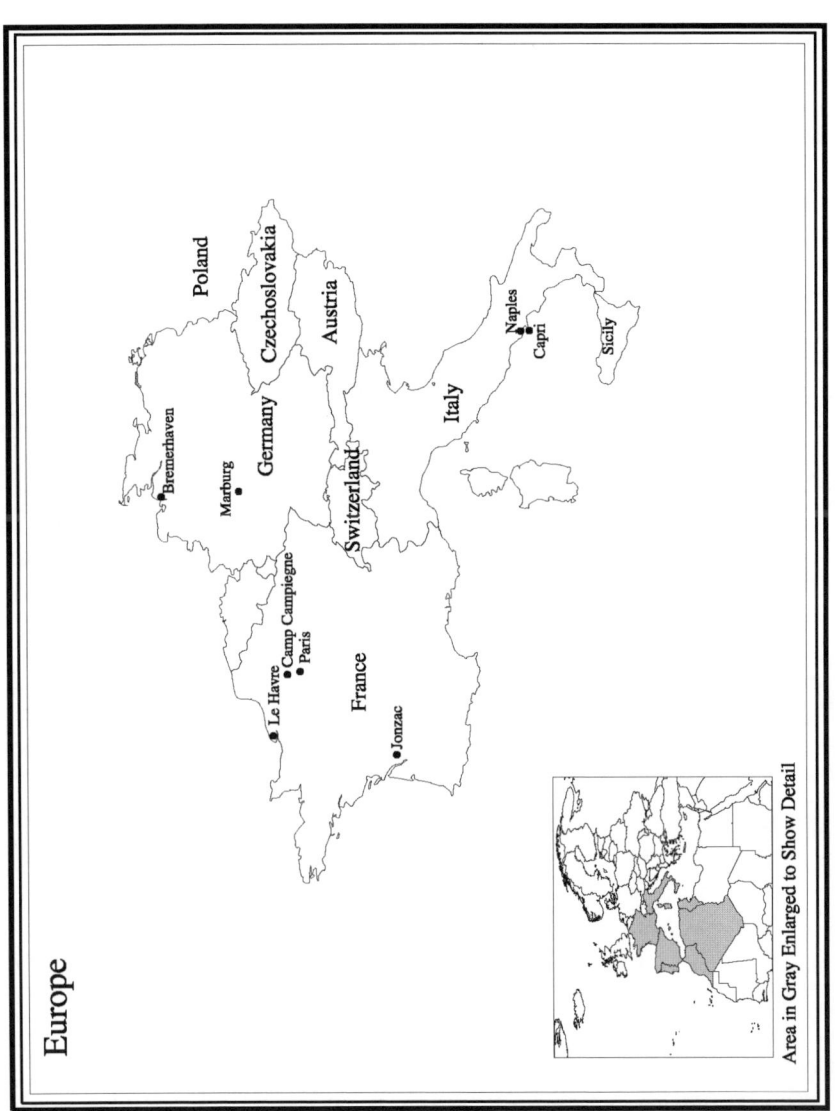